Relationship-Based
RESEARCH IN
SOCIAL WORK

of related interest

Relationship-Based Social Work
Getting to the Heart of Practice
Edited by Gillian Ruch, Danielle Turney and Adrian Ward
ISBN 978 1 84905 003 6
eISBN 978 085700 383 6

Innovations in Social Work Research
Using Methods Creatively
Edited by Louise Hardwick, Roger Smith and Aidan Worsley
ISBN 978 1 84905 585 7
eISBN 978 1 78450 145 7

Handbook for Practice Learning
in Social Work and Social Care
Knowledge and Theory
Third Edition
Edited by Joyce Lishman
ISBN 978 1 84905 571 0
eISBN 978 1 78450 010 8

Challenging Child Protection
New Directions in Safeguarding Children
Edited by Lorraine Waterhouse and Janice McGhee
ISBN 978 1 84905 395 2
eISBN 978 0 85700 760 5

Domestic Violence and Protecting Children
New Thinking and Approaches
Edited by Nicky Stanley and Cathy Humphreys
ISBN 978 1 84905 485 0
eISBN 978 0 85700 875 6

Relationship-Based RESEARCH IN SOCIAL WORK

Understanding Practice Research

Edited by
GILLIAN RUCH AND
ILSE JULKUNEN

Foreword by Irwin Epstein

Jessica Kingsley *Publishers*
London and Philadelphia

First published in 2016
by Jessica Kingsley Publishers
73 Collier Street
London N1 9BE, UK
and
400 Market Street, Suite 400
Philadelphia, PA 19106, USA

www.jkp.com

Library of Congress Cataloging in Publication Data
Names: Ruch, Gillian, editor. | Julkunen, Ilse, editor.
Title: Relationship-based research in social work : understanding
    practice-near research / edited by Gillian Ruch and Ilse Julkunen.
Description: Philadelphia : Jessica Kingsley Publishers, 2016. | Includes
    bibliographical references.
Identifiers: LCCN 2015032613 | ISBN 9781849054577 (alk. paper)
Subjects: LCSH: Social service--Research. | Interpersonal relations--Research.
Classification: LCC HV11 .R395 2016 | DDC 361.6072--dc23 LC record available at
http://lccn.loc.gov/2015032613

British Library Cataloguing in Publication Data
A CIP catalogue record for this book is available from the British Library

ISBN 978 1 84905 457 7
eISBN 978 1 78450 112 9

Printed and bound in Great Britain

MIX
Paper from
responsible sources
FSC
www.fsc.org   FSC® C013056

CONTENTS

FOREWORD

Irwin Epstein, PhD

Having reached the ambiguous stage of 'semi-retirement', I suddenly find myself being asked to write forewords. Always flattering, I can't help thinking about what it means existentially. And since *reflexivity* and the dismantling of *subjective/objective dichotomy* are central themes in this book, I feel free to ask myself – both privately and publicly – why this book?

The question becomes even more provocative when I note that neither Ruch nor Julkunen, nor any other of their contributors, cite any of my writings on practice research. I know; I checked. It's what old (and I suspect young) academics do when they read a new book or article. Start with the index or bibliography. Did I influence anyone's thinking? Negative or positive? But what, if they didn't even cite me?

Further reflection is revealing beyond the narcissistic wound. In this book, Ruch and Julkunen expertly chart different streams of *relationship-based* practice research in the UK and in Finland, floating exemplars from each country and from multiple practice settings with different sets of stakeholders and service users. By first launching and then docking them conceptually, Ruch and Julkunen help us see what is common to their European origins, methods and destinations.

Though not their intended purpose, the book helps me understand the differences between practice research as I witness, support and promote it in my own and other countries and what it means in Europe.

At the same time, these European exemplars feel strangely familiar in that several of them are conducted by passionate, social-justice motivated doctoral students, in the process of transitioning from practitioner to practitioner researcher. Thus they remind me of many of my former PhD students. Other contributors, like Ruch and Julkunen, are academics like me, committed to exploring and extending the multiple meanings and applications of practice research in social work.

Posing the original question more broadly (and less embarrassingly), how is social work practice research different in the USA than it is Europe? Reading this book, I see four major differences.

First, virtually all of these European practice-research exemplars are qualitative and while the co-editors do advocate 'multi-method' practice research, the varietals they display are all essentially qualitative. By contrast, in the USA, practice researchers are as likely to use quantitative as they are to use qualitative methods and may be more comfortable than their European compeers in combining the two. American practice researchers do this with little concern about epistemological contradictions. Pragmatists more than epistemologists, they simply mix and match.

Second, the studies presented in this book rely primarily on original data collection, whereas American practice researchers are more likely to use available administrative data. More commonly, they collect original quantitative data. Or, as I have advocated in my writing about clinical data-mining (CDM), they convert qualitative case information into quantitative data (Epstein 2010). Though not widely known or employed in Europe, academic colleagues and I have demonstrated the value of CDM in practice research in the USA as well as in Australia, Hong Kong, Israel and New Zealand (Lalayants et al. 2012). Qualitative analysis of available practice data is possible, but unexplored everywhere (for a rare exemplar, see Cordero and Epstein 2005).

Third, the studies presented by Ruch and Julkunen are theoretically pluralist. Those from the UK are unapologetically informed by psychoanalytic theory. And, given the emphasis on process and self-reflection in European practice research, psychodynamic theories of causation or interpretation are as likely to be applied reflexively to the authors themselves as to the subjects of their studies. Not so in the USA, where behavioural theory is much more influential and Freud is caricatured in social work schools as a vestige of a bygone and scientifically invalid era. (For a rare   practice-research exemplar of qualitative CDM informed by psychoanalytic theory and conducted in the UK by an Australian social worker, see Jones, Statham and Solomou 2006.) The Finnish studies, on the other hand, represent several theoretical approaches including critical realist, psychodynamic and systemic perspectives. Despite these differences, every exemplar study is explicitly informed by theory. More pragmatic American practice research studies conducted for purely formative evaluation purposes tend to be a-theoretical (or at least pretend to be), staying closer to the data. Practice research PhD dissertations more closely resemble the Finnish studies in their use of theory.

Finally, the practice-research studies in this book utilise the power of metaphor to advance their meanings and practice implications. As a result, they are especially rich and vivid in what they convey. In their published studies, American practice researchers, writing for journals that emphasise evidence-based writing styles, steer away from metaphorical allusion.

Allowing myself a metaphor, Ruch and Julkunen's European practice researchers remind me of courageous kayakers paddling their graceful but seemingly fragile ships to places that big boats (and most academics) are unwilling to go. Like skilled kayakers, they remain close to choppy or even turbulent practice waters; remarkably resilient and sure of reaching a valued destination, even when the landing point is not what was originally intended. The kayak turns over? No problem. The kayaker hangs in, rights her/himself, shakes off the unwelcome but exhilarating water and with minor but necessary course correction proceeds on the journey. Sometimes the point of the journey is the journey itself. In each case, however, the trip is worth the effort and experience matters in ways that are inherently meaningful to future practice.

Like all metaphors, mine is imperfect. Unlike solitary kayaking, Ruch and Julkunen remind us that practice research in social work is an entirely human endeavor. Consequently, *relationship*, of one kind or another, is recognised in this book as essential in starting, maintaining and concluding the trip. In some exemplars, the relationship includes multiple polyvocal sets of stakeholders. In others the journey depends on the negotiation of dyadic relationships between practitioners and supervisors or administrators. In many, *relationship* is based on a constant and continuing internal dialogue between practice and research principles *within* practice researchers' own heads.

11

A common impediment to both European and American practice research is the shadow of evidence-based practice and, in the US at least, the disparagement of practitioners' research capacities by research academics. (For a glimpse of that dysfunctional relationship in the USA, see Epstein 2011.)

No longer supervising PhD students myself, Ruch and Julkunen's exemplars recall the academically 'dangerous' conceptual, methodological and truly dangerous places my former PhD students have taken me – places I never would have had the courage to go on my own. Qualitative practice-research studies of child soldiers and female abductees in African and Latin American countries experiencing civil wars, of the plight of Philippine domestic workers in New York City, of the use of 'Nuyorican' poetry in working with Puerto Rican male adolescents in a community-based mental health programme, of homeless LGBT adolescents who for their own safety prefer to live rough on the streets of New York than in abusive foster care settings and, in an unusually refined location for social workers to go, of the use of metaphor in understanding and healing conflicts among classical string quartets members.

How telling that the final dissertation I supervised is an auto-ethnographic study, informed by Goffman's symbolic interactionist theory applied to the student's own transition from female to male social worker; his 'presentation of trans' in his everyday life and his own practice (Nealy 2014).

My point here is that relationship-based practice research, as Ruch and Julkunen would define it in Europe, is alive and well in the US, primarily because fearlessly creative students take us there. These journeys are also beholden to mutually trusting, appreciative and working *relationships* between students and their dissertation advisors.

Returning to the awkward question with which I began this brief written journey, full disclosure requires that I met both Gillian and Ilse at the second International Conference on Practice Research in Helsinki in 2012 where I gave a plenary on CDM and the importance of context in interpreting CDM findings.

In 2014, I was privileged to Chair the third International Conference on Practice Research in New York City. Together with other members of the Conference Planning Committee, Ilse and I co-authored the 'New York Statement on the Evolving Definition of Practice Research' (Epstein *et al.* 2015). So it's no big surprise (though it remains an honour) that I was asked to write the Foreword to this stimulating, insightful and provocative collection. A fourth International Conference will take place in Hong Kong in 2017. Yet another set of meanings of practice research in Hong Kong, Singapore, China and India are likely to be articulated there.

This current collection of illuminating European practice-research studies convinces us that, rather than being bogged down by a weighty and illusory 'gold standard' of quantitative experimental research, if we allow our students and ourselves to closely follow the many and evolving streams of social work practice globally, we may be heading toward a 'golden age' of practice research. Ruch and Julkunen are to be congratulated for calling our attention to one exceedingly important route to that destination.

REFERENCES

Cordero, A. and Epstein, I. (2005) 'Refining the practice of family reunification: "Mining" successful foster care case records of substance abusing families.' In G.P. Mallon and P.M. Hess (eds.) *Child Welfare for the Twenty-first Century: A Handbook of Practices, Policies and Programs.* New York, NY: Columbia University Press.

Jones, S., Statham, H. and Solomou, W. (2006) 'When expectant mothers know their baby has a fetal abnormality: Exploring a crisis of motherhood through qualitative data-mining.' *Journal of Social Work Research and Evaluation 6,* 195–206.

Epstein, I. (2010) *Clinical Data-mining: Integrating Practice and Research.* New York, NY: Oxford University Press.

Epstein, I. (2011) 'Reconciling evidence-based practice, evidence-informed practice, and practice-based research: The role of clinical data-mining.' *Social Work 56,* 284–287.

Epstein, I., Fisher, M., Julkunen, I., Uggerhoj, L., Austin, M.J. and Sim, T. (2015) 'The New York statement on the evolving definition of practice research designed for continuing dialogue: A bulletin from the 3rd International Conference on Practice Research.' *Research on Social Work Practice 25,* 711–714.

Lalayants, M., Epstein, I., Auslander, G., Chan, W., Fouche, C., Giles, R., Joubert. L., Hadas, R. and Vertigan, A. (2012) 'Clinical data-mining: Learning from practice in international settings.' *International Social Work 56,* 775–797.

Nealy, E.C. (2014) 'The Presentation of Trans in Everyday Life: An Autoethnographic Exploration of Gendered Performance.' Unpublished PhD dissertation, City of New York Doctoral Program in Social Welfare.

Chapter 1

INTRODUCING THE BOOK

Gillian Ruch

The germination of the book took place when the editors were exploring ideas concerning practice research. Out of these conversations it became apparent we were both aware of colleagues and doctoral students who were engaged in innovative research in a wide range of social work settings. Our interest in exploring in more depth how relationships shaped these research activities took hold and has come to fruition in this book. The book brings together two important and complementary strands of research – relationship-based research and practice research – from two distinctive European national contexts. While discrete and different, what these two approaches share is their commitment to research that, first, positions people (researchers and the research participants) as critical constituents of the research process and, second, recognises the parallels between research processes and practices and professional social work practices.

THE RESEARCH CONTEXTS

Given the European perspectives that the book embraces, it is important and necessary to briefly outline distinctive features of the two national settings in which the research being presented was conducted.

United Kingdom

Over the past 40 years social work research in the UK has developed a reputable and expanding presence in the social sciences and professional practice arenas, but the pace of this growth has been slow and interrupted. Historically, most social work research has been predominantly qualitative, reflecting the intrinsic people-orientated nature of the professional and its interest in understanding how people experience social work (Shaw and Holland 2014). This is not to say that quantitative studies had not been conducted in this field, but they certainly have been, and remain, in the minority. The growing strength of social work research, however, has been undermined by constant attacks on the knowledge base of social work (Briggs 2005). Consequently, in comparison to other professional research domains, social work lacks a coherent and consistent epistemological foundation on which it can build its research profile. In addition, the impact and significance of social work research has been compromised by top-down policy, as opposed to practice-driven research initiatives. The government-led, evidence-based practice movement that took hold in the 1990s, in particular, has presented difficulties for social work research, with its emphasis on narrow definitions of research evidence and a preoccupation with determining 'what works' in practice from a positivistic epistemological perspective. One of the biggest challenges associated with this initiative has been its privileging of particular research methodologies, most notably randomised controlled trials, which 'seek to drive a wedge between professional experience and research' (Briggs 2005, p.18). As Briggs goes on to say:

> The hammer which drives home this wedge is a methodological one, so that aligned on one side, representing EBP [evidence-based practice] are quantitative, positivistic, experimental and quasi-experimental, while on the other side are qualitative, observational, naturalistic methods. Thus the EBP movement has tended to nullify research that is important to social work, and which aims to connect quantitative and qualitative, validation and discovery, comparison and in-depth understanding. (2005, p.18)

In 2004 the Social Care Institute for Excellence published a knowledge review of how research was taken up and used in social work (Walters *et al.* 2004). It recommended that a whole system approach be developed to create closer synergies between those designing and those taking up research. Such an approach is premised on the belief that 'the system will work best if all parts of the system work together in complementary ways' (Walters *et al.* 2004, p.iv). A subsequent significant developmental landmark in the history of social work research took place in 2009 with the appointment of a strategic adviser (Professor Elaine Sharland) by the Economic and Social Research Council (ESRC), the government-funded research council that deals with most social work research applications, to conduct a review of the current state of play in social work research. The rationale behind the review, informed in part by the slowness in the growth and variable quality of research in this academic and professional domain, was to invite recommendations about how the capacity of social work research could be developed, expanded, enhanced and consolidated:

> There needs to be a fundamental step change in breadth, depth and quality of the UK research base in social work and social care... The knowledge base to underpin existing social care services, to support their improvement and to make judgments about cost-effectiveness in their delivery is currently inadequate. Despite some notable exceptions, social work and social care policy and practice have developed largely without an adequate, closely connected research evidence base. It is essential that a stronger connection is made and that the social work and social care research can then deliver high quality evidence to the policy and practitioner communities. High quality, high impact research requires capacity to produce it; at present capacity levels fall far short of what is required. (Sharland 2009, p.3)

Following on from this report, published in 2009, which recommended a comprehensive investment programme, social work research has continued to develop an increasingly distinctive and more confident profile, albeit slowly.

Over the years several attempts to promote and develop practice research have taken hold but have had difficulty in getting a solid purchase on the social work research terrain (Broad and Fletcher 1995; Fuller and Petch 1995; Shaw and Lunt 2011). Unlike in Finland (see below) there has not been a government-funded initiative to support the development of practice research across the UK in a more coherent and systematic way. Consequently, its expansion has been piecemeal, contingent on the energy and interest of individuals and their networks (see the Salisbury Forum 2009). Most recently, Shaw and Lunt (2011, 2012) have begun to further explore understandings of practice research, particularly from the practitioner perspective. They argue that:

> The elements of practitioner research have to be understood as being interwoven and bringing together and containing different career and life concerns that otherwise might remain scattered. The implications of this research suggest that practitioner research should not be seen as a less or more comfortable add-on to everyday core practice, but as a multiform activity that challenges the taken-for-grantedness of practice, mainstream academic research, management and, in all likelihood, the experience of receiving services. (Shaw and Lunt 2012, p.197)

Briggs (2005, p.24), addressing recent developments in social work research, refers to 'emergent methods' that arise out of practice and practitioners' interests and challenge the restrictive characteristics associated with positivistic research orthodoxy. A crucially distinctive feature of these emergent approaches, according to Briggs, is their solid theoretical foundation, in this instance drawn from psychoanalysis. As we will see in the subsequent chapter, theoretical underpinnings are a key characteristic of the studies being discussed. One of, if not the, biggest challenge to this agenda, however, is maintaining the momentum when government and other funding bodies are not always 'on board' with qualitative approaches to research that, in their view, do not deliver robust and rigorous science. It is misinformed positions, such as this, that this publication seeks to confront, challenge and confound, in order to strengthen the academic community's conviction about and commitment to these invaluable approaches to research.

Finland

There have always been different views about what form of knowledge production is needed in social work. Different research paradigms and research positions are often linked to how one sees social work and its tasks in society. Critics claim that when the social work research field is scrutinised it appears to be rather one-sided, consisting of predominantly qualitative studies. Although there are quantitative studies, they are not often recognised in the social work debate. Critics also claim that the social care and social welfare field – even at the societal level – is left aside and not acknowledged, leaving the research field rather narrow (Mäntysaari 2013; Hämäläinen 2014). On the other hand, the research field has been claimed to be rather diffuse and under-defined.

These conflicting perspectives reveal the difficulty currently faced in Finland in getting a comprehensive picture of the research field of a discipline that is young and has a dynamic developmental trajectory. There are interesting new developments in critical realistic approaches that tackle the many societal levels interacting in people's lives: critical discourse analysis, dialogical approaches, practice research, mixed methodologies and indeed cross-sectional national surveys on attitudes towards welfare and professional welfare. Perhaps what these trends reveal is that social work, as a complex field of professional practice, needs hybrid approaches. Social work as a discipline, however, is still struggling to decide what exactly it is that makes it distinctive and there are competing views about the added value of social work research.

Most recently in the Finnish context, multi-professionalism and multi-disciplinary approaches have challenged this issue of distinctiveness, as recent research politics have 'forced' the research community to forge broader collaborative approaches, in order to be competitive enough to creative new knowledge that builds on the existing cumulative knowledge base. This puts pressure on social work. On the other hand, there is a search for strategic knowledge – knowledge that may have a societal impact and offer innovation in social welfare services (Academy of Finland 2015). Here, social work may offer a competitive partner with direct access to practice.

One of the strengths in the Finnish social work research is collaboration in national networks. The Finnish National University Network of Universities (Forssén *et al.* 2011) has recently identified social work research needs and themes and concluded that one of the greatest challenges for social work is the digital era, which for social work means new competencies and requirements of broader collaboration across disciplines and practices. Another strength is the collaboration in social work research across Nordic societies, which has lead to numerous shared conferences and common doctoral programmes.

What is distinctive in relation to the Finnish context is that in recent years there has been a strong political interest in developing social work as a modern academic discipline and as a key part of the social political infrastructure in society (Hämäläinen 2014). Since the 1980s the concepts of research-oriented social work, research in practice and practitioners as researchers have been central in the Finnish debate on social work education. Karvinen-Niinikoski's (2005) argument that the qualifications for a competent social worker should be at masters level has led to a strong emphasis on the production of research-oriented practitioners and on establishing an impressive field of social work research and methodological development in Finland. As a direct consequence of these successful debates there is a strong emphasis on research-oriented social work. Much of this research orientation stems from the professional interest in both making social work an academic profession and in generating reflexive expertise that contributes to the production of new and innovative knowledge for society (Fook 2004; Karvinen-Niinikoski 2005). Over time this vision has developed into a closely inter-woven social work–practice research relationship, as Mirja Satka outlines:

> Today it is possible to argue that social work research has been and continues to be a very important influential factor in developing new social work practices, and vice versa, social work practice has become a very essential context for research and practice [also defines] research. One conclusion of the Finnish situation is that only now, at the beginning of the new century, the real social work research has [come] into existence. By that I mean research that is relevant for practice and [also takes] place either in actual social work practices or in close connection with them. (Satka 2001, p.15)

The formation of practice research networks such as the Heikki Waris Institute and the Mathilda Wrede Institute, a joint research and development structure of municipalities and the discipline of social work at the Helsinki University, has been very important in facilitating and developing the practice research framework in social work and has provided a safe and supportive environment for researchers. These forms of collaborative networks with broad international connections are crucial forums for learning and knowledge production and for enhancing the emergent developments in practice research in social work.

They are also in line with the demand for strategic and open expertise in a knowledge society.

As the Helsinki Forum (2014) for practice research in social work stated, we need to engage a wider audience of interested practitioners and researchers around the relevance of social work practice research and move towards validating such research findings in larger and external networks.

INTRODUCING THE CHAPTERS

Opening chapters

Chapters 2 and 3 develop some of the themes touched on in the preceding section. In Chapter 2 we outline the developments in research that have enabled more relationship-based approaches to research to emerge, and consider the distinctive features such approaches encompass. Chapter 3 explores the emergence in recent years of practice research and the central position of relationships in how such research is developed, designed, delivered and disseminated.

Contributions from the UK and Finland

The eight chapters that comprise the core of the book are written by practice researchers from the UK and Finland and provide rich and diverse accounts of practice research conducted in a wide range of social work settings. The four UK-based chapters (Chapters 4, 7, 8 and 11) adopt, in comparison with the Finnish-based chapters, a more psychoanalytically informed perspective on relationships in the research process as each of the authors undertook their research as part of a psychoanalytically informed professional doctorate programme. The four chapters from the Finnish context (Chapters 5, 6, 9 and 10) employ several theoretical approaches to understanding research relationships, including critical realist, psychodynamic and systemic perspectives. In so doing, they serve to enrich the dialogue between these different approaches and illustrate the breadth of theoretical perspectives that can inform understanding of the research relationship.

In Chapter 4, Judy Foster provides insightful psycho-socially informed ethnographic accounts of practice in three adult services teams. Judy pays careful reflexive attention to her early encounters in, and perceptions of, the team and to the on-going, seemingly incidental, exchanges and experiences she engaged with. In so doing, she provides a compelling account of the role that contextual and relational characteristics associated with each team play in determining the capacity of practitioners to think *and* feel and to survive *and* thrive.

Similarly researching in team settings, Laura Yliruka and her colleagues from Finland outline in Chapter 5 the developments of a new research-based approach to practice improvement – the Mirror method. Adopting a polyvocal approach, Laura narrates, alongside her co-researchers, how the Mirror method was utilised as both a research method and a practice improvement initiative. Notable in Laura's chapter is the attention paid in practice research to co-constructing the research from beginning to end. At the outset the research brief responded to a practice need, which it was hoped would be of benefit to practitioners. And in disseminating the research, the commitment to the practitioner experience is powerfully demonstrated in the co-authored nature of this chapter.

In Chapter 6, Harry Lunabba draws on his ethnographic accounts of boys in a secondary school more generally, and of two boys in particular – Peetu and Santu – to explore how research relationships are established and how they unfold in the course of a research project. Harry's account provides a vivid insight into the intricacies of establishing, maintaining and negotiating research relationships where power dynamics are so tangibly felt, and also reveals the strong parallels that can be drawn between research and professional relationships.

Helen Hingley-Jones' research in the UK social work context, reported in Chapter 7, concentrates on observing adolescents with learning disabilities in their family setting and brings to our attention the delicate sensitivities involved in negotiating a pathway through relationship-based research. Adapting for research purposes a clinical method of infant observation, Helen demonstrates the need for the researcher to be responsive to hidden, 'beneath the surface' dimensions of behaviours and researcher-researched relationships. As a researcher with practice experience in this field, Helen highlights the importance of vigilance with regard to appropriate research-practice boundaries and to managing the transference in the research relationship.

Chapter 8 provides a candid account of the experiences of Gavin Swann, a senior manager in children's services, who conducted an action research project in his own workplace. Gavin identifies the 'prerequisites, opportunities, complexities and challenges in achieving relationship based research' and emphasises the need for a sustained reflective stance if the full potential and efficacy of the project is to be realised. In particular he notes the importance of ensuring relationships are secured and sustained in all directions within the organisation – up and down the hierarchy and across the practice domain – and that the significance and impact of the diverse characteristics and inter-sectionalities of the people engaged in the project are held in mind.

A creative approach to researching practice is outlined in Chapter 9. Katarina Fagerström uses novels and autobiographical literature for the purposes of widening professional perspectives on alcohol misuse among families. Katarina observes in the focus group sessions, which involve the differential engagement of practitioners with the stories, how the group produces distinctive and at times challenging reflections. The lively group dynamics required a reflexive stance on the part of the researcher that could accommodate and respond to them as required.

Elina Virokannas' research in Chapter 10 offers the reader the opportunity to reflect on how the processes involved in conducting secondary analysis can provide opportunities for the researcher to think about the emotional material embedded in pre-existing research data. Utilising a form of clinical data-mining and an explicitly reflexive stance, Elina explains how she analysed peer supporters' reflections of their work in the field of substance misuse in order to elicit the emotional dimensions of their work, as expressed through their written reports. For Elina, conducting experience-led, bottom-up research is important in its own right for giving voice to marginalised individuals and groups, plus it makes an invaluable contribution to the development of experience-based knowledge in social work education.

Researching fathers' experiences of diagnoses of testicular cancer is the focus of Kathleen Russell's research in Chapter 11. As an experienced hospital social worker in the field of oncology, Kathleen provides a compelling account of how qualitative methods in general, and psycho-social methods in particular, can counter more positivist research paradigms associated with medical settings and generate invaluable insight into the experiences of fathers. Using the biographical narrative interview method and interpretive phenomenological analysis, Kathleen displays the power of these reflexive research approaches to identify defended responses and bring to the surface powerful hidden emotional responses.

Conclusion

Drawing together the ideas explored in the book, Chapter 12 is where we reflect on the emergent, common themes that have arisen in the course of writing, editing and compiling this book. The chapter simultaneously highlights both the enormous creative potential of relationship-based, practice research and the not inconsiderable challenges inherent in such approaches. This edited collection will make an important contribution to our expanding understanding of the centrality of relationships in all aspects of research and professional practice.

REFERENCES

Academy of Finland (2015) 'Strategic Research Funding' and 'Research and Science Policy.' Available at www.aka.fi/en/research-and-science-policy/strategic-research-funding, accessed 17 September 2015.

Briggs, S. (2005) 'Psycho-analytic Research in the Era of Evidence-based Practice.' In M. Bower (ed.) Psycho-analytic Theory for Social Work: Thinking under Fire. London: Routledge.

Broad, B. and Fletcher, C. (1994) Practitioner Research into Social Work: From Experiences to an Agenda. London: Whiting and Birch.

Fook, J. (2004) 'What Professionals Need from Research: Beyond Evidence-based Practice.' In D. Smith (ed.) Social Work and Evidence-based Practice. Research Highlights in Social Work 45. London: Jessica Kingsley Publishers.

Forssén, K., Hämäläinen, J., Juhila, K., Kuronen, M., Laitinen, M. and Rauhala, P. (2011) 'Sosiaalityön Valtakunnallinen Tutkimusohjelma.' Available at www.sosnet.fi/Suomeksi/Tutkimus/Sosiaalityon-tutkimusohjelma, accessed on 2 December 2015.

Fuller, R. and Petch, A. (1995) Practitioner Research: The Reflexive Social Worker. Milton Keynes: Open University Press.

Hämäläinen, J. (2014) 'Tiedontuotanto Sosiaalityön Rakenteellisena Kysymyksenä.' In A. Pohjola, M. Laitinen and M. Seppänen (eds) Rakenteellinen Sosiaalityö. Sosiaalityön tutkimuksen vuosikirja. UniPress: Kuopio.

Helsinki Forum (2014) 'Helsinki Statement on social work practice research.' Nordic Social Work Research 4, 1, 7–13.

Karvinen-Niinikoski, S. (2005) 'Research orientation and expertise in social work.' European Journal of Social Work 8, 3, 259–271.

Mäntysaari, M (2013) 'Yksipuolista tutkimusta.' Noste 3, 80–81.

Salisbury Forum (2011) 'The Salisbury Statement on practice research.' Social Work and Society International Online Journal 9, 1. Available at www.socwork.net/sws/article/view/2/12, accessed on 19 November 2015.

Satka, M. (2001) 'Research, knowledge and the development of social work.' The Finnish example. Intervenção Social 23–24. Available at http://revistas.lis.ulusiada.pt/index.php/is/article/viewFile/1011/1132, accessed on 19 November 2015.

Sharland, E. (2009) Strategic Adviser for Social Work and Social Care Research Main Report to the Economic and Social Research Council Training and Development Board. Swindon: ESRC.

Shaw, I. and Holland, S. (2014) *Doing Qualitative Research in Social Work.* London: Sage.

Shaw, I. and Lunt, N. (2011) 'Navigating practitioner research.' *British Journal of Social Work 41,* 1548–1565.

Shaw, I. and Lunt, N. (2012) 'Constructing practitioner research.' *Social Work Research 36,* 3, 197–208.

Walters, I., Nutley, S., Percy-Smith, J., McNeish, D. and Frost, S. (2004) *Improving the Use of Research in Social Care.* London: SCIE.

Chapter 2

DEVELOPING RELEVANT AND RESPECTFUL RESEARCH RELATIONSHIPS

Gillian Ruch

REFLECTING ON A RESEARCH ENCOUNTER

In the course of a research project exploring how social workers thought about and understood their practice, I undertook ethnographic observation in a social work children's support team. The observations lasted approximately four months and involved me spending several whole days per week observing practitioners in their team settings. At the outset of the research I had explained my role in the team as a non-participant observer, but emphasised that I was more than happy to be engaged in conversation and did not see myself as the equivalent of a 'fly on the wall' observer. Towards the end of the research process in the team I undertook individual interviews with each of the practitioners. When I asked at the conclusion of these interviews how each practitioner had experienced the research process, I was surprised by one response in particular: 'I didn't think I could talk to you. I thought I would affect your objectivity.' This response, implying that if she talked to me it would somehow contaminate my research, was particularly surprising as the practitioner concerned was a social worker and a systemic therapist, whose systemic training had emphasised the significance of multiple narratives and subjective perspectives.

WHAT SORT OF PEOPLE ARE WE? UNDERSTANDINGS OF SUBJECTIVITY AND OBJECTIVITY

The significance of the research encounter, described above, has stayed with me for several years as it captures the powerful discourses that pervade the on-going debates surrounding what constitutes 'good' research. In this instance the practitioner concerned would have been imbued, through her social work and systemic training, with a clear sense of the intrinsically inter-subjective nature of social work encounters. One might have hoped too, therefore, that this understanding of the quintessentially subjective nature of social work 'realities' would have translated into her understanding of research in a social work setting. Clearly this was not the case and this is not, I would suggest, an unusual stance for social workers to hold. In his preface to Marion Bower's book *Psychoanalytic Theories for Social Work: Thinking under Fire*, Andrew Cooper captures these social work and research dilemmas in a different register:

> Social work in common with the profession of psychoanalytic psychotherapy has been reluctant and slow to engage with this new culture [evidence-based practice]. This is to be explained partly by the familiar (but again largely phoney) cultural tension between the clinical and practice 'arts' and the research and social policy 'sciences'. Good experimental research designs in the applied social sciences are notoriously hard to achieve, but this is not a reason to abandon the quest. Equally there is much we need to know about social work and psychotherapeutic practice that cannot be quantified. A rich and diverse tradition of qualitative, descriptive and clinically-based research methodologies has evolved in recent decades. For good philosophical reasons but also for reasons that have to do with intellectual defensiveness, creative interchange between different research paradigms has been hard to achieve. We need to advance beyond this state of affairs... (Cooper 2005, pp.xix–xx)

It is precisely these entrenched, perturbing and inaccurate representations of research in social work (and in other human service professions too) and the dilemmas associated with them, that this book seeks to challenge and recalibrate.

In the companion book to this publication, *Relationship-based Social Work: Getting to the Heart of Practice*, the changing fortunes of the relationship in the context of social work practice were traced. The book records the origins of social work in the early 20th century being firmly rooted in relationships and how, during the 1950s and 60s, the professional relationship became the defining characteristic of psycho-social casework. By the 1970s, however, the centrality of the relationship in social work had tailed off dramatically with the ascendancy of more politicised and anti-oppressive-focused approaches. More recently, the resurgence of interest in relationship-based practice and re-affirmation of its significance for effective practice have given grounds for optimism that more humane approaches are being rediscovered (Megele 2014; Ruch, Turney and Ward 2010).

In contrast, qualitative research is a relatively new phenomenon compared to the social work profession and has a different relational trajectory. Developing, as Hollway (2001, p.13) puts it, 'in the shadow of positivism', qualitative research has always had to struggle to justify its existence and its distinctive characteristics, one of which is the focus on relationships in the research process. Consequently, discussions regarding how relationships are understood in qualitative research have largely been determined by the dominant discourse of objectivity associated with positivism, which configures the researcher and research subject as separate, rational individuals. From this positivist standpoint, subjectivity and any notion of relationship are problematic. The overriding endeavour is to minimise their significance – their interference in the research process – by rendering objective, as far as possible, any hint of subjectivity or relationality. In this context, reflexivity, another distinctive feature of qualitative research, is simply a means to an end, that is, the means by which subjectivity can be rendered objective, rather than being understood as important in its own right as a different source of knowing. Hinshelwood (2014), in his comprehensive response to the challenge faced by psychoanalytic research, suggests that one of the issues or problems is how subjectivity is understood:

> The field of observation is a subjective one, yielding subjective data. But in addition the means of gathering data is via an instrument that is equally subjective, the person of the psychoanalyst. Without the objective data of natural science, Freud's claim that psychoanalysis can 'take its place as a natural science like any other' (Freud 1938b, p.158) appears to be defeated. It is perhaps a 'science of subjectivity' instead. (p.9)

Price and Cooper (2012), writing about research from a similar psychoanalytic perspective, but considering its application to a wider field of professional contexts, make a similar point. Referring to the idea of 'social scientific' research methodologies, they suggest that subjectivity needs to be embraced as a rich resource, rather than being perceived as an inevitable annoyance:

> Transference, countertransference, unconscious identifications and projection of unprocessed material into the research supervision arena should not be considered as problems, rather they are the richest and most valuable means of accessing the unconscious field of inquiry. The epistemological debates surrounding the status of such data are real, and we must be prepared to engage with them. But in our view the psychoanalytic observational method is just that – a systematic discipline for studying the subjective and unconscious life that can be acquired in the same way as any other qualitative method. (p.64)

And while these excerpts come from a particular theoretical perspective, we would argue that the issue of how subjectivity, and the research relationships that it accompanies, is addressed, is a central component of all qualitative research, regardless of its theoretical underpinnings.

Compounding this challenging epistemological backdrop has been the ascendency of the evidence-based practice (EBP) movement with all the positivistic trademarks that define it. Briggs (2005), describing this aspect of the contemporary research landscape, refers to EBP as driving:

> a wedge between research and professional experience. The hammer which drives home this wedge is a methodological one, so that aligned on one side, representing EBP are quantitative, positivist, experimental and quasi-experimental, while on the other side are qualitative, observational, naturalistic, methods. Thus the EBP movement has tended to nullify research which is extremely important in social work, and which aims to connect quantitative and qualitative, validation and discovery, comparison and in-depth understanding. (p.18)

In recent years, despite the powerful influence of this epistemological and methodological context, more nuanced and, in our view, more accurate, representations and understandings of the research subject and research relationships have emerged, and this book is a contribution to these developments.

UNDERSTANDING RESEARCH RELATIONSHIPS: SUBJECTIVE OBJECTIVITY AND OBJECTIVE SUBJECTIVITY

A distinctive characteristic of qualitative research, if not *the* distinctive characteristic, in all its diverse forms, is the role played by people, whether as participants or researchers, and the relationships that are created between them. According to Shaw and Holland (2014), approximately 70 per cent of qualitative research in social work involved researchers conducting interviews, with ethnographic observation being another popular and widely used qualitative method. Given the centrality and significance of relationships in qualitative research, their careful management from the outset to the conclusion of a project is vital if the full potential of the research is to be realised.

In a chapter by Gergen and Gergen (2000) entitled 'Qualitative Inquiry: Tensions and Transformations', published in Denzin and Lincoln's (2000) seminal *Handbook of Qualitative Research*, an optimistic and encouraging note is struck with regard to the actual and potential value of research relationships. In the section on 'Research as a Relational Process' they state:

> Experiments in reflexivity, literary form and multiple voicing, for example, have injected new vitality into the research endeavour. Yet there is good reason to press farther in such pursuits. Earlier we stressed the inextricable relationship between research and representation. (p.1038)

They go on to state, 'In this sense every form of representation – like a move in a dance – favors certain forms of relationship while discouraging others' (p.1038).

For Gergen and Gergen the reframing of research as representation, which generates communicative processes as opposed to fixed research outcomes, means that the overarching aim of research becomes the creation of productive forms of relationship.

It is how these relationships are created and sustained in the context of research and their significance for, or even as Gergen and Gergen would suggest, as, research findings in their own right, that is the focus of this book. Shaw and Holland (2014) refer to how in the process of co-constructing meaning the understanding of behaviour is mediated through a primary emphasis on what things mean to people and on how the meanings emerge through the research process, that is, through the research relationship. And, paradoxically, it is on account of the inevitable and unavoidable nature of these relationships that investigating and surfacing them can be problematic.

Adopting a devil's advocate position in relation to the debates regarding subjectivity and objectivity, Price and Cooper (2012, p.57) pose a rhetorical question: Can objective research 'unmediated by the human sensibilities and language of the researcher…ever really speak to the emotional dimension of a social setting?' Hinshelwood (2014), in his efforts to address the challenge of subjectivity in the context of the natural sciences, provides something of an answer in his suggestion that seeking to realise orthodox scientific status is a false aspiration. Instead he proposes a more realisable and realistic ambition: the promotion of the 'science of subjectivity' (p.9). Contributing to these discussions and debates, Hollway (2009, p.160) advocates that we need to go 'beyond the binary of realism and relativism by working rigorously through the implications of the principle of using researcher subjectivity as a way of knowing'.

Understanding the pivotal role relationships play in the research process requires careful attention being paid to them. The imperative for this is heightened given the criticisms of qualitative research that abound (Briggs 2005; Hinshelwood 2014). The significance of a trustworthy and comprehensive reflexive strategy is immediately apparent, although not necessarily easily achievable. Most research methodology books that explore qualitative research relationships and the crucial role of reflexivity configure it in rather narrowly defined ways, as a conscious and tangible phenomenon (Bryman 2001; Ritchie and Lewis 2003), and from this perspective it is operationalised in relatively straightforward ways, such as the production of a reflective diary. In contrast, the distinctive relationship-oriented approach of this book, which is significantly, but not exclusively, influenced by psychoanalytic theoretical frameworks, invites the reader to engage with the complex and contested ideas surrounding researcher subjectivity, objectivity and reflexivity. We seek to deepen and expand our understandings of how reflexivity operates to embrace the unconscious, invisible aspects of relationships, from which research relationships are by no means exempt.

THE PRACTITIONER RESEARCHER IDENTITY

Distinctive to the chapters that follow is the professional identity of the authors. All have been, or still are, social work practitioners and find themselves researching aspects of practice that have for some reason or other caught their attention. The practitioner researcher identity that arises out of this constellation of circumstances is in its own right a fascinating and complex phenomenon. In the chapter that follows, Ilse Julkunen explores how in recent years understanding of the centrality of practice research and the pivotal nature of the relationships that is established with research partners and participants.

Drawing on the language of ethnography, one of the challenges that practitioner researchers encounter is 'how to make the familiar strange'. In many instances, and the chapters in this book are no exception, practitioner researchers are researching familiar territory. Not only is it familiar, it is often quite ordinary, and hence requires a 'theory of noticing' and 'deep attentiveness' (Hollway 2001, p.6). Yet, paradoxically, as Hollway acknowledges, 'parochialism is universal' (Hollway 2001, p.6). Price and Cooper (2012, p.55) similarly recognise how the ordinary everyday is often initially perceived as uneventful, as if 'nothing happened'. But if, through careful observation, attention focuses on 'everything that happened', the ordinary becomes both interesting and extraordinary.

RECIPROCITY IN RESEARCH RELATIONSHIPS

It would be inexcusable to be considering the centrality of relationships in research processes without mentioning the place of ethics. In so much research literature discussions about conducting ethical research place considerable emphasis on the significance of research being non-maleficent (Ruch 2014). While an indisputably important feature of research, the preoccupation with not harming anyone has led to far less attention being given to the capacity of research to generate beneficence; and use of the term 'beneficence' alludes to something more than simply remuneration of individuals in cash or kind for their participation in a research project. It refers to the unexpected benefits that arise in the context of the research relationship. Writing about this elsewhere (Ruch 2014), I highlighted both the intentional and unintentional benefits that can arise for participants in research projects. Developing these ideas led to the recommendation that prior to the commencement of a research project consideration needs to be given to all potential forms of beneficence. Drawing on Bion's (1962) psychoanalytic concept of 'containment', it is possible to design and conduct research in ways that address the relational and emotional dimensions of the research process from the outset and throughout a project's life. Acknowledging the significance of relationships in research from the start maximises the likelihood of them contributing to more informed findings specifically and to more beneficial relational experiences in general:

> According to Hollway and Jefferson (2012) attention to 'process' brings with it recognition, respect and containment. This processual stance acknowledges the ongoing ethical responsibilities that are central to psycho-social research and to 'containing' research relationships, referred to by Clarke and Hoggett (2009, p.22) as 'relationality'. For alertness and attentiveness of this order to be sustained, researchers need a willingness to become vulnerable themselves through exposure to the challenging experiences that research generates. In addition it requires researchers to possess the reflexive skills and strategies to make sense of these embodied dimensions of the research process. The creation of 'containing' research relationships, with the capacity to facilitate the development of relational benefits that permeate beneath the surface of the research, requires researchers who are morally active and contextually situated (Shaw, 2008; Hugman, 2010) and who are themselves well contained. (Ruch 2014, p.535)

I go on to say:

> Currently containment is conceived primarily as an unexpected 'benefit' arising from the research relationship. The findings from this research suggest that it is possible to explicitly design research with the potential to be containing and capable of generating relational benefits, with the associated positive implications for

the research process and outputs. A note of caution and realism is necessary too. It is not inevitable that research designed to offer containment will do so. Nor is it a foregone conclusion that 'containing' research will automatically generate relational benefits. It is imperative, therefore, that our understanding of these complex but potentially enriching dimensions of the research process is expanded. Therein lies the challenge for qualitative researchers. (Ruch 2014, p.536)

It is perhaps the potential of reciprocal relationships that Gergen and Gergen (2000) are also alert to:

The researcher ceases to be a passive bystander who generates representation products communicating to a miniscule audience. Rather, he or she becomes an active participant in forging generative communicative relationships in building dialogues and expanding the domain of civic deliberation... with this challenging re-conceptualisation of research we can and should become progenitors of relational practices. (p.1039)

MAKING AND SUSTAINING RELATIONSHIPS IN RESEARCH

The chapters that follow provide diverse and lively accounts of relationships with a wide range of individuals and groups. Common to them all, however, is the capacity of each researcher to engage sensitively with not only their research participants but also with key gatekeepers and significant 'others' in the field who had influence over how/if the research was commenced, how it was conducted and how it was concluded. These accounts reinforce for the reader the importance of researchers being mindful of the *breadth* of relationships, in terms of who needs to be approached in order for the research to progress, and of the *depth* of the relationships with regard to the often intimate and sensitive issues they can evoke. Negotiating access, entering the research field and leaving it require attention to detail and a thoughtful, reflective mind-set, qualities abundantly displayed in the subsequent chapters. Without these relationships the research that is reflected on in the following chapters would not have got off the ground.

REFERENCES

Bion, W. (1962) *Learning from Experience.* London: Heinemann.

Briggs, S. (2005) 'Psycho-analytic Research in the Era of Evidence-based Practice.' In M. Bower (ed.) *Psycho-analytic Theory for Social Work: Thinking Under Fire.* London: Routledge.

Bryman, A. (2001) *Social Research Method.* Oxford: Oxford University Press.

Clarke, S. and Hoggett, P. (2009) 'Researching Beneath the Surface: A Psycho-social Approach to Research Practice and Method.' In S. Clarke and P. Hoggett (eds) *Researching Beneath the Surface: Psycho-Social Research Methods in Practice.* London: Karnac.

Cooper, A. (2005) 'Foreword.' In M. Bower (ed.) *Psycho-analytic Theory for Social Work: Thinking under Fire.* London and Didcot Parkway: Routledge.

Freud, S. (1938b) *An Outline of Psycho-analysis: The Standard Edition of the Complete Psychological Works of Sigmund Freud,* Vol. 23. London: Hogarth.

Gergen, M. M. and Gergen, K. J. (2000) 'Qualitative Inquiry: Tensions and Transformation.' In N. Denzin and Y. Lincoln (eds) *Handbook of Qualitative Research.* Thousand Oaks, CA: Sage.

Hinshelwood, R. D. (2014) *Research on the Couch: Single Case Studies, Subjectivity and Psychoanalytic Knowledge.* Didcot Parkway: Routledge.

Hollway, W. (2001) 'The psycho-social subject in "evidence-based practice".' *Journal of Social Work Practice 15,* 1, 9–22.

Hollway, W. (2009) 'Applying the "experience near" principle to research: psycho-analytically informed methods.' *Journal of Social Work Practice 23,* 1, 461–474.

Hollway, W. and Jefferson, T. (2012) *Doing Qualitative Research Differently.* London: Sage.

Hugman, R. (2010) 'Social Work Research Ethics.' In I. Shaw, K. Briar-Lawson, J. Orme and R. Ruckdeschel (eds) *The Sage Book of Social Work Research.* London: Sage.

Megele, C. (2015) *Psychosocial and Relationship-based Practice.* Glasgow: Critical Publishing.

Price, H. and Cooper, A. (2012) 'In the Field: Psychoanalytic Observation and Epistemological Realism'. In C. Urwin and J. Sternberg (eds) *Infant Observation and Research: Emotional Processes in Everyday Lives.* Didcot Parkway: Routledge.

Ritchie, J. and Lewis, J. (2003) *Qualitative Research in Practice: A Guide for Social Science Students and Researchers.* London: Sage.

Ruch, G. (2014) 'Beneficence in psycho-social research and the role of containment.' *Qualitative Social Work 13,* 522.

Ruch, G., Turney, D. and Ward, A. (eds) (2010) *Relationship-Based Social Work: Getting to the Heart of Practice.* London: Jessica Kingsley Publishers.

Shaw, I. (2008) 'Ethics and the practice of social work research.' *Qualitative Social Work 7,* 4, 400–414.

Shaw, I. and Holland, S. (2014) *Doing Qualitative Research in Social Work.* London: Sage.

Chapter 3

DOING PRACTICE RESEARCH THAT MATTERS

BUILDING RELEVANT AND SUSTAINABLE RESEARCH RELATIONSHIPS

Ilse Julkunen

INTRODUCTION

There are many studies that confirm that research relationships are essential if we are to increase our understandings of effective dynamics in social work practices, find more sustainable solutions for practice and develop welfare policies and practices within the complex dynamics of the social work field (Dal Santo *et al.* 2002; Julkunen and Karvinen-Niinikoski 2014; Marthinsen *et al.* 2012; Shaw and Lunt 2012). However, few studies have critically examined how relationships are formed and sustained in research and how they impact on the research findings. Ethnographic studies have shed light on the researcher's access to the field and action research approaches on multi-voiced and heuristic research processes. Social work, however, may be unique in representing a field of complex dynamics associated with global and local practices that meet the challenges of the prevailing social and political domains (Dominelli 2012; Wrede *et al.* 2006). This responsibility raises the issue of how we can build up a knowledge base that is socially robust and goes beyond the question of how effective social work is (or evidence-based knowledge). White and Stancombe (2003), for instance, argue from a practice-based perspective in social work for the importance of acknowledging the knowledge and experience that the immediate actors in frontline practices and in policy implementation obtain while carrying out their decision making and interventions. Sirpa Wrede and her colleagues, from a research perspective in the field of health care, similarly (2006) argue for context-sensitivity in research processes, emphasising the capacity of multi-voiced practice and experience to generate robust knowledge for practice.

This book tries to dig into the productive forms of research relationships in practice-based research in social work and give examples of studies in real-life settings where these relationships have been scrutinised. Hence, the focus is not only on the research process and research findings but also on an actor relational approach for understanding the relationship formations in practice-based research processes. I will start by explaining what I mean by practice-based or practice research and present some theoretical foundations for analysing the dynamics of the research relationships. I argue that these may increase our understanding not only of the impact relationships may have on research findings but also on the relationship-formation processes that are relevant in practice-based social work research. In dealing with relationships in practice-based research settings, I seek to emphasise sustainability. Sustainability is important but in a complex sense. It refers to looking for sustainable spatial solutions, which are well embedded locally and historically, and to sustainable social solutions, which are broadly supported (see, for example, Boelens 2010).

REFLECTING ON PRACTICE RESEARCH

Being involved in practice research involves curiosity about practice. It is about identifying effective and promising ways in which to help people and it is about challenging troubling practice through critically examining it in order to then develop new ideas in the light of experience. It involves a commitment to locally based collaboration between researchers and research settings and practitioners and practice settings in the planning, generating and disseminating of research, and a participatory and dialogue-based research process designed to develop practice while also validating different types of expertise within the partnership. Practice research in social work is an evolving approach with much of its recent development based on an international discussion, which started with the Salisbury Forum group in 2008 (Salisbury Forum 2011). The Forum comprised an international group of researchers convened to reflect on the evolving definition of practice research and issues involved in negotiating practice research activities with multiple stakeholders.

Practice research strives to create a reflective relationship between practices in different contexts and the prevailing conceptions and theories in the social sciences. The research process is attached to the practice and its development and is focused on increasing the visibility of social work, not only in terms of describing the practice but also attempting to continuously re-evaluate how it is conceived (Saurama and Julkunen 2011). It is a question of epistemic practices (Knorr-Cetina 2001), critical reflection and thinking (Fook and Askeland 2007; Ruch 2009), dialogic processes as a source of knowledge production (Bakhtin 1981; Engeström 2014; Shotter and Gustavsen 1999) and socially distributed expertise (Nowotny, Scott and Gibbons 2001) for testing concepts and theories, as well as for validating the results in multiple and natural settings.

The process of capturing the real-life settings of professional practices and welfare policies can be designed in various ways and with various methodological approaches. The methodological dimensions of practice research include a reliance upon academic research standards and an in-depth understanding of the concrete and pragmatic issues of social work practice. Alongside this is the capacity to challenge practice in new ways (empirical, exploratory, emancipatory and theoretical) and the interpretation and dissemination of findings through dialogue with service users and practitioners that reflects a learning process (Austin *et al.* 2014). Building on the work of the Salisbury Forum, the Helsinki Forum (2014) discussed the principles and values of establishing partnerships and relationships between research and practice, highlighting the importance of the negotiation between the various partners as a specific element of the practice research process. In this context, practice research partners are equal, but different, and share different interests within the collaborative process.

Practice research is not reflected in a single philosophy or methodology but rather seeks to define practice-based knowledge through shared understandings. Uggerhöj (2014) has described it as a meeting point between practice and research that needs to be negotiated every time and everywhere it is established, because real operational change requires the involvement and participation of several different stakeholders and actors. The crucial issue in practice research is that involvement is required throughout the different phases of the research process. This emphasis on interaction and a balanced discussion between different parties provides opportunities for people to change and gain meaning through interacting. The interaction enhances the process of co-operation and collaboration in the convergence of practice and research methods (Julkunen 2011; Miettinen, Samra-Frederichs and Yanow 2009).

CLOSE INTERACTION OF SOCIETY AND SCIENCE

Practice research brings together the daily practice of practitioners and academic researchers with tools of research and may form a purposeful blend between different contexts of practitioners and researchers (Engeström 2015, p.129). What is critical and interesting in practice research is an exchange of perspectives and knowledge. Practitioners are not meant to become researchers and researchers are not meant to become practitioners. The knowledge coming out of the negotiation will challenge traditions and understandings both within practice and within research; moreover, it will challenge the participants' collaboration skills as both partners will not only meet their usual partners but also others – with different interests (see, for example, Uggerhöj and Julkunen 2015). The partners both construe their inter-subjective understanding and at the same time they remain unique individuals who sustain and defend their independent positions within their inter-dependent relationships (Bakhtin 1981; Engeström 2014).

Drawing on a science of the concrete (Flyvberg 2001) and contextualised knowledge (Nowotny et al. 2001), practice research places itself in a position between academia and professional practice. Flyvbjerg discusses the science of the concrete and phronetic science and points out:

> research focuses on values, the authors get close to the people and phenomena they study, they focus on the minutiae and practices

that make up the basic concerns of life, they make extensive use of case studies in context, they use narrative as expository technique, and, finally, their work is dialogical, that is, it allows for other voices than those of the authors, both in relation to the people they study and in relation to society at large. (p.63)

The science of the concrete includes dialogue with those who are studied, with other researchers, and with decision makers as well as with other central actors in the field; it thus shares the notion of co-evolving science as Nowotny *et al.* (2001) have put forward. The starting point is that knowledge is formed through interaction with people when people are able to encounter one another. Knowledge cannot be apprehended solely as a commodity to be transferred from one person to another irrespective of its origin. Nowotny (for example in 2003) addresses the issues of how to organise spaces of translation, claiming that validity should be repeatedly tested not only within the practice but also outside the community in different networks. It necessitates interaction that takes place in public spheres and involves an interaction between many actors, each of whom represents different interests and contributes a variety of competences and attitudes. It is this emphasis on within and outside that is interesting from a relationship-based approach.

UNDERSTANDING RESEARCH RELATIONSHIPS: AN ACTOR RELATIONAL APPROACH

Working with practice research issues for a decade in a university, community and practice setting at the practice research unit of Mathilda Wrede Institute in Helsinki, I have come to the conclusion that the key ingredient for practice research in social work is getting clued up on research issues, by which I do not simply mean that the translation of research into action goes through close collaboration. Being clued up means something more:

- Being well-informed, possessing reliable information on a particular subject.

- Being shrewd, having or showing keen awareness, sound judgement and often resourcefulness, especially in practical matters.

• Possessing a sharp intelligence, hardheadness and often an intuitive grasp of practical considerations.

And this is where I want to draw attention to what we may mean by research use. Do we look at research as dissemination and thereby put all our efforts into organising smooth translations? We tend to forget that translating practices into research and research issues into practice is not a static process but involves significant shifts in how we as actors interpret, construe and relate to each other.

Much of the need for practice research has focused on the disconnection between research, practice and policies, especially the limited use of research findings by practitioners and policy makers who fail to see how research can contribute to the development of practices and policies. In evaluating the dissemination and utilisation of practice research, Dal Santo *et al.* (2002) emphasised the importance of organisational and community factors in enhancing research utilisation. For research to be utilised, the knowledge generated by research must be relevant to the dilemmas facing practitioners and policy makers. At the same time, the nature of the communication channels between researchers and practitioners needs to be taken into account when assessing the likelihood of research utilisation. They concluded that the most important factors in enhancing research utilisation are to establish clarity in the early stages of defining the problem at hand and to strengthen communication in the agency researcher partnership during the whole process, especially noting the importance of identifying potential conflicts between the different actors involved.

With regard to the complexities of linking research to practice and practice to research, Latour (2005) reminds us that ideas are spread by people who are *interested in the idea*; therefore, we need to critically assess and take into account how actors are involved within these research and development contexts. We also need to identify who the actors are that we need to involve.

By focusing on *leading* actors, Luuk Boelens (2010) draws upon the ideas of Latour (2005). For Latour the facts are realised and distributed only because an increasing number of actors become interested and involved through sustainable and flexible alliances. Building on the concepts of 'leading or focal actors' emerging out of evolutionary economics and urban sociology (Boschma and Frenken 2006; Yeung 2005), Boelens argues that it is possible to make their interests coincide on meaningful issues. The more they coincide, the more durable they will be. So, instead of pushing towards objectivity and representative democracy, Boelens pinpoints power and subjectivity as central themes in the actor-relational approach. Furthermore, he draws on Michel Calloon's (1986) translational approach or a participant engagement framework. Calloon developed this well-known framework while studying the anchorage of scallops in the Mediterranean area. He was concerned to find answers to how scallops could be anchored again in the area and he understood that he needed the assistance of key local actors: the team researcher, the fishermen and the scallops. By including the scallops Calloon made way for including the human and non-human elements in practice. In the beginning these three universes were separate and had no means of communication with one another. At the end a discourse of certainty had brought them into a relationship with one another in an intelligible manner. This would not have been possible without the different sorts of displacements and transformations, negotiations, and the adjustments that accompanied them. It was also possible because at the outset no a priori category or relationship was used. Calloon himself was overwhelmed by the process, but only afterwards. He asked: Who at the beginning of the story could have predicted that the anchorage of the scallops would have an influence on the fishermen? Who would have been able to guess the channels that this influence would pass through? These relationships became visible and plausible only after the research.

This example mainly shows that the distribution of roles (the scallops that anchor themselves, the fishermen who are persuaded that the collectors could help restock the Bay, the research colleagues who believe in the anchorage) is a result of multi-lateral negotiations during which the identity of the actors is defined and tested. The process started with a problem definition and with conflicting expectations, and ended in new conceptualisations and shared meanings. These processes display changing relevancies inscribed in the activities people came to know through practice (Engeström 2014).

Calloon found that four key questions needed to be asked in order to scrutinise the elements of the complex process. These can be summarised as follows:

1. *Problematisation:* It is important to ask what the issue and phenomenon are that require a solution and how the problem is identified by the different actors.

2. *Interest:* How invested are the different actors in the solution to the issue and how do they conceptualise their roles and responsibilities?

3. *Visions:* Here it is crucial to analyse how the different actors see their role in a new setting and how they can be encouraged to change and have new visions.

4. *Mobilisation:* The anchorage of new working models and what forms of allies are mobilised.

These four stages are comprised of critical elements for both understanding, organising and analysing the research relationships. Although this framework seems to hold a specific structure, a prerequisite for research relationships is openness and flexibility towards actor identification. The actors may live, spend time or work in the locality and have an involvement with the issues in question. However, Boelens points out that actors who are distantly connected may also be involved. The only criterion, he says, is that the actors are able and willing to act like leading actors. This is consistent with the view that actor-network associations are fundamentally open and cut across different universes. Innovation often emerges from these crossovers.

Engeström (2014) has interestingly added a new dimension in looking at the interplay in research in practice by focusing on the process of meaning construction. With an emphasis on dialogue her starting point is that the object of human conduct is reflexively constituted, being outside and inside at the same time. Humans choose aspects of things that are relevant for them emotionally and cognitively, but the meaning construction cannot be presupposed; rather the focus should be put on the actors' awareness of boundaries to be crossed. She claims that we need to pay more attention to the subjective mechanisms that allow actors to enter an extensive space where the potential for the developments of new insights and new knowledge can be found.

DISCUSSION

Karin Knorr-Cetina (2001) has emphasised that the emergent phenomena of the modern knowledge society challenges traditional ways of understanding the meaning and nature of practices. She refers to the concept of epistemic practices as open, question-generating and complex, appearing to have the capacity to unfold indefinitely. A central understanding in this is emergence. Phenomena, events and actors are viewed as mutually dependent and mutually constitutive, and they actually emerge together in dynamic structures, as Tara Fenwick (2010) discusses in relation to the complexity of researching professional collaboration. For a professional practice, such as social work, this means that the embedded relationships – both human and non-human – emerge through the continuous rich and recursive interactions among these elements. It means also that we need to understand that real-life settings are 'criss-crossed by other places and temporalities, as well as by absent third parties' (Engeström 2014, p.122). From a research perspective the focus should be on tracking inter-relationships among different levels and dimensions.

More concretely, it implies an openness to the dialogue and negotiation process. To be able to establish negotiation processes throughout a practice-based research project, each partner needs to be open to critical assessment regarding the traditions associated with doing research and/or social work practice. Emergence not only enables continuous adaptive change, it also enables self-organisation (Fenwick 2010), just as Calloon's example showed us.

In order to build a more unified understanding of the focus of practice research, the collaborative or co-productive knowledge production processes require a process of managed communication between different stakeholders (Nowotny 2003). Calloon (1986) pinpointed critical elements of a careful initial analysis of the present problematics being focused on and the importance of negotiating actor relations throughout the process. Practice-based research starts and defines the processes by recognising the importance of relationships that promote respect and understanding among the other partners, as part of a negotiated and shared struggle.

Boelens' notion, building on the translational approach of Calloon of leading focal actors, suggests that the problematisation phase includes and describes a system of alliances and associations between different actors, thereby defining the identity of the process and what the different actors 'want'. The critical issue is to identify possible actors or stakeholders who are ready to invest in the exploration of opportunities and possibilities. It is more a 'bottom-up' perspective, engaging actors both from within and outside of the professional practice, thus emphasising both power and subjectivity. This may open up sustainable, trusting and long-lasting relations, which take on important significance in practice-based research.

The complexities embedded in epistemic practices, such as social work, urge us to trace the on-going dynamics that both reveal and create 'what matters'. The chapters in this book all scrutinise practices in social work and by doing so try to trace the inter-relations and dialogues embedded in it that have significance for both the research process, as well as the research findings.

REFERENCES

Austin, M., Fisher, M., Julkunen, I. and Uggerhöj, L. (2014) *Practice Research*. Oxford Bibliograhies in Social Work. Oxford: Oxford University Press.

Bakhtin, M. M. (1981) *The Dialogic Imagination: Four Essays* (ed. Michael Holquist, trans. Caryl Emerson and Michael Holquist). Austin and London: University of Texas Press.

Boelens, L. (2010) 'Practice and practising theory: Outlines for an actor-relational-approach in planning.' *Planning Theory 9*, 1, 28–62.

Boschma, R. and Frenken, K. (2006) 'Why is economic geography not an evolutionary science.' *Journal of Economic Geography 6*, 273–302.

Calloon, M. (1986) 'Some Elements of a Sociology of Translation: Domestication of the Scallops and the Fishermen of St Brieuc Bay.' In J. Law (ed.) *Power, Action and Belief: A New Sociology of Knowledge*. London: Routledge.

Dal Santo, T., Goldberg, S., Choice, P. and Austin, M. J. (2002) 'Exploratory Research in Public Social Service Agencies: An Assessment of Dissemination and Utilization.' *Journal of Sociology and Social Welfare 29*, 4, 59–81.

Dominelli, L. (2012) *Green Social Work*. Cambridge: Polity Press.

Engeström, R. (2014) 'The interplay of developmental and dialogical epistemologies: Outlines.' *Critical Practice Studies 15*, 2, 119–138.

Fenwick, T. (2010) 'Complexity science and professional learning for collaboration: A critical reconsideration of possibilities and limitations.' *Journal of Education and Work 25*, 1, 141–162.

Flyvbjerg, B. (2001) *Making Social Science Matter: Why Social Inquiry Fails and How It Can Succeed Again*. Cambridge: Cambridge University Press.

Fook, J. and Askeland G. (2007) 'Challenges of Critical Reflection: "Nothing Ventured, Nothing Gained".' *Social Work Education 25*, 5, 520–533.

Helsinki Forum (2014) 'Helsinki statement on social work practice research.' *Nordic Social Work Research 4*, 1, 7–13.

Julkunen, I. (2011) 'Knowledge-production processes in practice research – Outcomes and critical elements.' *Social Work and Society 9*, 1, 60–75.

Julkunen, I. and Karvinen-Niinikoski, S. (2014) 'Socially Robust Knowledge Processes of Local and Global Interest in Social Work.' In T. Harrikari, P. Rauhala and E. Virokannas (eds) *Social Change and Social Work.* Aldershot: Ashgate.

Knorr-Cetina, K. (2001) 'Objectual practice.' In T.R. Schatzki (ed.) *The Practice Turn in Contemporary Theory.* London: Routledge.

Latour, B. (2005) *Reassembling the Social: An Introduction to Actor-network Theory.* Oxford: Oxford University Press.

Marthinsen, E., Julkunen, I., Uggerhöj, L., Rasmussen, T. and Karvinen-Niinikoski, S. (2012) *Practice Research in Nordic Social Work: Knowledge Production in Transition.* Critical Studies in Socio-Cultural Diversity. London: Whiting and Birch.

Miettinen, R., Samra-Frederichs, D. and Yanow, D. (2009) 'Re-turn to practice: An introductory essay.' *Organization Studies 30,* 1309–1327.

Nowotny, H. (2003) 'Democratising expertise and socially robust knowledge.' *Science and Public Policy 30,* 2, 151–156.

Nowotny, H., Scott, P. and Gibbons, M. (2001) *Re-Thinking Science.* Cambridge: Polity.

Ruch, G. (2009) 'Identifying the "critical" in a relationship-based model of reflection.' *European Journal of Social Work 37,* 659–680.

Salisbury Forum (2011) 'The Salisbury Statement on Practice Research.' *Social Work and Society International Online Journal 9,* 1. Available at www.socwork.net/sws/article/view/2/12, accessed on 2 December 2015.

Saurama E. and Julkunen I. (2011) 'Approaching Practice Research in Theory and Practice.' *Social Work and Social Sciences Review 15,* 2, 57–75.

Shaw, I. and Lunt, N. (2012) 'Constructing practitioner research.' *Social Work Research 36,* 3, 197–208.

Shotter, J. and Gustavsen, B. (1999) *The role of 'dialogue conferences' in the development of learning regions: doing 'from within' our lives together what we cannot do apart.* Stockholm: Centre for Advances Studies, Stockholm School of Economics.

Uggerhøj, L. (2014) 'Learning from each other: Collaboration processes in practice research.' *Nordic Social Work Research 4,* 1, 44–57.

Uggerhöj, L. and Julkunen, I. (2015) 'Guest editorial: Negotiating practice research.' Special Issue on Teaching Practice Research. *Journal of Teaching in Social Work.* In press.

White, S. and Stancombe, J. (2003) *Clinical Judgement in the Health and Welfare Professions: Extending the Evidence Base.* Maidenhead: Open University Press.

Wrede, S., Benoit, C., Bourgeault, I., Teijlingen, E., Sandall, J. and De Vries, R. (2006) 'Decentred comparative research: Context sensitive analysis of maternal health care.' *Social Science and Medicine 63,* 2986–97.

Yeung, H. W. C. (2005) 'Rethinking relational economic geography.' *Transactions of the Institute of British Geographers New Series 30,* 37–51.

Chapter 4

ETHNOGRAPHY ON THE 'FRONT LINE'

WHY SOME TEAMS STRUGGLE AND OTHERS THRIVE

Judy Foster

INTRODUCTION

My interest in finding out what impacts on our ability to think in pressured situations was stimulated when seeing young children flourish with sympathetic teachers but falter with others. My own thinking can be obliterated by strong emotions – particularly fear, anger or anxiety – or when I am confused by worry and preoccupations. I noticed the different effects on staff performances when introducing the qualities of a 'learning organisation' into a social services department. My own capacity to think is considerably affected by service users and their worlds, managers, colleagues and the current policy and working environment. What is it like for others?

During the last 40 years society has moved away from a co-operative and community-based approach to one based on individualised risk and reward. Social work practice has reflected this trend, reducing its attempt to help the excluded to re-engage with their communities. However, in assessing users for services, treatment or intervention, social workers still tacitly acknowledge Donald Winnicott's definition of social work as 'largely counteracting disintegrating forces in individuals, families and in localised social groups' (Winnicott 1965, p.227). The complexity of the relationship between the worker and service user, which both constrains and illuminates professional thinking, is little considered by current inspection and regulatory regimes.

Relationship-based practice has two main components: the external relationships between client and social worker that provide practical support and service user empowerment, and the internal relationships that hold the intellectual and emotional content. Social workers need to hold both aspects in mind during their working day. Inspired and intrigued by my own experiences, and particularly in light of the poor public view of social workers following the Victoria Climbié Inquiry (Department of Health 2003), I registered on a doctoral programme. My motivation was to see for myself what went on day-to-day in an ordinary social work team. In order to explore this I posed the question: 'What happens to social workers' ability to think on the job?' I thought the most productive methodology would be to take an ethnographic and psychodynamic approach to observation, followed by interviews with participants to further explore their relationship with clients. Alongside these methods I intended to use my reflexivity skills to interpret what I observed, both intellectually and emotionally. In the course of my research I observed how social workers in three inner city adult services teams spent their time, and explored the relationships that they formed with service users.

THE THREE TEAMS

The District team

This team worked with younger adults with chronic illness. The team had 21 staff including three on maternity leave (the deputy manager, one of three senior social workers and an administrator). Two respected locum social workers left during the research, which added to the pressure on staffing. It was a permanent challenge to meet government timescales for conducting assessments. I made six observation visits, ten informal visits for interviews, and undertook 20 interviews with volunteer staff members over a four-month period.

FIRST IMPRESSIONS OF THE DISTRICT TEAM

The team was focused on people whose adult lives had been disrupted by crippling illness, strokes or brain damage. Two years earlier the District team had inherited 250 unallocated cases following a restructuring and had a real fear of drowning in the work. They counteracted this by investing heavily in the duty system to prevent the demands from accumulating, referring to the need to 'keep the work flowing', to 'unstick any blockages' and to make sure 'nothing is lurking in the cupboard'.

Both they and their clients were worried about being ignored. The team welcomed my research, with comments such as 'nobody comes to see us!' The team was based on the outer boundary of the borough, ironically inaccessible to their chronically sick or disabled service users. When I looked from the window and saw the cemetery beyond, I thought, 'That says it all – society wants to bury them!' At my introductory visit I became increasingly uncomfortable with the amount of time the area manager was spending with me, but found it difficult to break into his torrent of words. I felt I was drowning under the flow of information – just like the team itself.

The Hospital team

This team arranged the discharge of isolated elderly people into residential or nursing care within a two-day deadline under the Delayed Discharges Act 2003. There were 22 staff in the team at the start of my research. Departmental restructuring and sickness led to vacancies in all four management positions by the end of the period. I made six observational visits, eight further visits when interviewing, and held six interviews with social workers who volunteered to talk to me. The research took place over three months, with a break after the first month while I obtained further ethics approval from the NHS.

FIRST IMPRESSIONS OF THE HOSPITAL TEAM

The team had agreed enthusiastically to my research after my visit to a team meeting to describe its purpose. However, the service manager in my first meeting had warned: 'I always say to new applicants "Forget about hand holding – it's a conveyor belt here." We are always under pressure from hospital targets so I have recruited two locums to take up the flack [sic].'

I thought her Freudian slip between 'slack' and 'flack' exposed her feelings of vulnerability, and the sense of being in a war zone under fire. Identifying her major concerns, she said: 'Staff sickness and staff retention – we are all so stressed and tired, I don't know how much more we can cope with.'

When walking through a long, 28-bed ward, an old lady, like a little sparrow, had pushed her chair out from the bedside to catch people, repeatedly asked in a distressing way, 'Are you the Doctor? I want to go home.' Her cotton robe was hanging open at the chest and I felt confused as to whether to stop and straighten it. But what would I do when she clung to me? And would that make it worse? I walked on to the meeting room, disturbed by the scene as well as the sense of desolation and despair.

The specialist multidisciplinary
Community Mental Health team

This team worked with homeless mentally ill adults. The team volunteered to take part in the research in response to my letter to mental health service managers across the city. There were 18 staff members, eight of whom were part-time, including the job-sharing managers. I made six observational visits and a further eight visits for interviews, when I interviewed 11 staff who volunteered. I completed the research in two months.

FIRST IMPRESSIONS OF THE HOMELESS MENTAL HEALTH TEAM

The team was in a different part of the city. It had been established with extra funding in the late 1980s to provide specialist mental health services for homeless mentally ill people. This followed the shocking murder of a commuter by a vagrant. After meeting the staff, I was accepted on condition that I did not observe supervision sessions. This turned out to be an early indicator of their ambivalence to being observed, which was a major feature of the research.

The Mental Health team's most defining features were its gritty 'front-line' feel and its professionalism. The sensation of being in the middle of a dirty, noisy and somewhat dangerous district was illustrated on an early visit:

I found a Securicor van half-blocking the office door. Its lights were flashing and loudspeakers were broadcasting 'Help! Securicor driver requires assistance – call the police!' I saw a dishevelled woman inside the van speaking on her mobile. When I gestured towards her she shook her head, not wanting help. Once I was inside the office, the building seemed to shake with the racket and there was no way of escape.

DOING RELATIONSHIP-BASED RESEARCH

The rationale for using ethnography and interviewing

I was aware that pressure from a decade or more of inspections and audit had blurred the veracity of factual presentations. I was convinced for the purposes of my research that I needed to be present rather than rely on staff keeping time sheets of activities. It was the only way to understand what went on day-to-day in a social work team. Ethnographic techniques felt like an appropriate research method for this multiple-case study since, as White notes, 'by attending to how work actually gets done, rather than to how it should be done, ethnographic data can form the basis for fruitful dialogue between research and practice' (White 2001, p.114).

Rather than spending six months to a year immersed in the chosen organisation, Shaw and Gould (2001) refer to 'a range of structured, time-limited approaches to ethnography which can be relevant to the pragmatic character of social work programmes and practice' (p.140). More recently, an analysis by the Behaviour Insight team (Department for Education 2014) of initial decision making in children and families services confirmed the confidence gained after only one or two observational visits to five local authorities generated by 'seeing for oneself'.

Most researchers feel nervous when seeking out participants, and negotiating a working relationship with individuals and the group. Most groups also feel apprehensive at the thought of being observed for a prolonged period of time. Shaffir and Stebbins (1991) warn that 'Fieldwork…is usually inconvenient, sometimes physically uncomfortable, frequently embarrassing, and to a degree, always tense' (p.1).

Familiar with a formal observer role (having earlier trained in organisational, group and individual consultancy), I knew about the need to keep an eye on the objective events happening, the emotional atmosphere, and my own inner experiences (Hinshelwood and Skogstad 2000). This would allow for awareness of 'the disintegrating forces' that the social workers were struggling to counteract. I limited the 'psychodynamically informed' observations to six for each team –

as many as the teams and I could tolerate. But waiting in the office to interview volunteer members of staff provided another valuable source of information to answer the question: 'What happens to thinking opportunities at work?'

Interviews with staff were essential to gain insights into the pressures and rewards of work with each client group. They helped understanding of the major dynamics in the team and correlation of information across the three teams; for example, assessing the coherence of policies, the amount of professional development going on, the opportunities for mental space, and the way that the work was handled.

My concerns on the need to prove objectivity were modified by Cooper's (2009) view: 'good practice-near research seems to me to *depend* upon subjectivity and emotional engagement with the subject of the research' (p.438). This indicates that accurate analysis depends on researcher reflexivity, the use of the minds of others (in writings or discussion) and a constant ethical watch from the third position. Regular research seminars and supervision provided opportunities to challenge my interpretations and broaden my vision of the findings.

Negotiating access

After a few false starts, one senior manager said she was minded to allow me access as the research 'made few demands on the social workers, it was unusual to have someone interested in seeing actual work and the research might help the social work field in the future'. She invited me to a meeting with her managers. The social workers competed for my attention: one offered the chance to observe 'the tension between the hospital's need for acute beds and the patient's need for a timely discharge'; another ended his pitch rather sadly saying that 'no one ever visits us!' I realised that turning down his offer would come over as a rejection not only of him and his staff but of his service user group (adults aged 19–64 years who had an acute or chronic illness or disability and their families). I agreed to research both teams to counteract society's marginalisation of this group. But I was acutely aware there would no longer be time to research a children and families team.

I recruited the third team by writing to all the district mental health managers across the city. From 120 teams I had just one response, which I quickly followed up.

All three team managers invited me to a team meeting to explain the research proposal to staff, letting me know later their unanimous agreement. But, that was only the start of the negotiations. My reception varied dramatically. For instance, in the District team there was little delay between their agreement and my arrival; the open plan office had spare chairs to sit on and a wide group to observe; I was shown the kitchen and invited to make a coffee there (though the hostility to my eating there was palpable); one of the team leaders identified with the project and informally took charge of my involvement. He suggested observation opportunities, teased me over unexpected absences, and was interested in my past experience. His colleague was more suspicious, so I was careful to sponsor his charity run to encourage his agreement to allow me to sit in on his duty morning the following week.

This was in complete contrast to the Hospital team where, after three visits, I found that any open debate took place at the Multi-disciplinary team (MDT) meetings on the wards. Hence, I needed NHS research approval to continue, causing a three-month gap between initial visits and the main body of the research. Staff sat in a number of small rooms, the manager was away sick, no one offered me a chair or showed me around – understandable perhaps from a group dedicated to 'moving people on'. My only welcome was from the newest and most temporary administrator, who greeted me and found me a coat peg. By my second or third visit staff curiosity was aroused and people approached me to be interviewed, allowed me to sit nearby and observe them at work, or accompany them to their wards for the weekly multidisciplinary meetings.

The Homeless Community Mental Health team was based above a medical surgery, with the majority of staff in an open plan office. The social work team leader had recently started a job share with the permanent team leader, who was a community psychiatric nurse. Given my experience with the Hospital team, I encouraged him to introduce me to other team members, find me a desk, have a coffee together and share his feelings, which transpired to be mainly of apprehension. This helped considerably my informal interaction with team members. Given some later challenging and hostile episodes, I was relieved and grateful that we had managed the start so well.

In order to develop trust and form a working relationship, I asked for advice from managers and social workers – how would it be best to go about something? I said I genuinely welcomed their help and also asked for their advice on the suitability of attending different meetings. If they were not happy, I accepted their decision. It was also helpful to be able to reassure team members that their working practices were acceptable. I was often asked to compare current practice with some past golden era – 'You must find the work we do so different?' I could respond that while an individual case may have received more attention, there had also been considerable inequalities in service provision.

Reflexivity in the field: Undertaking observations

The simplest way to involve everyone was to observe a team meeting, so I did that first with each team. But there were still surprises. In the District team, the manager confirmed that the meeting the following day began at 9.30 am. I arrived at the office at 9.10 to find the meeting had already started. I had been completely wrong-footed. At least I was able to sit behind the group and gradually recover. The manager spoke for two hours without a break, handing over to the assistant director to explain management restructuring for another hour. Despite questions and discussion before she left, it felt like a gruelling experience.

In contrast, the Hospital team meeting was participative, well-chaired and included some case discussion. It was held in a large room where I could again sit behind the group. The team meeting in the Mental Health team was equally well run. However, the group of staff and the room were much smaller, which contributed to a disconcerting intensity. I found that while the team discussed a violent and unpredictable applicant for a hostel vacancy, I had an unpleasant memory of a conflict that morning at home that had left me feeling damaging and incompetent. This stray thought may have been a counter-transference experience (Ogden 1982) giving insight into one of the group's concerns and an illustration of the 'disintegrating forces' they grappled with.

Due to a tightening of NHS and Higher Education Ethics approval, and a reluctance to involve service users, the closest I could observe social workers with clients was on duty in the District and Mental Health Teams, in the hospital during MDT meetings on the wards and additionally in case discussions in the Mental Health team.

Consequently I sat in on two duty sessions in the District and Mental Health teams and two Multi-disciplinary ward meetings in the hospital.

In the District team I experimented with separating the observation from my interpretation. This was intended to allow the reader to use his or her own judgement on both the observations and the analysis (Skogstad 2002). During one Friday afternoon's course of duty I made notes about the staff actions, as follows:

> The administrator, Sara, leant over and said that Mrs Y had rung back and cancelled the care service, because she intended to commit suicide and would not need it. The duty senior, Leroy, rang Mrs Y again, emphasising that his service could not collect her children. He sounded supportive but clear. She repeated her threats and put the phone down.

> Meanwhile, there was a line-up of staff who had come to voice their protest to the area manager about taking on a 'no recourse' case from another borough (Mrs H, a destitute asylum seeker and her daughter).

> At the same time, the duty senior was insisting that Kath, the duty social worker, should follow up that morning's abortive visit to Will, a brain-damaged chronic alcoholic, to assess his situation.

> A man rang Sara to say that his 50-year-old wife, who had cancer, was back in hospital.

> The duty senior, Leroy, rang about a referral from housing about Mr and Mrs Z. He told me that they had been worried about the wife, who was in a wheelchair with a degenerative disease, but her husband would not let anyone into the house, and when they had offered an assessment, Mr Z had refused it. While they were wondering what to do, Mr Z had a massive heart attack. He was now in hospital with severe brain damage at only 38 years old. Now they needed to arrange emergency respite care for his wife.

That evening I wrote up these researcher reflections:

> There were now a number of situations taking place, any one of which demanded careful thought. The duty senior's ability to contain the anxieties of referrers, service users and staff was a major factor throughout the afternoon. His ability to prioritise accurately

and to think carefully were essential, faced with a hysterical mother, a destitute mother and child, and a brain-damaged alcoholic – all needing attention.

Mrs Y, whose need for help and assistance had been recognised, had made two hysterical threats of suicide during the afternoon.

Mrs H may have been mentally competent, but as a destitute person she had no voice in the plans being made for her, and we were uncertain as to her motivation.

Will was a chronic alcoholic with brain damage. The red alert on his file indicated that he was potentially violent and abusive too.

Initially, I felt sad for the man who had made the effort to let us know that his wife with cancer was failing fast.

This feeling was then displaced by the shocking reminder that heart attacks and strokes do not happen only to the very old – here was a service user (Mr Z), who had just suffered severe brain damage at the age of 38, and his disabled wife was mentally alert but physically unable to care for herself. There was also a sinister undertone to this case. Why had Mr Z refused anyone admission to the house? What was his relationship with his wife? The primitive notion that his heart attack was some form of retribution crossed my mind.

I was aware that I was picking up just small fragments of information overheard from telephone conversations, or heard from the other side of the room. It was surprising to realise how vividly I could construe a story on such little evidence, as with Mr Z.

As well as reflecting on the emotional content of the work in the duty team, I later analysed from my records how many person hours were spent trying to interpret policies and procedures or were wasted in the search for the latest correct form and so forth. During the afternoon one social worker spent half an hour trying to identify the current version of a form – she was eventually advised to ring a colleague in another office for a definitive answer. Members of the team spent time throughout the afternoon debating how to handle the difficult 'No Recourse' case of a homeless mother and child. The time added up to a surprising five person hours – the Service manager two hours in the lead; a team manager half an hour; the duty manager one hour; the senior social worker who then took on the case one hour; and two other social workers, who briefly took part in the debate, half an hour.

In the Hospital team I attended three multi-disciplinary team meetings. I found my first, which followed my walk through the 'geriatric' ward, unbearable:

> The meeting did nothing to cheer me. The consultant questioned the ward doctor on the patients while the other nine staff from all disciplines sat in silence for two hours (18 person hours, equal to two and a half days' work). My notes were as monosyllabic and lifeless as the meeting.

My second meeting, with an experienced social worker and ward sister, was more accessible as they ran through the register:

> *Nurse:* You heard about this next man who came in not eating or drinking. He has a history of a number of things including TB. He came from a nursing home. The nursing home basically wants him transferred somewhere else. He's not for 'resusc'.

> *Social worker:* That home is usually pretty good – what is the matter?

> *Nurse:* I don't know. They say that he has behavioural problems. He is fine in hospital but is a problem for the nursing home. He is quite anti-social. He pees into cups. He also does other pretty horrible things. So they want him to have an EMI [Elderly Mentally Infirm] assessment.

> *Social worker:* We need some further investigation there. Gail might know.

The influence of psychoanalytic theory on the observer

Kleinman (1991), a professional ethnographic researcher with no particular knowledge of psychoanalysis, makes a clear link between a fieldworker completing a naturalistic study and the work of psychoanalysts such as Ogden: 'Fieldworkers do not think of feelings as disturbances that impede objectivity and thus should be overridden. Rather, feelings become resources for understanding the phenomenon under study' (p.184).

Ogden (1999), along with Bollas (1987) and Armstrong (2005), argues that the observer's subjective thinking, reflection, reverie and rumination are in part prompted by unconscious elements in the individuals, organisations and groups with whom they work. This is equally true for an observer researcher, and these feelings provide important data – whether they are considered as counter-transference or subjective.

Ogden (1999) explored the reverie and thoughts that he had in analytic sessions with his patients, and linked them to the work of the session. Everything that happens in an observation is pertinent. Valuable unconscious insights may become evident if these musings are considered rather than ignored. A focus on his own emotional state can induce 'a feeling of intense emotional immediacy and a resonance with the patient's unconscious experience in the present moment' (p.77). This was occasionally my experience in the field and underlined the need to maintain trust.

For instance, in the District team I often felt that the activity in the office seemed to form a thick, impenetrable surface, like ice on a pond or a heavy fire blanket, trapping all the repressed and unpleasant aspects of the community under the surface (think of a painting by Hieronymus Bosch). I felt that the workers alone stood between this 'hell' and the local residents. At the end of my time with the Hospital team I noted my reflections:

> I had an unpleasant sense of vertigo, as if I was on the edge of a cliff or volcano and everything was falling away around me. Was it due to too much pressure and rush? Or was it my worries at home? I did not know. I wanted to distance myself from the hospital and all that it stood for. The next day I learnt that the last remaining manager was not returning from sick leave. My sense of vertigo *had* related to the team – its management really was falling apart.

Speck (1994) refers to times when over-identification with a client can strain one's professional boundaries and sense of reality. I was probably over-identifying with the team and in my unconscious equating this task of holding everything together with my family's task of holding my just-widowed mother-in-law's world together.

The Mental Health team projected a lot of anger and hostility onto me. I reflected:

The quick talk became quicker and Ed made a sharp in-joke about Fraser, which I missed. Everyone looked at me to see how I'd reacted. I said, 'I missed that', and put down my pen and stopped writing. The meeting came to an end. I mentioned that it was the end of Part One of my research and there would no more observation.

The group eventually pressured me to stop making notes. I felt compelled to put my pen down, unable to continue recording due to the intensity of feeling in the group. The group used Ed (a young white psychiatrist) with his sharp tongue to attack me as the outsider, just as they used him to express their frustration with their clients and each other. I could not continue. I told them that this was my last piece of observation. That evening a friend asked me, 'Have you finished your surveillance yet?', articulating the team's emotions. Perhaps their defensiveness was to hide unacceptable attitudes that had begun to emerge.

Interviews

The 'semi-structured' interviews provided the opportunity to hear about the rewards and frustrations of working in each team. This opportunity to speak confidentially was important for the staff. One member of the District team, who had asked to be interviewed early in the process, refused to allow senior staff into the room until we had finished. As he closed the door on them he said: 'You were asking about decision making. Well, no one is allowed to make decisions round here!'

After describing cases, the interviewees mentioned what thinking space they had; how they had joined the team, the opportunities they saw for getting support and help in the team, what further training they had undertaken and what their plans were for the future. I made a digital recording of each interview, transcribed with voice recognition software. I completed random checks for accuracy on each transcript against the initial recording. By setting an informal atmosphere – my first question was 'Tell me about a case that's been giving you grief' – interviewees enjoyed offloading and sharing some of their experiences. For instance, a specialist placement officer in the Hospital team talked of the daily confusion in the district on discharging patients:

The consultants shout that they want acute beds. Nurses panic. Doctors panic. They don't fill out an assessment. They don't understand the procedure. They don't understand that to arrange a discharge, a social worker has to go to the hospital, assess the patient, come back and do a load of stupid paperwork.

Members of the Mental Health team were quick to say how well they handled conflict, but several interviewees had examples of where they had disagreed with a superior or colleague:

My supervisor thinks that we should do a mental health assessment. But I'm really not happy – I don't see any justification to do that. He is just one of those interesting characters who do not really fit into any niche.

Another told me bitterly how colleagues refused to let her second-year social work student attend the staff support group. She said that nursing students who came for six weeks did not attend, but her student was there for six months. An experienced professional, and one of the few black members of staff, was shocked on return from holiday to find that a white colleague was working with the middle-aged black woman whom she had assumed was her client.

When asked to describe a case they were really pleased with, some tales of exceptional negotiating skills emerged. In the District team a recently qualified social worker successfully challenged the Department's eligibility criteria with the Assistant Director:

I bumped into Sue out shopping with her carer last week. She goes once a week now. That's superb – she hadn't stepped out of her house at all for four years. She was in a terrible situation physically. I tried everything. Then I got her to wear socks and parked right outside the shop so she could get some shoes. That's what I did. It was the only way I could think of to get her out.

ANALYSIS

At the end of each fieldwork period I had three sources of material: observation records, interview transcripts and consistent records on both of researcher reflexivity. I had set out to find out 'what supported and what impeded thinking on the front line'. This provided a natural start to the data analysis. I used a qualitative data analysis software program (MAX QDA) designed to support the development of bottom-up findings, such as those used to develop grounded theory. I could put the material together in a variety of ways using different codes, and add memos to capture passing thoughts and connections in order to enrich the analysis.

My initial coding covered all the incidents that appeared to support or inhibit mental space for the social workers from both interviews and observations. I coded all interactions either as 'supportive' (for example, asking and receiving advice from a manager or neighbour) or 'inhibiting' (such as interrupting someone in the middle of another task – for example, the business manager while she calculated invoices). I looked at how they spent their time, such as dealing with concerns about continuing care funding, or arranging accommodation and transport for a mother with no recourse to public funds. These codes produced visible and tangible surface factors that influenced their thinking.

I structured the material, drew clusters of what was appearing, and gradually developed and defined some bridging concepts. I identified a further four areas in addition to my initial proposition of mental space that contributed to the thinking of the teams and creative capacity. I drew these areas out of the material and confirmed them through past professional experience and published research (Fetterman 1998). I examined all the metaphors, similes, adjectives and actions people used in interviews or in observations for meaning, and noted how they often reflected the unconscious world of their clients. I looked at the different ways the staff group let me operate in the team as an indication of how the group dealt with external uncertainty. I searched for issues that took the workers' focus away from service users and found wide variations between the teams in the need to interpret legislation, handle internal procedures such as complaints, provide supervision and other forms of mental space, encourage autonomy to motivate people in their work, promote continuous professional development, use staff imaginatively to provide support structures in the team, and hold regular, well-attended, participative team meetings.

The use of tables (Miles and Huberman 1994) easily demonstrated the differences between the three teams and proved useful in analysing specific areas, such as the different policies that each team had to respond to.

TABLE 4.1 HIGH-CONFUSION AND HIGH-IMPACT POLICIES

Policy	District team	Hospital team	Mental Health team
NHS and Community Care Act 1990	HU LC	HU LC	nil
No Recourse to Public Funds	HU HC	nil	MU HC
Community Care (Delayed Discharges) Act 2003	nil	HU LC HI	nil
Continuing Care	HU HC	HU HC	nil
Direct payments	HU LC	nil	nil
Adult Protection procedures	HU MC HI	MU MC HI	HI
Fair Access to Care Services (eligibility)	HU LC	HU LC	nil
Adult complaints procedures	HU MC HI	nil	nil
Rough Sleepers Initiative	nil	nil	HU LC
Mental Health (Amendment) Act 1983	nil	nil	HU LC

TABLE KEY
HU High use **HC** High confusion **HI** High impact
MU Medium use **MC** Medium confusion
LU Low use **LC** Low confusion
Nil = researcher not aware of use of this legislation in the team

The research findings were summarised in one pentagon:

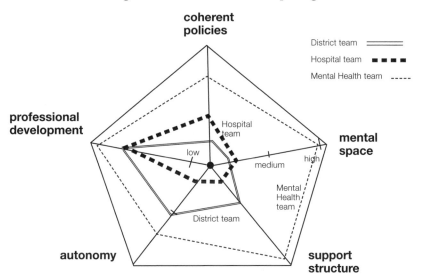

Figure 4.1: Five enabling factors

In this research the District team were two managers down; and while the three remaining managers provided a supportive environment for the staff, there was little formal mental space. The majority of the team remained well-motivated and by all volunteering to be interviewed, the team used the researcher's presence to bring about change in the office structure and to introduce more reflective space through regular case discussions.

The Hospital team operated within strong policy guidelines, were keen to develop professionally and used what little mental space there was, but they had appalling administrative support and no autonomy at all. They were on a factory conveyor belt. Not surprisingly, they had the weakest relationships with their service users.

In contrast, the Mental Health team worked within a clear legal framework, with the ability to prioritise effort and continuously reflect on progress with service users, involving close interaction between experienced members of staff and those newer to the field. The degree of autonomy and mental space allowed the team to maintain morale in challenging situations. The research demonstrated the importance of having all five of the identified factors underpinning a successful team.

CONCLUSION

This chapter has set out how research into relationship-based practice was applied in a study of the working and thinking practices in three different social work teams in an inner city. The choice of particular research methods required commitment from the teams and assurance that the demands on them would enhance rather than detract from their work and would be limited in time. Successful relationships with teams required catching and holding their interest and involvement. This worked well with the District team and slightly less well with the Mental Health team, where some members remained defensive, but was more problematic in the Hospital team – reflecting the degree of engagement achieved.

The value and veracity of psychodynamically informed observation in understanding a group's behaviour became increasingly apparent as the research progressed, and it was further tested by discussion of emerging findings in regular research seminars and supervision. The separation of observation records from the interpretation allowed effective reflection on the emotional content of the work observed, as in the extract from the duty team. Semi-structured interviews facilitated useful open comment from staff being interviewed. The full verbal records of the interviews were checked for accuracy and annotated with reflections of the researcher's reactions. Valuable insights were made by reflecting on my own emotional state during the observations and interviews, showing how the observer's stray thoughts may be used productively by understanding how counter-transference can give insight into the concerns of a group. Ultimately, however, the success of this research depended on keeping the 'research objects' at the centre of the project through continuous consultation and explanation.

REFERENCES

Armstrong, D. (2005) *Organisation in the Mind. Psychoanalysis, Group Relations, and Organisational Consultancy.* London: Karnac.

Bollas, C. (1987) *The Shadow of the Object. Psychoanalysis of the Unthought Known.* London: Free Association Press.

Cooper, A. (2009) 'Hearing the grass grow: emotional and epistemological challenges of practice-near research.' *Journal of Social Work Practice 23*, 4, 429–442.

Department for Education (2014) *Clinical Judgement and Decision-making in Children's Social Work: An Analysis of the 'Front Door' System.* Consultation Paper. London: DfE. Available at www.gov.uk/government/publications/clinical-judgement-and-decision-making-in-childrens-social-work, accessed 19 September 2015.

Department of Health (2003) *The Victoria Climbié Inquiry*. Report. London: DoH. Available at www.gov.uk/government/uploads/system/uploads/attachment_data/file/273183/5730.pdf, accessed 19 September 2015.

Fetterman, D.M. (1998) *Ethnography: Step by Step*. London: Sage.

Hinshelwood, R. and Skogstad, W. (eds) (2000) *Observing Organisations: Anxiety, Defence and Culture in Health Care*. London: Routledge.

Kleinman, S. (1991) 'Field-workers' feelings: What we feel, who we are, how we analyse.' In W. Shaffir and R. Stebbins (eds) *Experiencing Fieldwork: An Inside View of Qualitative Research*. London: Sage.

Miles, M. and Huberman, M. (1994) *Qualitative Data Analysis*. London: Sage.

Ogden, T. (1982) *Projective Identification and Psychotherapeutic Technique*. New York: Jason Aronson.

Ogden, T. (1999) *Reverie and Interpretation: Sensing Something Human*. London: Karnac.

Shaffir, W. and Stebbins, R. (eds) (1991) *Experiencing Fieldwork: An Inside View of Qualitative Research*. London: Sage.

Shaw, I. and Gould, N. (2001) *Qualitative Research in Social Work*. London: Sage.

Skogstad, W. (2002) 'Psychoanalytic observation – The mind as research instrument.' *Organisational and Social Dynamics 4*, 1, 67–87.

Speck, P. (1994) 'Working with Dying People: On Being Good Enough.' In A. Obholzer and V. Z. Roberts (eds) *The Unconscious at Work*. London: Routledge.

White, S. (2001) 'Auto-ethnography as Reflexive Inquiry: The Research Act as Self-surveillance.' In I. Shaw, and N. Gould (eds) *Qualitative Research in Social Work*. London: Sage.

Winnicott, D. (1965/1990) 'The Mentally Ill on your Caseload.' In D. Winnicott *The Maturational Processes and the Facilitating Environment*. London: Karnac.

Chapter 5

COLLABORATIVE KNOWLEDGE PRODUCTION IN RESEARCH PRACTICE

THE DEVELOPMENT OF THE 'MIRROR' METHOD IN TEAM SETTINGS

Laura Yliruka, with Jonna Vanhanen, Outi Jaakkola and Erja Saurama

INTRODUCTION

This chapter addresses research and knowledge production in social work and the research relationships that evolved while developing a reflective method for practice: the 'Mirror'. The Mirror is a method that I developed in co-operation with my social work team in 2003 in order to support reflection on and evaluation of our own work (Yliruka 2006). At the time, I was a social worker in adult care.

In this chapter I describe how I asked a social work team that has been one of the co-developers of the method to reflect on the use of the method and the development of the model, as the approach has required a reflective partnership between the researcher and social work teams. This relationship has been crucial in my PhD study, which has been conducted as a participatory action research process. In my study I have analysed the development process and the consequences of adopting the model in the social work teams (Yliruka 2015).

In this chapter I analyse how the social workers see the Mirror method supporting their expertise by creating a mental space (see Foster in Chapter 4 in this book) and reflective structure (Yliruka 2015). By reflective structure I mean practices that support learning and working, and that target knowledge creation in social work as a means to enhance the flexible, open and critical expertise of social workers. I am also interested in what kind of concrete knowledge production can be enhanced by the Mirror process.

There are three different data used in this chapter. The first source is based on a focus group interview in spring 2014, where I interviewed one social work team, including the co-writers, about their experiences of using the Mirror method. This is also part of the body of research data in my PhD study. The second source is my PhD research data from the so-called 'Hand Mirror Forms', where members of the teams using the Mirror method reported their immediate experiences from Mirror peer evaluation meetings during the pilot project in 2006–2008. The third data source is from a social work team that has been writing observations during 2013–2014 about what we refer to as the 'Weak Signals' in the Mirror process.

It is important that the participatory action research or practice research underpinning this work strengthens the agency of the participants. One way of achieving this is by writing an article together, as we have done here. My co-writers are Jonna Vanhanen, a senior social worker, and Outi Jaakkola, a social worker, and they have analysed the focus group interview data from their perspectives. Erja Saurama, Professor of Social Work at the University of Helsinki, has analysed the Forms of Weak Signals.

In the nexus of this chapter is a child welfare social work team, which I was working with as a researcher and which has been actively using and reshaping the Mirror for its own needs. Throughout the years, I have had contacts with the team on a regular basis. I have been interested in their work with the Mirror method. My involvement with the Mirror method has been twofold: primarily I have been co-developing the method, and, therefore, have been interested in the method itself. In addition, I have been interested in the implementation processes of the Mirror method in different social work organisations. Through those processes I have looked at how different reflective structures are constructed in practice and what they enable/produce in social work organisations.

I will start by giving a brief outline of the initial development phase of the method. By asking questions about the different phases of the development and research process, my co-writers contribute their thoughts and observations. A crucial phase of all development processes is when a method is applied and anchored within a setting (Koivisto 2006; Yliruka and Hänninen 2014). Jonna and Outi describe how further development of the Mirror method within a child welfare working team has had an impact on carrying out child welfare work. They talk about building a mental space (see Foster in Chapter 4 in this book) as part of the team's everyday work.

Erja Saurama explores her collaboration with the team as a professor of practice research. This has not been part of my PhD process and has made a valuable contribution in showing how to create knowledge on the basis of observations done in the Mirror process by the child welfare team. Erja's contribution has opened up a horizon for knowledge creation in co-operation with social workers and a researcher using the Mirror method. She encouraged the team to collect thought and insights that they considered important but which were not yet on the agenda.

My chapter shows how the joint development and use of reflection methods for practice and research purposes have made it possible to produce qualitative information on social work in order to enhance practice. The Mirror method and its processes challenge individuals and their peer groups to ask themselves again and again, at different points, what is important in their work, what feelings the work evokes and what they can learn from their reflections. This is a story of an inspiring and fruitful co-operation that harnesses knowledge creation in the best interests of social work practice.

CREATING A MIRROR

In 2003 I was working as a social worker in a social services unit focusing on providing financial support for adults with a group of social workers interested in developing their own work to bring about a more holistic professional orientation. I had just finished my own master's thesis relating to tacit knowledge and self-evaluation in social work and my new working community had a positive atmosphere towards further development. We started to work together to create a continuous evaluation model suitable for our own work, inspired by reflective evaluation ideas (Shaw 1998). The team developed a method that would help us do our work in a more reflective manner. We wanted to gain a better understanding of our work and the phenomena involved. We initially started out with self-evaluation, but we soon discovered the strengths of a peer-based approach and the importance of tapping into the diverse range of experience available in a working community. We wanted to reinforce an analytical and critical approach towards our own work and we wanted to analyse the structural factors and parameters that have a bearing on how we do our work (Yliruka 2006).

Through experiential learning (Dewey 1938), we were able to develop a self- and peer-evaluation method, which we named the 'Mirror'. In theoretical terms, we could define the Mirror as being a type of evaluation method that supports reflection and combines individual learning processes with collective learning, thus also promoting transformative learning (Mezirow 2000). Subsequently, the method has been tested and piloted in many different social work contexts, such as school social work and child welfare services. The method has been built on a research process that has included research into the requirements of service users and professional communities (Kivipelto and Yliruka 2012; Yliruka 2011, 2015; Yliruka and Hänninen 2014; Yliruka and Karvinen-Niinikoski 2013).

The Mirror method is based on the use of a series of self- and peer-evaluation forms, guiding individual workers and teams towards reflection (see Yliruka 2011, 2015 for more specific guidance on using the forms). The way I see it is that instead of being about whether to use structures in social work, the method is about how to use structures in subtle ways, so as to retain the individuality of workers and individuals. It thus builds on different forms to be filled in, which structure the individual as well as the collective reflection. Research has shown that dialogue-intensive use of the Mirror strengthens both the cognitive and emotional capabilities of working communities. Its open themes – the analogy is easily found in qualitative group interviews or discussions – challenge users to make sense of and reflect on their own work from several angles. The shared structure of trust reinforces the ability of a working community to deal with the different service user situations and challenges that it faces (Yliruka 2011).

The Mirror method has evolved in recent years to incorporate the service user perspective more strongly than the previous version (Yliruka 2011). Service user evaluation was developed in Jonna and Outi's team. The newest application is a Service User's Mirror in adult social work (Pitkänen 2012).

The Mirror process consists of five main steps (see Figure 5.1):

1. *Self-evaluation* of the social worker's own work and preparation for the peer evaluation meeting (Mirror Hall Form).

2. *Service user evaluation* (Service User's Mirror Form).

3. *Peer evaluation discussion* within the social work team and assessment of further work (Internal Mirror Form).

4. *Follow-up* in formative or summative evaluation meetings (Rear-View Mirror Form).

5. *Drawing conclusions:* This includes the team's conclusions on the parameters of social work and on specific themes requiring monitoring or improvement (Weak Signals Mirror Form) (Jaakkola 2012; Yliruka 2011, 2013) or Prism (Yliruka 2011).

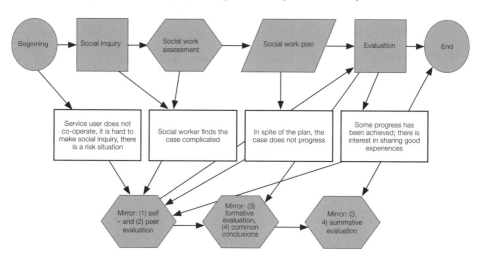

Figure 5.1: The Mirror process supports the social work process

The metaphorical name of the form, Mirror Hall, refers to reviewing one's own work from various aspects in a certain context. When using the Mirror Hall self-evaluation form, according to Yliruka (2011, p.122), the social worker reviews several elements:

1. Any opportunities and obstacles for change in the service user's life situation;

2. The established internal and external factors;

3. Resources and risks;

4. Social work targets;

5. Working method choices;

6. Assumed impacts on working methods;

7. The employee's experience of interaction with the service user;

8. His or her expertise-orientation in the service user relationship;

9. His or her role as a social worker in the service user relationship; and

10. Assumptions on how the situation may be influenced by factors related to self (gender, values, attitudes), previous experiences, or the current situation of the service user relationship under review or structural factors facilitating or hindering client work (such as the service system, established social work practices, legislation and resources).

Initially, the Mirror method was developed to facilitate client work in situations where a social worker wished to receive more support from colleagues to outline a service user situation:

> I'd like to have a discussion about how other team members perceive the service user's situation, how they would come up with some sort of prognosis and raise critical or essential factors that are significant in terms of the service user's future. (A social worker's comment from a Hand Mirror)

In typical cases, social workers have been working with a certain service user for a long time but have not been able to make progress for some reason or have reached a point where they feel stuck and unsure how best to proceed. The cases generally brought to the Mirror process are somehow seen as perplexing; they may involve considerable work and make workers especially anxious. They perceive such cases as being difficult to analyse, incomprehensible, sometimes downright dangerous. They put their own resources to the test and feel that the case gets under their skin. A service user may also have some characteristics that are personally new or strange to the worker. As a result, the Mirror builds on peer supervision but it is structured such that it can be used to identify knowledge elements and factors in support of professional development that go beyond individual service user cases. In such cases the Mirror takes on a slightly different role; it becomes a shared channel for knowledge creation and collective learning within social work:

> I wanted to inspire thoughts and discussions about how [...] families' different ways of living and thinking about issues are taken into account in social work. To what extent should we do so? And are there any issues where differences due to cultural backgrounds should not be accepted? (A social worker's comment from a Hand Mirror)

The Mirror may expand to become a forum for a more general discussion about the role of social work in society, inviting critical points of view. Such a working style may be unfamiliar to individuals or teams, which is why methods such as the Mirror method are vital to promote new ways of operating.

THE MIRROR METHOD IN A WORKING COMMUNITY – BECOMING AN ANCHOR OF DEVELOPMENT IN CHILD WELFARE WORK

Jonna Vanhanen and Outi Jaakkola are child welfare social workers in a team that started to pilot the Mirror as part of a broader dissemination project (2006–2008) for the method (Yliruka 2011). I was the researcher of the project and through these pilot groups knowledge was collected and produced as the core data for my doctoral thesis. It is interesting that I did not know Jonna and Outi at the time their pilot project started. They were not members of the piloting team at first. They became members of the team after the dissemination project had ended. The team invited me to hear how they had developed the method over many years and wanted to start to co-operate with me. I heard that they were very proud of their team and what they had accomplished by using the Mirror method. As a case this was extremely interesting and inspired me to dig further into what the use of the Mirror meant for the working community. I encouraged the social workers to write about their process. That is why we decided to do a focus group interview. Here Jonna and Outi base their analysis on the views raised in a focus group interview with the entire team.

Over the years, the team has developed its use of the Mirror method further in response to changes in the parameters of their work and new professional challenges. The municipal child welfare service system in Helsinki has been going through major organisational changes. Child welfare social work has been split according to the phase of the process in a child's needs assessment, community social work and social work during placement.

Of the original team that introduced the Mirror into child welfare services, only two social workers are still part of the team. Nevertheless, the Mirror has been carried along with the team all the while and new members have also gradually adopted and reshaped it. At present, the team using the Mirror method is carrying out short-term social work in child welfare needs assessment.

Nowadays, it would be fair to say that the role of the Mirror method in child welfare work does more than simply provide immediate support for working with service users. Use of the Mirror shines the spotlight on the interactions taking place in different relationships. Through analysing the focus group interviews we found three critical elements: *a shared professional mind-set, a broader scope for social work informed by structural perspectives and a focus on knowledge creation.* The team has become open to dialogue, recognising the importance of continuous improvement of social work in child welfare services. The Mirror method helped the team reflect on the ways that we and others carry out our work. We noticed that it strengthens our professional identity at an individual level and at the level of the whole team's shared understanding of social work within child welfare services.

A shared professional mind-set

The Mirror method has gradually become part of a shared professional mind-set, present in workers' ways of speaking, patterns of thought and professional actions. Workers have become more confident as communication partners, more active in surfacing and sharing problems and sometimes even becoming critics by questioning professional working methods both in client work and in relation to the team and the professional community.

> The Mirror is not just a method but a way of thinking, operating and doing this work. It's visible in day-to-day work in how people discuss, bring up issues in the team, even in a critical tone. Sometimes you notice in some other context that you are being misunderstood, when your own opinion is taken as criticism, while you are used to that sort of conversation style where you can throw your thoughts out there in the sense that my opinion is no more correct than yours, but the shared view is created through joint discussions. (Focus Group, social worker 3)

The team describes how the Mirror helps individuals to understand different ways of carrying out child welfare social work. It steers thoughts away from making light of other people's work and makes room for more appreciation and respect. In the Mirror process, providing and receiving feedback on personal work is wrapped up in encouraging and appreciative words. If workers are used to working in pairs and discussing their own roles and division of work, it is also easier for them to open up their own work as part of a larger team. Mutual trust between team members builds a foundation for bold reflections, involving plenty of revelations about personal choices, values and emotions, as well as articulation of the circumstances of a service user family.

The team shares the experience that the Mirror helps social workers to analyse the personal emotions induced in them by client work. Feelings become an acceptable part of a child welfare social worker's professional identity. The Mirror enables social workers to stop and get in touch with their emotions, reflect on them together and carry out a personal way of working with their own clients, with better awareness of the presence of emotions. As the Mirror also reveals service users' emotions about child welfare work through the Service User's Mirror, workers can mirror their own feelings in relation to individual service users' emotional experiences. Emotions are analysed in relation to one's self, one's professional role and the work performed by colleagues, as well as to what service users have revealed.

And what's good about this Mirror in my opinion is that it brought to the fore those feelings that arise from situations. You should bear in mind at work how your own reactions and feelings may influence how you operate, so that you should be able to analyse them. (Focus Group, social worker 2)

In child welfare work, it is important to recognise that some service users and their circumstances will touch workers more strongly than others. Empathy involves the ability to share the feelings of another, to understand and articulate the emotions involved (Shulman 1999). The presence of empathy in client work is increased by the fact that social workers consciously aim to put themselves in the service user's position. In child welfare work, the client is the child(ren), even though the work targets the family as a whole. In general terms, the Mirror examines a service user situation from a social worker's own professional perspective, but the method also makes it possible for workers to put themselves in the position of a family member during peer evaluation.

We assigned listening roles [during self-evaluation] so that some [workers] looked at the situation from the child's perspective and others assumed the parent's viewpoint. It was quite interesting, as it made the differences between those perspectives quite visible and raised the family's internal conflicts to the fore, helping us understand how to tackle things and work on issues such as why it was difficult for the parent to see the child's needs. Like, when you put yourself in the parent's position during the Mirror session, it actually opened up the service user's personal experiences in a different way. (Focus Group, social worker 5)

Child welfare social work is loaded with ample negative and positive emotions. A social worker should never forget to look at a service user family's situation from many sides. The Mirror method may help the social worker to broaden their perspective to cover the needs and experiences of a child or a parent and their mutual relationship. With the Service User's Mirror, the Mirror process also indirectly presents the experiences of a service user, which means that the worker's thoughts and reflections are also influenced by the service user's own emotions and the impression formed of the service user. The service user perspective introduces a certain interactive element into the discussion, where the service user is present in the form of impressions, as a source of emotions and as a person relating his or her experiences.

Broadening the scope and strengthening expertise

The team describes the Mirror as a method that makes more equal the mutual relationships between team members as it allows them to express different opinions, ways of thinking and ruminations on working methods. As a structure, the Mirror brings together reflections that support the worker who has performed self-evaluation in making choices concerning their way of working. The reflections that team members have produced as part of the Mirror process serve to guide their understanding of child welfare social work towards a coherent interpretation of ethical and high-quality social work that helps service users in an effective way. This includes work done at the individual service user level and collective structural social work level.

> There are different levels, there's the level of knowledge that develops in everyone who is present at a meeting, about what types of methods there are, what the people are like, what their thought patterns are like, about the team's joint way of working, and then there's information about services and phenomena that is specifically recorded, so that's also being created, but not all information is written down, instead it's stored by those people who are present. (Focus Group, social worker 3)

The Mirror provides the team with a chance to sit back and reflect on issues in the midst of hectic client work. Reflection calls for time and space. The worker's self-evaluation heard at the start of the Mirror meeting frames and structures joint reflection among team members. After the self-evaluation, the worker reads the questions included on the Service User's Mirror Form and the service user's answers to the team. The self-evaluation is thus supplemented at the Mirror meeting by hearing the personal thoughts of the parent service user or the young service user, albeit as conveyed by the worker. The service user's thoughts about his or her own situation are present at the Mirror meeting as the service user's concerns and resources, which the service user associates with him- or herself, his or her family, the work carried out by child welfare services as well as the structures of society, according to the themes of the Service User's Mirror Form.

In the Mirror method, the service user indirectly becomes part of the team's joint knowledge creation process. When the team took up the Mirror method, its focus was on self- and peer evaluation relating to client work and the content-related questions of work. Through the Mirror method the team provided individual members with concrete suggestions in support of client work and feedback on their professional work. It was only at a later stage that the team members were also able to perceive the benefits of the method from a societal as well as an individual perspective.

> Perhaps it yielded the most in terms of client work to begin with, how to do client work, but it gradually moved perhaps more towards how it supports you in professional development. You also started to see the structural side and phenomenal level that became involved in this Mirror at some point. (Focus Group, social worker 3)

The team faced the need to develop the Mirror such that the method would also guide them more clearly towards societal reflection on phenomena relating to social work. At the same time, the team discussed ways in which the knowledge created as part of the Mirror process could be put to use in structural social work, including social reporting. That is how we realised that we needed a Mirror of Weak Signals. Over the years the team has been very active and has used several ways of raising debate (Yliruka and Karvinen-Niinikoski 2013).

Knowledge production through the Mirror

As a result of many years of development, the team has shaped two different roles for peer evaluation, which define each worker's perspective. Some workers mirror their reflections from the perspective of the questions included in the weak signals role on the Internal Mirror Form, while others do so from the perspective of the questions included in the systematic work role on the Internal Mirror Form. In the weak signals role, the underlying assumption of analysis is guiding the worker's thinking towards phenomena linked to the situation of a service user family as well as towards successes and shortcomings relating to society or child welfare work. In the systematic work role, the worker's reflections focus on the evaluation of work carried out with the service user family and on planning future work. With this division of roles in peer evaluation, the workers listen to their colleague's self-evaluation from a certain perspective, thus introducing two different dimensions into peer evaluation – the client work level and the societal level.

The Mirror method helps social workers analyse *the impact of organisational changes* on their own work and its parameters as well as the ways in which the changes reflect on service users' chances of getting help in child welfare social work situations. It is natural that changes involve a wide variety of feelings for and against. The Mirror provides an opportunity to take some time as a team to think about the altered nature of child welfare work and how social work will be carried out in a new operating environment. The team considers that the Mirror makes it possible to produce important, current and even anticipatory information to support organisational management and decision makers. Social work is about working alongside service users through various life crisis situations, while also taking a front-row seat to pick up what kinds of reflections a complex modern society introduces into the everyday lives of families with children.

> Well, if you think about the professional code of ethics for social services workers, there are definitely lots and lots of elements about how you ought to make a difference in society and intervene in the living conditions of children and young people and families, and this Mirror definitely offered lots and lots of resources for this, but it's quite a different thing, of course, to what extent we are able to promote it. (Focus Group, social worker 10)

The Mirror method makes use of various forms, which are filled in by workers at different phases of the process. These forms have also been used as research data (see for example Pulkkinen 2011). The Mirror is used to produce systematically collected information about everyday child welfare work, which could be put to use when studying the practices of social work within child welfare services.

> But then again, purely as research data, these Mirror sessions with the Service User's Mirror Forms and the Weak Signals Mirror Forms as materials, would be completely ready for use as data. (Focus Group, social worker 10)

It is possible to adopt a research-oriented and self-evaluative approach towards work in child welfare social work. Curiosity and a desire to learn from one's own work together with the team or service users will help carry out ethically sustainable social work within child welfare services. Professional confidence will also make room for other points of view. Service user feedback and joint discussions will make it possible to study one's own work as a natural part of the service user relationship in day-to-day work.

REACHING THE SOCIETAL LEVEL

After developing the Weak Signals Mirror Form, which was a new adaptation of the method, the team became more interested in tackling ethical dilemmas embedded in welfare. At that time, another university researcher, a professor of practice research in social work, Erja Saurama, became involved. Throughout the years, she participated in the team meetings, which were more and more heading towards societal questions and social reporting.

Here Erja Saurama describes the knowledge production process she was involved in with the team. She was particularly interested in how the weak signals were actually operationalised. In the next section she analyses her writings over two years.

Saurama on the Weak Signals Forms

The reason for my involvement was in the idea that as experts in everyday life, social workers have antennae for identifying new issues. When social workers complain that their work has become increasingly difficult, this partly goes to show precisely that social work is faced with new phenomena ahead of time and, at least to some extent, without the means to address them. This situation should be given its due; social workers can make use of their bridgehead in society as observers of everyday life and initiators of social debates. They also have the means to analyse their observations thanks to their research training in social sciences. According to the code of ethics for social workers, they can use their advocacy and empowerment skills in service system networks. Instead of dealing with the issues of individual service users, various collective initiatives are possible. I encouraged the team to collect thought and insights that they considered important but which were not yet on the agenda. We started to call them 'weak signals'.

The team produced the Weak Signals Mirror as an example of structural social work. I describe the Weak Signals Mirror as being a means of identifying, naming and recording weak signals in everyday work and passing them on. The aim is to draw attention to social phenomena that are yet to reach the awareness of the general public or that will become problems requiring solutions. It may also be used to raise important questions that have already been recognised and have gained meaning as part of the Mirror process. Regardless of the intended use, however, the decisive point is that the Weak Signals Mirror goes partially above and beyond individual targets of social work, thus opening up opportunities to discuss phenomena emerging with the times. The Weak Signals Mirror is like a kaleidoscope that produces different viewing angles, depending on the context. Although the Mirror is used to examine current phenomena in a proactive manner, the observer is not looking at a *tabula rasa*. The types of scenarios that open up depend on the prior experiences to which workers have become attuned. As part of the Mirror method, the social workers recorded different observations, which described the process and provided a wider subtext for the case in question. The importance of this innovation is that at the same time the social workers are able to work in multifarious levels in a very efficient way. This provides organisations with an opportunity to obtain direct information for structuring preventive actions. Help provided at an individual level must be structured as social reporting material to be communicated to the organisational management, decision makers and/or wider audiences. This calls for changes in operating methods and attitudes.

Observations documented systematically may serve as a collective wake-up call or as a messenger for the organisation or political decision makers. They may also be a key element that allows social workers to express their ethical concerns about pressures and issues relating to their service users. As such, they make the work more meaningful and expand its perspective out of the office into society. In the Weak Signals Mirror, social workers may have an effective tool for preventive work relating to their ethical duty to report any deficiencies observed both in people's circumstances and in operating practices, which is included in the professional status of social workers.

In the example case described here, the observations of weak signals is part of broader structural social work carried out within the framework of municipal social services. This way, the observations produced are also clearly connected to child welfare operating practices, 'inside' child welfare services. Gradually, the amount of completed Weak Signals Forms increased and we analysed the data and could form three different themes for attention: *inter-generational service user relationships and invisible children; the significance of being heard, recognised and touched in child welfare work; and dysfunctions in development of the service system.*

THEMES RAISED AS TARGETS OF ATTENTION
Inter-generational service user relationships and invisible children
In recent years, social work discourse has emphasised the resources of local communities when assessing the needs of children within child welfare services. Help has been sought from children's close relationship networks and extended families by means such as family group conferences. Likewise, there has been a keen desire to acknowledge children's resilience and active agency. This has been a reaction to old-fashioned, authoritarian and patronising social work, which has been based on taking children into care and severing family ties, as families and relatives have been perceived as being sources of problems rather than solutions. In its one-sidedness, however, this resource-focused positive discourse and aspiration to reverse social responsibility has led to developments such as dismantling institutional care.

The Mirror process made it possible to reveal the problematic role of service user families and relative networks. The untreated mental and substance abuse problems of parents become visible through their children's difficult behaviour and growth patterns. Workers are forced to consider the influence of traumatised parents and grandparents on children.

> A single family may cause society really high costs in the inter-generational chain. How could we break the vicious circle of problems being passed on from one generation to the next? There is a considerable need to develop methods geared towards families with inter-generational child welfare service needs or those with multiple problems. (Mirror of Weak Signals)

Maintaining a child-centred work approach becomes very challenging when parents' own disappointments and experiences of missing out build up a strong shield that prevents outside help from being channelled to the children of the family. A powerful need to keep up appearances leaves the children's plight unnoticed, making them gradually invisible. The children are only brought into the spotlight through teenage rebellion and/or attempts to break away, which is often unnecessarily late. Even children growing up in the same family have different mechanisms and chances of survival, but it is difficult to work with children living under threat of physical or mental violence.

The significance of being heard, recognised and touched in child welfare work

Another major theme that I identified in the Weak Signals Mirror entries concerned the basic set of problems involved in client work and its role as a relationship-based social work that recognises the importance of hearing the service user. Social workers do not always come to think of the fact that creating a confidential relationship also requires them to open up to their clients about their own work. In many cases, the guilt experienced by parents is also reflected in child welfare work relationships. Acknowledging emotions is vitally important, but it is also very difficult. It is easy to focus on facts at the expense of speaking up about emotions and children's rights. It would be important for a social worker to articulate the experiences raised by a service user, thus making sense of them for the service user. A parent may indeed lack the ability to recognise and express emotions, which has been reflected in family interactions. Sometimes service users even wish for actual physical touch as a gesture of compassion. Social workers, in turn, may be afraid that they will violate service users' integrity and are all too ready to retreat into an official role, which service users perceive as emotional coldness. However, these are situations where it is advisable to aim to listen to an individual service user's emotional state with a very keen ear. To put it bluntly, when you fear excessive emotional intimacy, you do not dare to relate to people at all.

Building confidential relationships also calls for a frank and outspoken approach. This is another area in which social workers feel that they have insufficient training. Is this another example of too narrowly defined boundaries of the professional role, which social workers dare not even test although it might lead to good results? Could working in pairs make it possible to find solutions to problems that seem insurmountable when working alone? When considering the difficulty of service users' circumstances, it is also necessary for social workers to turn their eyes to their own way of working: 'Why is this particular situation and this service user relationship so difficult for me?'

Dysfunctions in development of the service system

In recent years, the operating system of social work has been in a state of turbulence. Organisational changes have followed one after another, testing the resilience of both service users and staff. As an objective, providing better services under conditions of chronic labour shortages has translated into work processes being segmented, making it increasingly difficult to manage the whole. In addition to actual client work, resources are currently drained into compensating for the drawbacks caused by the system itself. The objectives that were meant to bring improvements have, in fact, turned into nuisances and perhaps even aggravated the situation even more.

The demand for fast responses in child welfare work situations does not always meet the needs of individual families and children. Building trust and achieving results make for a slow process. It can be asked whether the rate of progress is sufficient for staff – and how about management? For whom are the objectives actually created? It is still important to set objectives in order also to define the means by which objectives can be reached. In a fragmented service system, it is all the more important for all parties to adopt a conscious goal-oriented and systematic approach, as service users are forced to get used to constantly changing working conditions. Numerous transition points increase the need for attention. Each break and transition is also a risk point.

Service user relationships call for continuity and a holistic approach. In addition to breaks in the process, staff turnover and variability in working methods affect the quality of child welfare work. A continuous relationship with the same social worker can be seen to have a positive effect on the quality of work. However, the Weak Signals Mirror reveals that the deteriorating working conditions in child welfare services also accelerate staff turnover. It is difficult to demand commitment from service users while the level of commitment among staff is weak. It is often the case that service users may fall within several services, none of which has assumed overall responsibility.

DISCUSSION

In this chapter we discussed the knowledge production enhanced by the Mirror process and its structure. We went on to show how joint development and use of reflection methods made it possible to produce qualitative knowledge on social work in support of exerting influence. When social work has structures in place that allow staff to systematically deal with the cognitive, reflective and emotional elements of their work, it creates opportunities to produce information tested in several processes, thus also providing a sustainable and credible foundation for efforts to exert influence in support of the work carried out by staff.

It is the joint production of knowledge that is essential, as it benefits many parties and is also relevant in terms of making a difference. The critical question has been how we can manage to build reflective work and research practices successfully (and so as not to consume too much time) in the midst of hectic daily routines, in order to support professional social work and social workers' professional development; and how we can make them almost intrinsically serve as a means of influence as well? After all, people's willingness to make a difference may even increase when they are involved in this way of working and as part of the working structures. The experience of making a difference may already have developed through participation in joint discussions and knowledge creation efforts, which make important issues visible – the chance to speak about issues may already be a sort of precursor to making a difference, which in turn creates a natural transition into joint efforts to move things or messages forward on the basis of a shared and perhaps more structured understanding of reality.

It is worth noting that the observations and issues that social workers and service users raised have been perceived as if they were forbidden themes in recent years. However, teamwork based on mutual trust also brings about the power of acting together. It is important to keep the forms simple enough and to acknowledge that it is acceptable to record quick, as yet unanalysed entries, in order to ensure that workers keep on collecting them for further processing. It has been possible to be flexible enough and structured enough so that the Mirror method can co-exist along with social workers and their clients. Social work needs words, a vocabulary for describing its essential features as a profession and as a discipline. The Mirror users want to internalise and update this vocabulary so that it better fits their purposes. On the other hand, I am also interested in ensuring that the core content of reflective knowledge production in social work will not disappear.

REFERENCES

Dewey, J. (1938) *Logic: The theory of Inquiry.* New York: Holt and Co.

Jaakkola, O. (2012) *Lastensuojelun käsikirja: Kuvastin-malli.* Helsinki: Terveyden Ja Hyvinvoinnin Laitos. Available at www.thl.fi/fi/web/lastensuojelun-kasikirja/tyomenetelmat-ja-valineet/tyomenetelmat/kuvastin-malli, accessed on 20 April 2014.

Kivipelto, M. and Yliruka, L. (2012) 'Mirror Method as an approach for critical evaluation in social work.' *Critical Social Work 13,* 2, 102–118.

Koivisto, J. (2007) 'What evidence base? Steps towards the relational evaluation of social interventions.' *Evidence and Policy 3,* 4, 527–537.

Mezirow, J. (2000) *Learning as Transformation: Critical Perspectives on a Theory in Progress.* San Francisco, CA: Jossey Bass.

Pitkänen, N. (2012) 'Tuntuu tyhmälle, että pitää vielä erikseen todistella, että on köyhä.' Asiakaspeili Aikuissosiaalityön Asiakkaiden Kokemuksien Sanoittajana. Julkaisematon Käytäntötutkimuksen Opintojakson Raportti (unpublished practice report). Helsinki: University of Helsinki.

Pulkkinen, K. (2011) *Asiakkaiden kokemuksia lastensuojelusta. Asiakaspeili tiedonmuodostuksen välineenä. Käytäntötutkimus opintojakson raportti* (unpublished practice research report). Helsinki: University of Helsinki. Available at www.socca.fi/praksis/opiskelijoiden_kaytantotutkimuksia/kaytantotutkimuksia_vuodelta_2011, accessed 21 September 2015.

Shaw, I. (1997) *Be Your Own Evaluator: A Guide to Reflective and Enabling Evaluation.* Wrexham: Prospects Publications.

Shulman, L. (1999) *The Skills of Helping Individuals, Families, Groups and Communities,* 4th edition. Itasca, IL: Peacock.

Yliruka, L. (2006) Kuvastin reflektiivinen itse- ja vertaisarviointimenetelmä sosiaalityössä (Working Paper No. 15). Helsinki: Stakes. Available at www.julkari.fi/handle/10024/75124, accessed 20 January 2016.

Yliruka, L. (2011) 'The Mirror Method: A Structure Supporting Expertise in Social Welfare Services.' In E. Marthinsen and I. Julkunen (eds) and L. Uggerhoj and T. Rasmussen (co-eds) *Practice Research in Nordic Social Work: Knowledge Production in Transition.* Critical Studies in Socio-cultural Diversity. London: Whiting and Birch.

Yliruka, L. (2015) *Self-evaluation as a Reflective Structure. Workability, Adaptation and Development of the Mirror Method.* The Heikki Waris Institute Research Series 1. Helsinki: Unigrafia.

Yliruka, L. and Hänninen, K. (2014) Sosiaalityön arviointimenetelmän käyttöönotto toimijaverkkona. *Yhteiskuntapolitiikka 3,* 278–290.

Yliruka, L. and Karvinen-Niinikoski, S. (2013) 'How can we enhance productivity in social work? Dynamically reflective structures and dialogic leadership for transformative expertise.' *Journal of Social Work Practice: Psychotherapeutic Approaches In Health, Welfare and the Community 27,* 2, 191-206. Available at www.tandfonline.com/doi/abs/10.1080/02650533.2013.798157#.UxWw6CRE0t4, accessed 22 September 2015.

Chapter 6

EXPLORING RELATIONSHIPS THROUGH ETHNOGRAPHY
A RESEARCH STUDY OF BOYS IN SCHOOL
Harry Lunabba

INTRODUCTION

In this chapter I discuss how social encounters can be analysed and how boys' talk can be interpreted using critical realist thinking (Bhaskar 1986; Layder 1997) and the theory of social bonds (Scheff 1997). The chapter draws upon an ethnographic study (Lunabba 2013) that I conducted in two upper-level compulsory schools in Helsinki during the school year 2008–2009. The study focused on how boys' (aged 13–16 years) need for support is manifested in the everyday life of classrooms and how encounters between adults and boys are conditioned by adult-boy relationships.[1] The analysis that I present is a reflective examination of my relational processes with two 14-year-old boys, whom I have named Peetu and Santu, who I observed and interviewed during fieldwork in an eighth-grade class. I draw parallels with the relational processes I experienced as an ethnographic researcher with the relationships experienced by the teachers and other adults working in school, even though I recognise that there

---

1   The data consisted of field notes of everyday life encounters between adults and boys in schools in five different classes, as well as ethnographic interviews. During fieldwork, 34 boys, 11 girls (aged 13–16 years) and 18 adults working in school were interviewed.

are some crucial differences in the relational interplay between an ethnographic researcher and boys and that between teachers or school welfare professionals and boys. An ethnographic researcher's position in school is negotiated through different means than a teacher's position or the school social worker's position. The professional adults working in school and researchers also have differing motivations and responsibilities. My starting point is, however, that despite the obvious differences between the position of an ethnographer and a professional adult in a school, they also share some similarities that allow for comparison to be made.

First, an adult working in a school and an ethnographer conducting research in a school share the burden of being an adult. I am aware of how some ethnographic researchers have argued convincingly that a childhood ethnographer should try to establish at first hand a participatory or a childlike position in his relationship to the child informants (Epstein 1998; Kehily *et al.* 2002) in an effort to gain access to an inside child perspective. I, however, arguing from a critical realist perspective (Bhaskar 1975/2008; Danermark *et al.* 2003) would suggest that adulthood is a constitutional reality that exists beyond the social construction of individuals. My standpoint is that adults have in general different contextual resources (Layder 2006; Lunabba 2013) to children, and an adult's position is also conditioned by the institutional practices of the school. Even though an adult researcher implements a participatory approach with children (Berg 2010; Kehily *et al.* 2002), the researcher will evidently be socially categorised as an adult rather than as a child. A successful implementation of a child participant approach in an ethnographic study in school can generate a position of a atypical adult (Corsaro 1985) or a position of a least 'adult' adult (Epstein 1998), but will never amount to a full child position.

Second, an adult working in school and an ethnographic researcher studying students in school have a shared ambition to establish attunement in the relational interplay with children and young people. The concept of attunement refers to the work of Thomas Scheff (1997) and it stands for the conditions when a secure bond exists between two parties that enables mutual understanding of each other's thoughts, beliefs and feelings. I view the concept of attunement as a related term to what Kroll (2010) defines as rapport, that is, the implication of meaningful interaction where trust exists between two parties and enables a researcher to gain access to the informants' problems or difficulties. Attunement and rapport are about a genuine connection between two interacting individuals that enables an in-depth conversation and the possibility of acknowledging and sharing difficult and sensitive issues and concerns (Kroll 2010).

REFLEXIVE EXAMINATION OF RELATIONAL ELEMENTS

The use of reflexivity is often highlighted as a central process in ethnographic studies, enabling the researcher to describe and analyse how their identity, methodological approach and position, as well as their personal voice and values, influence and affect the research process (Brewer 2000). Reflexivity can be practised through various means. Gordon *et al.* (2007) presented a collective approach where the research team conducting research in various classes and schools held joint meetings that allowed them to reflect and share their experiences as well as to collectively develop analytical levels to define and describe the school setting. Ojajärvi (2015), who conducted ethnographic research in the Finnish army, describes how she used to have reflexive dialogues with one of her supervisors in the car when she travelled home from the army base. They had agreed to audiotape their conversations and some of these taped conversations were used in her analysis.

During my fieldwork I mainly worked alone even though I had the support of my colleagues working in the practice research institute.[2] I used to present my thoughts and tentative findings during our work seminars, but I also adopted the practice of audiotaping my reflections. In fact, I produced most of my ethnographic data by talking on tape during breaks in school or at a parking lot in my car after a school day. I found that the practice of talking and audiotaping my journal notes generated a high degree of emotional reflexivity in my field-data. Talking was less time-consuming and less tedious than writing and I believe that I produced more data by recording it on tape than I would have done by simply writing it down. At first it felt awkward talking to myself in my car – in an empty parking lot – but as time went by I got comfortable with the practice and allowed myself to be increasingly emotionally expressive on tape. The practice of talking on tape rather than putting my feelings down on paper was not something that I have developed for the sake of being more emotional or reflective. It started out as a convenient way for me to collect data but it proved to be far more than that and an important source of insights.

During the data analysis stage of my research I often chose to listen to the material from my tapes instead of reading it as I realised that listening to the tone of my own voice gave me more direct access to memories and emotional sensations of my experiences in school (Lunabba 2013). Even today when I listen to my field notes, I can with a high degree of certainty place myself in the immediate context and atmosphere of the situation when and where the recording took place. Hearing the recording made the actual incident being reflected on come to mind more quickly, vividly and powerfully than if I had read a transcribed recording. With the following short excerpt I illustrate how on occasion I expressed strong emotions when I reflected upon my experiences of conducting fieldwork with teenage boys in school.

Journal note (tape) 19th September 2008

Today I felt that I really should have intervened. I really wanted to confront Sauli and put an end to his behaviour. His manner towards me was totally unacceptable and I so would have liked to set him straight once and for all. What I did was that I just more or less let him insult me as I avoided being an authority in the situation. I know I rationalise this by the idea that I feel that I might have lost my child-centered position if I had been judgmental or authoritarian. What I am saying is that I wished that I could have been like that (judgmental) just this once. Set him straight. But I didn't. And a part of me feels that this avoiding strategy just does not work with a boy like Sauli. He shows no respect for me. And why should he if I just sit there and let him insult me. But then again, Sauli is an exception. He goes against every conceivable social norm, not just in relation to me but to everyone. He can be really insulting towards his classmates and teachers...

The extract reveals not just the event of me being questioned and ridiculed by a boy in class, but also some of the emotions, including frustration, that I experienced. As I will discuss further in this chapter, emotions are particularly revealing as they define the state of a relationship (Scheff 1994) and are therefore an important informative constituent of ethnographic data.

CRITICAL REALIST ACCOUNTS

Leaning on the work of Roy Bhaskar (1975/2008), Derek Layder (1997) and Thomas J. Scheff (1997), my starting point for the analysis is that social reality is an open system, involving complex elements that interfere with social activities and transform meanings of social actions. This foundational aspect of critical realism highlights that when assessing social work practices, teaching practices, research practices or any other social practices, contextual components need to be noticed. According to Bhaskar's (1986) transformative model of social activity, and what he describes as the fourth ontological limit of naturalism – social-relational-dependence – a relationship can be regarded as an ontological structure that influences the development of meaning in a social encounter. Relationships condition and contextualise the encounter, but according to a critical realistic standpoint, social structures and social relations are also reproduced and transformed through social activities (see also Archer 2003). Trustful relationships enable and insecure relationships hinder individuals in reaching out to one another, but it is also through joint activities and shared experiences that individuals can develop relationships that can go below and beneath the mundane (Kroll 2010).

To illustrate how I implemented critical realist thinking in my research, I want to introduce a short extract from an interview I conducted with the two boys I name Peetu and Santtu, both 14 years of age. I had developed a practice to begin my interviews with young people by discussing research ethics and the idea of informed consent. My starting point for this practice was that I wanted to have a standard procedure to make sure that the young people whom I interviewed participated voluntarily in the interview. I also wanted to inform my interviewees about confidentiality and how the data would be used. As the following interview excerpt illustrates, when I had this introductory discussion with Peetu and Santtu, something unexpected happened:

Harry: First of all, I want to say that your participation in this interview is voluntary; participation in any study should always be voluntary. If I ask a question you do not want to answer, you don't need to. You can leave this room any time you want. And the discussion that we have is confidential. I won't tell anybody what we talk about, with the exception of the two professors that supervise my work. They can get access to this. If I publish something, some texts about what we talked about, I will change your names and other things to make sure no one can identify that it is you who are talking...

Santtu: I don't care even if you didn't change my name.

Harry: Ok. So my question to you is: 'Do you participate in this interview voluntarily?'

Peetu: Yeah.

Santtu: No, you forced us to do this.

Harry: Come on, seriously, Santtu?

Santtu: Yeah, yeah, you did not force us.

I interviewed 45 young persons during the study, but Santtu was the only one who in any way indicated something other than assent when I posed the question: Do you participate in this interview voluntarily? Even though Santtu states later that I did not force him or Peetu to participate, it is fair to ask how I can be certain of what Santtu meant when he stated that I had forced him and Peetu to participate. It is also relevant to ask whether Peetu actually was genuine in his response to volunteer to be interviewed. How can I be certain that Peetu was not forced to participate? If I had been in a position to force him, as Santtu suggests, could he have given any other response than a conforming 'yeah'? As Epstein (1998) describes, school is a setting where adults tend to be in charge. Adults give permission to students about when they can talk, leave class for lunch or take a break (Robinson and Kellet 2002). Adults in school tend also to ask questions of children even though adults have all the right answers. From this viewpoint it is possible that Peetu gave me the answer he thought I, as an adult doing research in school, wanted to hear, in other words the 'right' answer. To examine the meanings of Peetu's 'yeah' and Santtu's 'No, you forced us to do this' I suggest we need to examine the interpersonal relational reality that existed between me and the two boys.

THE INTERLINKED ELEMENTS: POWER AND EMOTION

In the analysis I highlight two elements: the dynamics of power between me and the two boys and the emotional atmosphere that occurred in this particular moment of interaction. Based on Layder's (1997) thoughts, which are developed from Foucault's understandings of power, power and emotions are viewed as constantly existing behind-the-scene elements that occur in all social life – always there and always everywhere. Power and emotion are also interlinked elements, affecting and transforming one another. Where there is power, there is emotion and vice versa. Linking emotion and power helps to explain how power can both restrict and enable. When assuming that adults have power over children, an adult can use power to empower children and young people to speak out, or an adult can either deliberately or unintentionally restrict children from expressing themselves.

Pattman, Frosh and Phoenix (2005), who conducted interview studies with boys aged 11–14 years, describe their research strategy as young person-centered, with the aim to generate a non-judgmental and friendly atmosphere when interviewing boys. In the context of ethnographic childhood studies, many researchers have discussed at length various research strategies to overcome the obstacles caused by the unequal power dynamics in interplay with adults and children – assuming that adults rule over children (Berg 2010; Christensen 2004; Corsaro 2005; Epstein 1998; Hill 2004; Kehily *et al.* 2002). Much less attention has been given to the question of how to overcome situations where adults are in the position of the underdog, something I presume all adults working in upper-level compulsory school or in child protection social work have experienced at some time or another. Even though adults have more direct access to political, social and material resources in society and particularly in schools, within the domain of situated activity the power dynamics can be the opposite. As Goffman (1983) suggests, the encounter or the interaction order can be treated as a substantive domain in its own right. Within a particular encounter an adult can experience a young person as reluctant, disinclined, even hostile, and the power dynamics can be opposite to the usual power relations between adults and children. To give you a more nuanced idea of what my position was to the two boys presented here, I will give another example of one of my encounters with Peetu and Santtu.

> I was in between classes and decided to take a stroll around the school neighbourhood. As I turned a corner I saw a group of boys smoking. For a short moment I reflected upon how I should handle the situation. Just keep on walking and pretend that I had not seen

them, or should I confront the boys? Before I had decided, I hear Santtu shouting: 'Look guys, there is Mr Lunabba!' When Santtu shouts out my name I see how Peetu desperately tries to hide his cigarette. I can still picture the shame in his eyes. But, Santtu does not seem to mind me seeing him smoking. He looks straight at me, and smokes with a provocative confidence. Just as I had made the decision that I can't just ignore the situation, out of nowhere comes Lasse, teacher in technical handicraft. Before he has said his first word, all cigarettes are gone and the group of boys scatters.

Adulthood is not a standardised experience (Lee 2001); nor are relationships between adults and young people. The different ways people impact on one another can be defined as the level of influence they exert. I, as an ethnographic researcher, had a different kind of influence when approaching a group of cigarette-smoking boys to that of the technical handicraft teacher, Lasse. Influence can further be deconstructed in Goffman's (1983) terms to subjective and categorical influences. Subjective influence refers to the subjective power of an individual that enables a person to control others to act in their favour (Layder 2009).[2] Categorical influence refers to the power that is linked to a person's position in a contextual setting, such as the formal authority of a school teacher. It is also important to recognise the varieties of influence I had in relation to Peetu and Santtu. Santtu had a habit of questioning me and, on several occasions, showed a self-representation (Goffman 1958/1990) that could be described as obstinate. Peetu, by comparison, was more of a follower in his relationship with me. Whereas Santtu gave an impression that he was more or less indifferent to what I thought of him, Peetu was careful to maintain a positive self-representation in relation to me. After the smoking incident, Peetu wanted to reassure me that he was not a 'real smoker' and he made an effort to convince me that it was only on rare occasions that he had ever smoked. In relation to my level of influence on Santtu I did not believe that I was in a position to force him to participate in the interview, any more than I could prohibit him from smoking cigarettes in school. In fact, when Santtu said that I forced him to participate, it is a kind of a paradox, taking into consideration the level of energy I had to put into gaining his participation in the interview in the first place. When Santtu stated that he had been

---

2   Layder uses the term 'benign control'.

forced to participate, it resembled how we used to interact with one another. Santtu often said things to provoke me in an admirable, clever and frustrating way, such as when he reflected about the colour of my teeth or when he commented on what, according to him, were 'kinda queer looking shoes'. Peetu in return kind of admired me – which I have to admit was flattering. He was one of my most keen key-people who actively kept me up to date on what was going on in school. Peetu also showed a genuine interest in me, asking questions about both my study as well as intriguing details about my personal life: Is your wife good-looking? Did you use to drink and smoke when you were younger? I did not need to talk Peetu into participating in the interview. In contrast with Santtu, Peetu had announced early on to me and to his classmates that he wanted to be interviewed by me. Even though Santtu and Peetu were good friends Santtu kept a distance from me during the whole course of my fieldwork, whereas Peetu had a tendency of coming uncomfortably close, such as when he posed intrusive questions about my personal life.

TOO-LOOSE BONDS, TOO-TIGHT BONDS AND ATTUNEMENT

Scheff's (1997) theory of social bonds offers a practical model to define the variations in my relationships with Peetu and Santtu. The model is based on identifying secure and insecure bonds. In Scheff's view an insecure bond comes in two forms. A too-loose or an *isolated* bond is characterised by a lack of engagement or understanding of one another. A too-tight bond refers to what Scheff defines as an *engulfed* relationship: 'at least one of the parties in the relationship, say the subordinate, understands and embraces the standpoint of the other at the expense of the subordinate's own beliefs, values or feelings' (p.77). Emotion is the key ingredient for identifying the state of a social bond. Scheff suggests that there are two foundational social emotions: pride signals an intact social bond; shame, a threatened one. I, however, prefer Collins' (2004) concepts of positive and negative emotional energy, which you can also find in Layder's (1997, 2009) writing. Positive energy is a good supplement for pride, and negative energy for shame. Emotional bonds can, in my view, also be characterised by a lack of emotional intensity in circumstances where two parties experience one another as indifferent or meaningless.

Scheff and Starrin (2002) contend that if emotions are reflectively considered, it is possible to visualise what is invisible: the condition of a relationship. Defining the emotional atmosphere in the interplay that I had with Santtu enabled me to define what I, within the situational interplay, experienced as obvious. Santtu made a joke when he said that I had forced him to participate – it certainly felt like a joke. The situation did not involve any tension or other emotional elements of insecurity, threat or negative emotional energy, emotions that I experienced with some of my other interviewees. It was not uncommon that when I posed the question 'Do you wish to participate in this interview voluntarily?' some interviewees respond with a slightly higher tone of voice than they usually used. Some interviewees whispered their answer, and sometimes I could not always say what the subtle nuance was in a boy or a girl's voice or in their body language, but I knew that it indicated an insecure bond. When such insecure bonds existed, I experienced it as an obvious sensation of uncomfortable tension.

That kind of negative or uncomfortable tension did not exist in the interplay with Santtu. It was a different kind of emotional state. The relational challenge that I had with Santtu was not about whether I had deliberately or unintentionally forced on him my values and views. It was more about an opposite challenge, which resemble the challenge of a too-loose bond. Me saying, 'Seriously, Santtu?' was an attempt to tighten the bond, making the situation sufficiently serious so that Santtu, instead of deliberately misinterpreting my initiatives, engaged in the interplay seriously. The relational condition was to some extent the opposite with Peetu. Whereas my bond to Santtu needed to be tightened, I needed to be careful with Peetu in how to maintain a loose-enough bond to avoid engulfment, given that he was subordinated in his relation to me. I believe, however, I did manage to successfully gain their trust. As our discussion proceeded, we covered several issues, some more sensitive and challenging than others. We reached stages in our conversation that were serious, even though there was always a slight undertone of humour. At the end of the interview I also got comforting feedback from both of the boys. They expressed how I had become someone whom they could talk to and trust, and I had the ability to make accurate judgments about what they meant. This kind of judgement can be determined by insight. It was not solely about getting the boys to speak out. It was about reaching a position where one could confidently make qualified judgements about the meaning behind their remarks.

Peetu: We really should have someone like you at our school. Someone who helps out – like a school assistant. And who also talks about stuff, you know.

Santtu: We can't really say nothing to the social workers.

Peetu: But we could talk to you.

Santtu: Cause you, you understand what's a joke. Like if I say that I sell speed, you'll know it's a joke.

The concept of attunement fits well to describe the emotional and relational state that I believe we managed to develop during the interview process. We had reached the state of a secure bond that enabled substantial mutual understanding of each other's thoughts, beliefs and feelings (Scheff 1997). I had reached a position where I could tell what was a joke. Reaching attunement was not, however, about becoming equal. I was still the adult and I still had an adult position as the facilitator of the interview. I was in charge and I had the power to maintain a level of seriousness in our conversation. To some extent I also used my power resources to encourage Santtu and Peetu to speak out. I have come to reject the idea of adulthood or the element of power being an obstacle to gaining access to children's and young people's experiences. As a matter of fact, in my experience power is necessary to reach out to teenage boys like Peetu and Santtu. Without my responsible exercising of the power I held, they would probably have ridiculed the whole project.

A MODEL FOR SCRUTINISING RELATIONSHIPS

As a conclusion for this chapter I outline a model (Figure 6.1) that I have developed in the course of this research from my reflections of experiencing and observing relational interplay between adults and boys in school. In the model I highlight the three interwoven elements that I have referred to above: emotional energy, insight and influence. The foundational thought behind the model is that each of the three elements defines various dimensions of a relationship. The element of emotional energy refers to the emotional atmosphere that characterises the relational interplay. The element of insight refers to the aspect of recognition of the other. The element of influence refers to the aspect of power and control that two parties have in relation to one another. In the tradition of critical realist thinking, each of these elements form a condition for the encounter at the same time as the elements can develop or transform through face-to-face interplay.

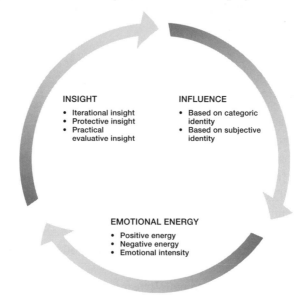

Figure 6.1: Model for scrutinising relationships

Emotions are regarded as the most revealing component when making judgments about the state in a relationship. All relationships generate emotions that can be manifested as positive or negative energy. Drawing on Collins' (2004) arguments, social encounters can either be energy-charging or energy-draining. Positive emotions create magnetism and draw people together; negative energy drives them emotionally or physically apart. Circumstances where the emotional energy level is low indicate a relationship that lacks mutual engagement. When assessing the effects and meaningfulness of a social encounter, it is crucial to recognise the emotional atmosphere. A negatively charged encounter, signifies lack of trust and easily leads to what Collins (2004) defines as energy-draining encounters. For an encounter to be meaningful or energy-charging it is necessary to develop some level of positive recognition, acceptance, inclusion and approval that enables two parties to reach out to and understand one other (Layder 2006).

Emotions are also of significance – when interpreting meaning in social encounters. The subtle insecurity when interviewees give assent, the lack of engagement of students in class as well as the irony in Santtu's response when he claimed that I had forced him to participate in the interview – is about invisible emotional energy. But emotional energy can be identified through reflection. Solely by identifying the atmosphere and whether it is positive or negative, or to acknowledge such circumstances where the level of emotional energy is low, helps to define the state of a research relationship.

Insight stands for the informative aspects in a relationship. Knowing someone indicates knowledge of the other's existence, but knowing someone well is indicative of a more detailed and broad sense of a person's subjective life (Layder 1997). Insight is a relative term, but I argue it is possible to make qualified judgments of various levels of insight, depending on the ability to interpret another's social actions. Emirbayer and Mische (1998) provide a helpful model for understanding three different dimensions of agency when interpreting social actions that can be linked to the concept of insight:

The 'iterational element' refers to the selective reactivation by actors of past patterns of thought and action that enable them to identify routines and identities, as well as institutional traditions of practice. Linking the iterational element to the interpretation of an individual's activities enables an understanding of how the current practice of actions is linked to previous patterns of actions. The iterational element enabled me to make a more nuanced judgment of Santtu's response in the interview, as I had shared previous moments with him and I could relate his sayings and doings in the interview with my previous experiences with him. In the same way, a teacher who has knowledge of a student's previous school achievements has a more nuanced perception of the same student's current achievements than a substitute teacher with a lack of insight into the student's past patterns.

In the 'projective element' Emirbayer and Mische (1998) highlight how social activities can be interpreted in relation to future desires and objectives. There is a qualitative difference in a relationship where one has insight or knowledge of someone's future hopes and desires compared with a relationship that exists only in terms of iterative practice. To actually gain access to another person's future dreams (why a person aims for some specific goals in life) calls for some level of mutual engagement, whereas knowledge of the past or categorical assumptions of future trajectories can at least to some extent be observed from a distance. A teacher who has knowledge of what a student aims for in life and why the student visualises a certain future trajectory also has an extensive ability to interpret current outcomes and activities. Insight into possible future trajectories can also obstruct, so that iterative expectations become engulfing. This can be the case in circumstances where previous events, such as past failures, dominate an individual's life trajectory. For instance, a student who has a bad reputation in school can be understood as someone whose iterative patterns engulf possible positive or constructive interpretations of the present, as well as possible constructive imaginative visions of the future.

Perhaps the most crucial ingredient of insight that Emirbayer and Mische (1998) define as the 'practical-evaluative' dimension of agency is the ability to contextualise social activities. The practical-evaluative dimension is both temporary and situated within the immediate domain of the present. However, as both Goffman (1983) and Layder (1997) have argued, it is not isolated from projections of the future, iterational patterns or the overall structural environment that exist beyond a situation or besides the immediate context. The practical-evaluative dimension of interpreting social activities enables nuanced judgments of actions in changing and emerging contextual situations to be made but also involves the ability to link the contemporary to a broader contextual reality. An example might be the ability of an adult in school to practically evaluate a student's present achievement and actions with a broader understanding of the student, as well as the ability to make judgments about the impact of contextual factors such as the class environment, emerging contextual changes or other possible conditions surrounding the student. Santtu's reflection on my and other adults' ability to understand what is a joke is an example of the practical evaluative element. Not understanding the social action as an act of irony or lacking the ability to act in proportion to the provocative act is about misinterpreting the bond between the contemporary acts with the immediate contextual surrounding.

Finally, the aspect of *influence* refers to how power dynamics constrain or enable meaningful interaction between two parts. I understand influence as Layder (2009) defines it – the aspect of being effective in a relationship. Layder argues that all relationships involve the feature of interpersonal benign control, which enables parties to influence one another. It is crucial to recognise the difference between benign control and malign control. Layder understands the latter as the negative use of power, such as manipulation, suppression or the use of other hostile control mechanisms. Benign control refers to the aspects of interpersonal control and power that entices recognition of action and the notion of understanding the interactive processes as significant or meaningful (Layder 2006). To lack the ability to influence in any way indicates the existence of too-loose a bond, where the parties are of no significance to one another. Conversely, relationships where there is a clear distinction between the dominant and the subordinate parts are indicative of a too-tight bond, leading to engulfment or malign influence. Based on Goffman's (1983) work, individuals can be identified both in terms of their category as well as their subjective position. A social worker, teacher or researcher can be viewed categorically as a specific kind of professional who impacts on an individual social worker or teacher's self-representation, as well as their ability to generate effectiveness in their relationship with students or service users. However, individuals also have personal power resources that can both strengthen or transform the categorical identity or position in a positive or negative way. When judging relational status, it is necessary to reflect upon how I, as a representative of my social category, am constructed in relation to the other, as well as how I, as a subjective person, am constructed in relation to the other. It is also equally important to understand the intersectionality of the self in terms of acknowledging how different categorical backgrounds can simultaneously portray various meanings in particular social moments. A person is never solely a particular social category – an adult, teacher, social worker or researcher – but a complex combination of both personal and categorical layers that form each individual into a unique person.

CONCLUSION

The three elements that I have presented above – emotion, insight and influence – are constant, interwoven elements in all social relations. Emotion is the key ingredient to reflectively examine the status of a relationship, but emotion can be further linked to the element of insight, as well as the element of influence. Whereas emotion is a practical element of all encounters that everyone can relate to, it is at the same time an abstract concept that often lacks transformative legitimacy when examined outside the immediate relationship or the immediate encounter.

The element of insight or knowledge and the element of influence or power in a relationship are, in my view, more practical terms that generate descriptions of relational limits and possibilities, which in turn legitimate whether the relationship has established rapport or attunement. Attunement is about the sense of balance of two sets of powers converging in an encounter between social agents. It is about reaching a state of harmony and understanding between different individuals in an unequal world – where power exists at all times and is always distributed unevenly. In such circumstances – which are the real circumstances of the social world – we cannot ignore how meanings are produced within the contextual reality of a relationship that is defined by power, emotion, insight and influence. Many have scrutinised this interpersonal reality. John Bowlby (1969) defined it as attachment, Erving Goffman (1983) referred to it as the interaction order and Thomas J. Scheff (1977) used the concept of the social bond. It might just as well be defined as a relationship, which is what Gillian Ruch et al. (2010) claim to be the very foundation of social work practice.

REFERENCES

Archer, M. S. (2003) *Structure, Agency and the Internal Conversation*. Cambridge: Cambridge University Press.

Berg, P. (2010) *Ryhmärajoja ja Hierarkioita. Etnografinen Tutkimus Peruskoulun Yläasteen Liikunnanopetuksesta.* Helsingfors: Helsingin yliopisto.

Bhaskar, R. (1975/2008) *A Realist Theory of Science*. London and New York: Verso Books.

Bhaskar, R. (1986) *Scientific Realism and Human Emancipation*. London: Verso.

Bowlby, J. (1969) *Attachment and Loss. 1. Attachment*. Harmondsworth: Penguin Books.

Brewer, J. D. (2000) *Ethnography*. Buckingham: Open University Press.

Christensen, P. (2004) 'Children's participation in ethnographic research: Issues of power and representation.' *Children and Society 18*, 2, 165–176.

Colllins, R. (2004) *Interaction Ritual Chains*. Princeton: Princeton University Press.

Corsaro, W. A. (1985) *Friendship and Peer Culture in the Early Years*. Norwood, NJ: Ablex.

Corsaro, William A. (2005) *The Sociology of Childhood*. Thousand Oaks, CA: Pine Forge Press.

Danermark, B., Ekström, M., Jakobsen, L. and Karlsson, J. Ch. (2003) *Att Förklara Samhället*. Lund: Studentlitteratur.

Emirbayer, M. and Mische, A. (1998) 'What is agency?' *American Journal of Sociology, 103*, 4, 962–1023.

Epstein, D. (1998) '"Are you a girl or are you a teacher?" The Least "Adult" Role in Research about Gender and Sexuality in a Primary School.' In G. Walford (ed.) *Doing Research about Education*. Brighton: Falmer Press.

Goffman, E. (1983) *The Interaction Order.* American Sociological Association, 1982 presidential address. New York, NY: American Sociological Association.

Goffman, E. (1959/1990) *The Presentation of Self in Everyday Life.* London: Penguin Books.

Gordon, T., Hynninen, P., Lahelma, E., Metso, T., Palmu, T. and Tolonen, T. (2007) 'Koulun arkea tutkimassa: Kokemuksia kollektiivisesta etnografiasta.' Presented in Lappalainen (*et al.*) *Etnografia Metodologiana: Lähtökohtana Koulutuksen Tutikimus.* Tampere: Osuuskunta vastapaino.

Hill, M., Davis, J., Prout, A. and Tisdall, K. (2004) 'Moving the participation agenda forward.' *Children and Society 18,* 2, 77–96.

Kehily, M. J., Mac An Ghaill, M., Epstein, D. and Redman, P. (2002) 'Private girls and public worlds: Producing femininities in the primary school.' *Discourse: Studies in the Cultural Politics of Education 23,* 2, 167–177.

Kroll, B. (2010) 'Only Connect… Building Relationships with Hard-to-Reach People: Establishing Rapport with Drug-Misusing Parents and their Children.' In G. Ruch (ed.) *Relationship-based Social Work: Getting to the Heart of Practice.* London: Jessica Kingsley Publishers.

Layder, D. (1997) *Modern Social Theory: Key Debates and New Directions.* London and New York: Routledge.

Layder, D. (2006) *Understanding Social Theory.* 2nd edition. London: Sage Publications Ltd.

Layder, D. (2009) *Intimacy and Power: The Dynamics of Personal Relationships in Modern Society.* New York: Palgrave Macmillan.

Lee, N. (2001) *Childhood and Society. Growing Up in an Age of Uncertainty.* Buckingham: Open University Press.

Lunabba, H. (2013) *När Vuxna Möter Pojkar I Skolan – Insyn, Inflytande Och Sociala Relationer.* Helsingfors: FSKC.

Ojajärvi, A. (2015 in press) *Terve Sotilas!* Helsinki: Nuorisotutkimusverkosto/Nuorisotutkimusseura.

Pattman, R., Frosh, S. and Phoenix, A. (2005) 'Constructing and experiencing boyhoods in research in London.' *Gender and Education 17,* 5, 555–561.

Robinson, C. and Kellet, M. (2002) 'Power.' In S. Fraser (ed.) *Doing Research with Children.* London: Sage.

Ruch, G. (2010) 'The Contemporary of Relationship-based Practice.' In G. Ruch (ed.) *Relationship-based Social Work: Getting to the Heart of Practice.* London: Jessica Kingsley Publishers.

Scheff, T. J. (1994) *Microsociology: Discourse, Emotion, and Social Structure.* Chicago: University of Chicago Press.

Scheff, T. J. (1997) *Emotions, the Social Bond, and Human Reality: Part/Whole Analysis.* Cambridge: Cambridge University Press.

Scheff, T. and Starrin, B. (2002) 'Skam och Sociala Band – Om Social Underordning och Utdragna Konflikter.' In A. Meeuwise and H. Swärd (ed.) *Perspektiv på Sociala Problem.* Stockholm: Natur och Kultur.

Chapter 7

USING OBSERVATION TO RESEARCH THE EXPERIENCES OF TEENAGERS WITH SEVERE LEARNING DISABILITIES

OBSERVING THE 'ORDINARY'

Helen Hingley-Jones

INTRODUCTION

> Daniel dipped his hands in the water in front of him and flicked the water, in the air. He seemed to have a variety of 'flicks', some soft, which kept the water spray fairly low down as it arched above the barrow, to medium and high flicks, when the water flew up a good few feet in the air, maintaining a droplet arch above the water surface… As I turned round, I saw that Daniel had now taken off all of his clothes and he was splashing about naked at the end of the garden. John shouted out, 'He's taken off his clothes, mum!'

As this fragment of data begins to illustrate, life for young people like Daniel and others who have severe learning disabilities and other challenges, such as autistic spectrum disorder, presents a wide array of experiences and daily ups and downs. Yet in my practice as a field social worker with disabled children and their families for a number of years, parents often said that professionals did not spend enough time with the families they were working with to really begin to comprehend that experience. What is life really like for parents, their disabled adolescent son or daughter and siblings? More particularly, I became interested in the ordinary experience of adolescent development and the shaping of identity from a psychosocial perspective; how is this experienced by severely learning disabled young people in the context of their family lives? Often it has seemed, in practice, difficult for families (and professionals) to hold on to the notion of development and growing separation and independence towards adulthood for young people with often profound impairments and considerable care needs.

This chapter describes a study I carried out for a professional doctorate in social work to research such experiences. I chose to carry out observations drawing on ethnographic traditions, but also by applying psychoanalytic infant observation methods. This combination of methods enabled the gathering of rich, detailed data that sought to capture the experience of the young people and their families, as psychosocial subjects, in some of their complexity. Observation does not rely on a traditional interview approach to data gathering so it can be a method that enables practitioner researchers to learn directly from and with people whose perspectives are often neglected. As such, I argue that it provides an empirically rigorous way of researching the lived experiences of both service users and their families, illuminating and informing professional social work practice.

First in this chapter, details of the study and its theoretical base in the psychosocial study of identity will be described and then the methodology and its roots in ethnography and psychoanalytic infant observation set out. After this, an extract from one of the four observation case studies will be included, followed by an explanation of the reflexive aspects of the research and data analysis process. Finally, perspectives on the ethics of observing and implications for practice are added.

THE STUDY

Participants

The study involved identifying four adolescents – Daniel, 12 years; Billy, 14 years; Carly, 14 years; Mohammed, 16 years (whose names I have changed), all of whom were attending schools for children with severe learning disabilities in an English city. I made contact with their families through a voluntary agency that works with disabled children and their families, using a process of purposive sampling (Silverman 2000). I carefully negotiated permission and consent to make observation visits to the families' homes, agreement to this having been obtained through university ethics processes. Visiting each young person for an hour a week, usually after school, the observations were conducted over a period of six months in each case. Following each observation, detailed records were kept. These data were analysed, theories built and case studies written.

Theoretical underpinnings of the study

Before describing the research methodology in more detail, it is important to set out some of the theoretical underpinnings and assumptions of the study. I was interested to draw on psychosocial ideas of human development, those that seemed able to capture the idea of the adolescent identity development as 'process'. To do this, the theory of subjectivation (Cahn 1998) was chosen.

This theory of identity development presents adolescence in a psychosocial light and it considers how young people 'become a subject' (Kennedy 2000); that is, they grow and develop on a number of psychological and social planes at the same time during this highly changeable stage of human development. Rather than being a linear progression from one state to another (childhood to adulthood), oscillation between different states and conditions can be detected in four domains: their inner world and unconscious state of mind; their interpersonal relationships; their bodily state; and in terms of them as members of society. They can, at times, be 'subject to' their own feelings and emotions, bodily conditions and external objects (parents, society and the outside world). At these times, their personal agency is weak and they are 'subject to' experiences and feelings in their lives; such feelings are often to do with the bodily changes of puberty as well as the developing sense of self. So the young person may feel unable to act; things happen to them and they can appear to feel disempowered, as though they are under the control of others.

This state oscillates, however, with times when young people can be more in charge. They embody a stronger sense of agency enabling them to be 'subject of' these experiences, able to act or to think in such a way as to empower themselves, to take charge and to really embody their own identity – to *be* themselves. This state of mind is associated with a movement towards developing adult subjectivity. Through the process of subjectivation, the young person gradually forms into a more settled adult subject, though following Klein's (1952) ideas there remain times when they may stumble and adults too may be 'subject to' events and experiences in their lives (see Briggs 2008 and Briggs and Hingley-Jones 2013 for further details).

I was interested to see how these ideas, shaped around normative adolescent development, may or may not be inclusive of the experience of the young people I was researching. The case study of Daniel, set out below, goes some way to illustrate, analyse and reflect upon these processes in action. Before introducing Daniel again, however, details of the research methodology will be set out.

METHODOLOGY

There are a wide variety of qualitative methodologies to choose from, but some are more suited than others to researching hard-to-reach communities and hidden topics that are not readily amenable to conventional interviewing. From a technical perspective, commonly used methods such as semi-structured interviews may be unsuitable; for example, for carrying out research with subjects who have significant cognitive and communication difficulties (Stalker and Connors 2003). For the young people with whom this study is concerned, an interview conducted with the support of symbols and other forms of communication aids would not have been the best form of data collection to explore their experiences as psychosocial subjects. Researchers have at times struggled to identify a research method appropriate for these circumstances, resulting in people with learning disabilities being excluded as they are unable to provide 'rational' answers to interviewers' questions (Lesseliers, Van Hove and Vanevelde 2009).

As an alternative, observation as a form of qualitative method can be a useful tool for researching in hard-to-reach areas of experience such as this, as it enables the gathering of accounts and interpretations that are close to the experiences of marginalised groups. This kind of method has been described as 'practice-near' in nature (Froggett and Briggs 2009), a term deriving from the work of Geertz (1974), who characterised, ethnographic work as either 'experience distant' or 'experience near'. His approach was to generate experience near, thick description of his encounters with those he researched, through detailed use of his ethnographic data and records. Rich, detailed accounts were written that capture Geertz's (1973) impressions and interpretations of the experiences of the social groups he encountered, written up in a way that stays close to the account of actual events.

In terms of researching severely learning disabled young people's experiences, a technique that stays close to experience and that aims to capture the young person's emotional and relational world seems particularly relevant. Sinason (1992, p.6), through her development of the notion of 'secondary handicap', comments that for learning disabled people, emotional intelligence is often 'left intact and rich' despite individuals having significant intellectual impairment. Research methods aimed at capturing emotions and relatedness are therefore potentially of great value as these can help the researcher to gain an appreciation of learning disabled people's experiences (Hingley-Jones 2013).

Before looking in more depth at psychoanalytic observation and its adaptation for this particular research project, it will be helpful to consider where it sits among the range of qualitative methodologies; in particular, how does it relate to the broader notion of ethnography?

OBSERVATION: BRINGING TOGETHER PSYCHOANALYTIC INFANT OBSERVATION AND ETHNOGRAPHY

Psychoanalytically informed observation research can be thought of as a form of ethnography (Price and Cooper 2012) allied to that carried out by anthropologists and sociologists. Both psychoanalytic observation and more traditional forms of ethnographic observation share certain characteristics: close attention to the experience of the individual in the context of their family, community and society and a commitment to the idea of spending considerable time with those who are being researched, developing relationships of one form or another with them, and learning from the researched (Atkinson *et al.* 2001). The way in which researcher reflexivity is conceived, however, is in the main quite different, each having its own ontology and history. As will be explained, psychoanalytic observation requires the researcher to be sensitive to unconscious processes, reflecting on what it feels like to be with others and thinking through what this might be telling us in terms of providing data. It can work outwards too, by considering how individuals' emotional states are shaped by and help to shape social processes. In contrast to this, ethnographers more usually remain at the surface level of society and culture, usually not venturing to explore the inner dimensions of emotion beyond what can be made explicit between researcher and subject.[1] Psychoanalytic observation thus provides a method for apprehending and properly researching psychosocial dimensions of human experience.

In order to set psychoanalytic observation in context, some key similarities and differences between this method and ethnography are now explored.

Ethnographic observation

Observation is a key element of the ethnographer's toolkit; it is what distinguishes ethnographic research from more generalist qualitative approaches that employ techniques such as interviews and focus groups (Atkinson *et al.* 2001). Atkinson *et al.* (2001, p.5) define 'ethnographic spirit': it incorporates a range of approaches that 'are grounded in a commitment to first-hand experience and exploration of a particular social or cultural setting on the basis of (though not exclusively by) participant observation'.

Contemporary ethnographers consider the postmodern turn in how observation is conceptualised. In earlier days, it was thought that the observer could visit a social group apart from their own, take in what was going on and be able to capture and pronounce on the key features of that culture. There was an idea that they were neutral and able to capture a scientific truth. With the postmodern turn, this 'privileged and totalising gaze' (Atkinson *et al.* 2001, p.3) comes

---

1   Some early ethnographers did use their work to question theories of personality development, however; for example, the universality of the Oedipus complex and Western notions of adolescent development (Malinowski 1927; Mead 1928; both in LeVine and New 2008).

into question. Just how representative of other cultures are accounts described by 'mainly male, mainly American' anthropologists (Spencer 2001, p.443)? So, for example, Mead (1928, in Spencer 2001) is criticised for not asking Samoan teenagers directly what they thought of her theorising about adolescence, when she characterised their experiences as mainly free of the turmoil of American teenage years. There is a move to a social constructivist position, questioning whether the researcher can ever really know what is in the mind of the other. Methods become more inclusive, negotiated between researcher and their subject, involving respondents' own views. As a consequence, the subjectivity of the researcher begins to take up a more central part in the research process, raising the importance of the notion of reflexivity and power differentials between researcher and their subject.

By becoming sensitised to the other, sadness, guilt and other feelings may be aroused in researchers as they uncover informants' uncomfortable personal experiences. Feminist researchers, for example, are encouraged to work at how such experiences are reflected on and represented in the text – described as 'working the hyphen between self and other' (Heyl 2001, p.375). Although it is acknowledged that it is difficult to feel what another feels, ethnographers are enjoined to try, in the effort to have a 'care-based ethical model' (Heyl 2001, p.379) of researching:

> I do not mean that a man with a home and family can see and feel the world as homeless women see and feel it. I do mean, however that it is reasonable and useful to try to do so. Trying to put oneself in the place of the other lies at the heart of the social contract and of social life itself. (Liebow 1993, in Heyl 2001, p.379)

Indeed, Kvale (1996) notes that good, close qualitative research can resemble a counselling relationship, with the researcher's ability to empathise with respondents seen as an essential component.

Psychoanalytic infant observation

Psychoanalytic observation, in contrast to traditional ethnography, specifically involves getting close to such experiences rather than shying away from them: to reflect closely on the kinds of feelings that emerge during encounters with others. Emanating from psychotherapeutic theorising and practice, it steps right into the emotional, relational field by using particular techniques that depend upon the observer's sensitivities to the emotional realities experienced by the 'other'.[2] Research that applies this kind of observational technique enables methods to be developed 'specific to their objects of study' (Rustin 2012, p.14). If the intention is to explore feelings, experiences and emotions, in the context of social forces (the full psychosocial realm), techniques to research these need to be evolved from practices where these are theorised and worked with, psychoanalytic observation and therapeutic practice being one such domain.

Infant observation has been part of the curriculum for trainees on the Child Psychotherapy course run at the Tavistock Centre since 1948. It was devised as a pre-clinical educational opportunity for students to witness the first two years of an infant's development at close hand, during weekly visits of an hour's duration. Students adopt a neutral, but emotionally alert observational stance so they can learn 'to conceive vividly the infantile experience of the child patients' (Bick 1964, p.558) and to make sense of the child's non-verbal behaviour and play in the context of their family setting. Another aspect is that the experience often has an 'intense emotional impact' (ibid) on the observer. As Urwin and Sternberg (2012) show, learning to make sense of the emotions aroused during an observation is seen as important for students in the development of the requisite capacities for psychotherapeutic practice. In particular, learning to take note of and then to make use of countertransference feelings as a therapist is particularly valued as such feelings are considered at least partly to be an unconscious communication of the patient's emotions.[3]

Infant observation has been adapted for use as a research method in many different research contexts in recent times: emotional labour in the classroom, Price (2001); the identity development of new mothers, Urwin (2007); older people (Davenhill et al. 2003); children in foster

---

2   Psychoanalytic concepts drawn upon include defences, such as projection and splitting, transference and countertransference and others. See Bower (2005) for a summary of these.

3   See Casement (1985, p.94) for an exploration of countertransference and how it may be experienced and understood by therapists:

   What most writers agree upon, in their differing ways, is that therapists are affected by their patient's impacts upon them, whether this be due to a patient's personality, a patient's transference, or a patient's manner of being. Often, the therapist's response to this may indicate something that has only to do with the therapist. At times, there may be elements also of unconscious communication from the patient. It cannot always be rigidly defined as countertransference or not, as pathological or not.

care (Wakelyn 2012). One criticism it has faced, however, concerns the use made by researchers of the countertransference. When discussing Wendy Hollway's (Hollway and Jefferson 2005, in Frosh and Baraitser 2008) description of her use of countertransference as a source of data, following an interview with a research subject called Vince, Frosh and Baraitser (2008, p.362), for example, suggest that what is uncovered says more about '*her* desire', therefore her transference to the research scenario, than it uncovers about Vince's unconscious world. The problem becomes how to untangle the researcher's own unconscious feelings and transferences from their own relationship histories (the researcher's 'stuff'), from those they may be detecting when with their research subjects.

To help move on from this position, Price and Cooper (2012, p.58) suggest that observational research can be thought of as sitting in a third place, 'between naive realism and constructivist realism'. They go on:

> Emotional and unconscious states are 'real', accessible to us as knowing subjects, but their 'meaning' is also inherently ambiguous and multiple. Multiple interpretations may be 'valid', but this does not apply to all or any interpretations. The observational 'facts' delimit the range of interpretive possibilities. (Price and Cooper 2012, p.58)

Drawing on the work of Hammersley (1992, in ibid), from an ethnographic tradition, Price and Cooper (2012) consider validity in relation to observational research. They argue that the psychoanalytic technique or 'craft methods' has something unique to contribute to critiques of 'researcher effects'; criticism that somehow the researcher's subjectivity will get in the way of getting close to finding truths about the experience of the research subject. To make sense of the psychic field in which research of this kind is conducted, the help of those less caught up in the fieldwork is needed in the setting of the research seminar; to think together about the emotional dynamics at play (ibid, p. 64). More will be said on reflexivity and the process of data analysis later, but before this a more lengthy extract from the observations of Daniel and his family will be set out, to illustrate the research process.

DANIEL: AN EXTRACT FROM THE OBSERVATION
AND ITS INTERPRETATION

Daniel is a 12-year-old white British boy who is on the autistic spectrum and who has severe learning disabilities. He lives with his parents and three brothers (Peter, 13; Andrew, 10; John, 6). Over the course of my observation visits to Daniel, at home, I became embroiled in some tensions the parents were having around how to respond to his behaviour. Daniel had revealed a preoccupation with playing with water in the garden and his mother, Kate, initially seemed content to allow this:

> Kate returned to cooking food for the boys' tea, calling out occasionally to the boys to try to keep them in order. I could see several lads bouncing on the large trampoline on the grass outside at the back. Daniel was at the far end of the garden, flicking water from the wheelbarrow as I've seen him before. Their activities were completely separate and I could see that there was at least one friend with Peter, and John also seemed to have a friend with him. As I went to go out of the back door, I noticed Kate behind me and she said, 'Daniel's enjoying the water. His dad tells me not to let him have it, but I can't see why he shouldn't.' She said that Daniel had pulled the hose off the tap while she was filling the barrow for him, which had been a bit annoying. She'd known he'd wanted the water to play with as he'd taken her to it as soon as he got home today.

After a while I become more involved in observing Daniel, with fascination, and over-step my role as observer.

> As I rounded the trampoline, I saw a wet-looking Daniel, standing over the wheelbarrow full of water at the raised area at the back of the garden...

> Daniel dipped his hands in the water in front of him and flicked the water, in the air. He seemed to have a variety of 'flicks', some soft, which kept the water spray fairly low down as it arched above the barrow, to medium and high flicks, when the water flew up a good few feet in the air,

maintaining a droplet arch above the water surface. With these higher flicks, he'd quickly raise his hands above his head and twiddle his fingers together. Once in a while he'd vocalise, making a noise which didn't resemble speech or singing, just a medium-pitched sound. Daniel's trousers were wet and he had no shoes on. He had drops of water on his face too...

I saw that he was flicking the water now onto the paddling pool, with a plastic, rattling sound and then onto the hardboard, with a wooden pattering. Then onto the concrete with a much 'deader' sound. The hardboard sound seemed preferable to Daniel, who speeded up the flicking, till he achieved a sound like falling rain on the wood. He repeated this a few times and whooped, enjoying the effect...

As I turned round, I saw that Daniel had now taken off all of his clothes and he was splashing about naked at the end of the garden. John shouted out, 'He's taken off his clothes, Mum!' Kate disappeared into the house, saying she'd fetch him some trunks. She came back and I offered to take them, carrying them over to Daniel to change into. She said, 'Give me a shout if you need help', and Daniel, slightly reluctantly, allowed me to help him step into the swimming trunks.

Kate continues to pair up with me, even when Daniel's father is disapproving of his behaviour, in week 11:

Kate seemed chirpy and said: 'Daniel's out in the garden, I think. Oh look, he's got nothing on!' At this, Ian stood to look through the kitchen window and shouted across, 'Daniel, put some clothes on!' quite loudly, but in no way loud enough to gain Daniel's attention right across the other end of the garden. Kate and I both became a bit jumpy about wanting to get Daniel clothed. I could see Daniel in the garden, looking slightly plump and pale in the distance. Dad retreated to the living room. As Kate came back towards the house, she said: 'Daniel's waiting for me to put the water on. Don't tell Ian as he hates it when Daniel plays with water.' Nevertheless, she walked down the side of the house extension to put the tap on.

Things changed a little over the next few weeks with Kate beginning to take up the father's position, questioning Daniel's activities:

> Just then, Daniel came flashing through the kitchen, having taken his clothes off upstairs. He ran through to the garden. Kate shouted after him as he ran 'put some clothes on!' His naked figure made it over to the back of the garden, to find some water to play with. Daniel looked comical as he'd left his black socks on – Kate drew attention to this dryly. I stood up and said, 'Shall I give him his swimming costume?' and she moved out of the room to find one for him. After a moment, she handed one to me and she speculated that she thought Daniel probably associated seeing me with taking his clothes off and heading to the garden to play with water. I laughed a bit nervously, thinking gosh, how is this going down in the family (knowing dad's view from last week) …I was still thinking about how I might be being seen to be encouraging Daniel to do this activity. I was left with questions about my role. Should I be trying to educate him or offer him some new activities I wondered?

By the next visit, things have moved further and Daniel is no longer allowed to play with water. I feel quite confused and guilty about the way I am associated with his 'problem' behaviour:

> Kate told me…that Daniel's dad had insisted he put his clothes back on yesterday, even though it was quite warm, when Daniel was playing with water… Kate was trying to work out whether Daniel just did this stripping-off and 'bathing' when I was around, I think. I felt awful at this – feeling that dad, who I've heard doesn't like the water playing or Daniel taking his clothes off, might associate me with actually encouraging Daniel to do these things.

I used supervision and the research seminar to help reflect on what I had been experiencing here: feeling guilty, as though I was causing Daniel's behaviour. Through discussion we were able to separate out my countertransference feelings of guilt (concern at 'using' the family for my research project, at possibly making things worse for them) from another possible explanation.

As I reminded myself, I had not encouraged Daniel's behaviour at all. In fact, I had continued to be sensitive to Kate's wishes in relation to where and how I positioned myself in the home. We began to explore whether in fact the parents may have been unconsciously projecting the 'indulgent parent' role onto me, so that they could unite in thinking about Daniel, overcoming the conflict between them. Perhaps they were making use of me to work out how they were feeling about Daniel as someone so reluctant to take steps towards independent, more age-appropriate subjectivity? The father seemed more able to conceive of Daniel as a young man, needing to develop more regulated and socially acceptable behaviour, while the mother had been happy to allow Daniel to continue with a more regressed, dependent state of mind.

It may be that the space this created enabled the couple to unite in communicating their expectations to Daniel, as he did seem a little more contained and connected to his siblings over the next weeks:

> Daniel had joined in at the edge of the trampoline and as an equal to the others, found his space effectively. Peter responded and faced him, the two of them coordinating the bounces. It was an unusual piece of joint play or activity.

• •

REFLECTIONS ON REFLEXIVITY

What becomes apparent from the presentation of this extract of the case study written following observations of Daniel and his family is that the research experience was very embedded and relational. I took on a flexible, open stance with families when making contact to negotiate a way to begin, with consent gained through working with parents/carers and where possible, involving the young person directly. This meant having to adapt the traditional psychoanalytically informed observational stance of the non-interacting observer to accommodate the family's wishes, to a greater or lesser extent in each family. I negotiated, in each case, a way to begin by stressing that I was hoping principally to observe the 'index' young person, but that the families should try as much as possible to carry on their normal activities.

During each visit, I did not make notes or attempt to record anything. Immediately afterwards, however, I wrote detailed 'process' accounts of the events of the observation hour as accurately as I could. These notes, which included factual description of what I saw, but also my subjective feelings, formed the research data.

As with an infant observation, a high degree of reflexivity is required when carrying out this kind of research, exemplified by the kind of close recording of experience following each observation. Where I found myself stepping out of the observer role – for example, into more of a helper or befriender of family members – I tried to reflect on what had led up to this. I asked myself whether it had made me feel better (for example, reducing my guilt about making a visit to such busy families and young people with high levels of need) or was I becoming caught-up with family dynamics (or 'used') in some other way?

Hunt (1989, p.43), who incorporates psychoanalytic concepts in her ethnographic work, looks at how such shifts in role for researchers can provide helpful data, providing some indication of the observed person's 'world of meaning'. A good example of this is shown in Daniel's observation, as the parental couple seem to be using the opportunity of having an emotionally receptive observer to help work out the tricky 'dance' of parenting an adolescent who is extremely resistant to giving up his usual way of relating to himself and others about him. Here, my role as observer seems to surface information about how his parents are dealing with Daniel's reluctance and difficulties in separating into an individual with the capability of some independence.

FROM REFLEXIVITY TO DATA ANALYSIS

There were several different elements to data analysis in this study: individual supervision to begin the process of reflection; research seminars to present and discuss data; and a thematic analysis that led to the writing of case studies on each young person.

First, to support me in reflecting on the experience of observing, I had regular supervision with a psychotherapist/social worker who has many years of experience of working with learning disabled people and their families. I also took part in research seminars, along the lines recommended by Price and Cooper (2012), where the observation records could be analysed and reflected upon. These processes were important in helping to triangulate the findings and themes that were emerging, as through close analysis and reflection, others were able to help me try to separate what might belong to my own experiences, my subjectivity, or personal countertransference, from conjectural exploration of the emotional/unconscious lives of those I was observing.

Being an emotionally engaged observer inevitably brings you closely in touch with the feelings experienced by those being observed and your own response to these. In terms of observing disabled young people with their families, the psychoanalytic literature describes how the emotional climate within the family can be fraught, particularly when there are hidden feelings of hurt, anger or damage experienced by family members (Simpson 2004). Bridges (1999, p.61) describes observations of disabled children and their families and how for the observer it can be uncomfortable: 'This pain and anguish stimulated by concentrated observation of children with very high dependency needs is almost indescribable... Watching can be a shocking experience.' Cooper (2009, p.432) describes this kind of encounter as 'the smell of the real' and warns of the danger of the researcher losing their way; struggling to untangle that which belongs to their own unconscious world and what they conjecture emerges from that of the observed person. The support of a supervisor and research seminar are therefore necessary when carrying out this kind of emotionally sensitive and intimate research, and close regard needs to be played to research ethics.

The third dimension of data analysis took place alongside presenting the field notes at supervision and research seminars when I undertook a thematic analysis of the field notes (Bryman 2012). By reflexively cross-referencing between these different levels or contexts of analysis, it was then possible to write case studies concerning each of the young people. These were written in broadly chronological fashion, while also maintaining a vertical thematic axis. This allowed the case studies to remain close to the observation data (as thick description); yet commonalities and distinctive features of each case could be highlighted to tentatively account for and make sense of (interpret) each young person's experience.

ETHICS

Given the highly subjective nature of the research method of observation, regular reflective supervision and taking part in the seminars was vitally important. I had to be constantly aware of the need to maintain certain boundaries with the families I visited, and clear about the length and purpose of the observations, in order to hold an ethical stance. One of the learning points for me as a researcher was just how active a process it is to do this. Families might feel disempowered by having a researcher visit their family, unable to activate their right to 'withdraw at any time' as we so blithely promise in our consent forms. With one of the four families – for example, Carly's – the observations were causing her mother some stress as I was visiting while Carly normally had her evening meal. Carly was reluctant to eat and her mother had to hand-feed her due to her physical and learning disabilities, as described in visit 3:

> The tune changed and Carly's eyes sought out the TV. Sonia [mother] slipped in another piece of cake and this time, Carly accepted it and began to chew it a little. At this, Sonia jumped into action and took a beaker of liquid, saying, 'Have a drink, Carly?' At first, Carly seemed to resist the beaker, shutting her lips tight. Then she allowed the liquid in a little and passively accepted the drink.

Over time, it seemed that my presence was distracting Carly, making it more stressful for her mother to carry out the feeding routine. Recognising this, we decided between us that I would visit at a different time, so that family routine would be less affected. Observing family life in this intimate way therefore required that I remained alert to the impact I was having on the family, even when it was not directly spoken about. There has to be great sensitivity towards how family members are experiencing being observed, while the researcher contains and holds on to anxiety this might arouse for them about having to withdraw. I found supervision invaluable as a place to air these issues, helping me find a way to process the guilt, anxiety and other feelings I had at times; enabling me to put the young person and their family first, despite my own wish to complete the work.

Although I did not do it myself during this study, there is also scope to share observation notes with those who have been observed, enabling them to comment on the data that have been generated and to involve them more directly in the research process. A benefit of this is that the research process is more open and equal. It does mean, however, that the researcher's interpretations of what they have been watching is open to close scrutiny; and where they may want to comment on the emotional dynamics they feel they have experienced, sharing data may act to inhibit their reflections, arguably limiting the knowledge generated. In practice, I found a way to respond as seemed appropriate in the case of each family. For example, one parent asked me to write a report on my observations for a school meeting about her son, which I was happy to do. In general, however, I did not offer to provide written notes to parents unless they asked me in this way. The findings do remain, therefore, the product of my own subjective experience of each family, though in each case the research seminar and supervision provided contrasting interpretations and triangulations that were incorporated into the writing.

IMPLICATIONS FOR PRACTICE AND RESEARCH AND CONCLUDING THOUGHTS

The extract from Daniel's case study provides an illustration of the ideas presented in this chapter. It shows the value of carrying out psychoanalytically informed observation in the relational, emotional field of the family while carefully maintaining an ethical stance, respectful of family members. Through researching in this way it is possible to get close to Daniel, someone whose perspective is not usually central to research, providing information and insights that can be useful in building the knowledge base for social work. In this case, it is tentatively suggested that the observer's experience may reveal how a particular family is able to draw in others to assist them in re-thinking their position as parents of a severely learning disabled adolescent progressing through the oscillations of this life stage. These are speculative ideas, but the reader is able to consider from the material itself whether it resonates with them. If they are working with young people who have similar needs to Daniel and his family, the need to engage with people on an emotional level is highlighted by this kind of insight, stressing the importance of the relational aspects of the social work role. As an adolescent with significant needs, it is not possible for Daniel to straightforwardly tell a researcher how things are for him, yet through the observation, elements of his personality and adolescent identity emerge, set within the web of his relationship with the people with whom he lives. Commonalities of experience are revealed between Daniel and his adolescent processing and other non-disabled young people.

Careful work is needed to ensure that the subjects of the research are treated ethically and there may, as indicated, be arguments for adding another layer to research of this nature by sharing observational notes with family members, where possible adding their commentary and reflections to the analysis. In any case, supervision and the support of a research seminar are important to provide alternative perspectives on the data and to contain the researcher.

REFERENCES

Atkinson, P., Coffey, A., Delamont, S., Lofland, J. and Lofland, L. (2001) *Handbook of Ethnography.* London: Sage.

Bick, E. (1964) 'Notes on infant observation in psychoanalytic training.' *International Journal of Psychoanalysis 45,* 558–566.

Bower, M. (2005) 'Psychoanalytic Theories for Social Work Practice.' In M. Bower (ed.) *Thinking under Fire: Psychoanalytic Thinking for Social Work Practice.* London: Routledge.

Bridges, G. (1999) 'Child observation as a training strategy: Social work with disabled children and their families.' *International Journal of Infant Observation 2,* 2, 51–66.

Briggs, S. (2008) *Working with Adolescents and Young Adults: A Contemporary Psychodynamic Approach.* 2nd edition. Basingstoke: Palgrave Macmillan.

Briggs, S. and Hingley-Jones, H. (2013) 'Reconsidering adolescent subjectivity: A "practice-near" approach to the study of adolescents, including those with severe learning disabilities.' *British Journal of Social Work 43,* 1, 64–80.

Bryman, A. (2012) *Social Research Methods.* 4th edition. Oxford: Oxford University Press.

Cahn, R. (1998) 'The process of becoming-a-subject in adolescence.' In M. Perret-Catipovic and R. Ladame (eds) *Adolescence and Psychoanalysis: The Story and the History.* London: Karnac.

Casement, P. (1985) *On Learning from the Patient.* London: Routledge.

Cooper, A. (2009) 'Hearing the grass grow: Emotional and epistemological challenges of practice-near research.' *Journal of Social Work Practice 23,* 4, 429–442.

Davenhill, R., Balfour, A., Rustin, M., Blanchard, M. and Tress, K. (2003) 'Looking into later life: Psychodynamic observation and old age.' *Psychoanalytic Psychotherapy 17,* 3, 253–266.

Froggett, L. and Briggs, S. (2009) 'Editorial.' *Journal of Social Work Practice 23,* 4, 377–82.

Frosh, S. and Baraitser, L. (2008) 'Psychoanalysis and psychosocial studies.' *Psychoanalysis, Culture and Society 13,* 346–365.

Geertz, C. (1973) *The Interpretation of Cultures.* New York: Basic Books.

Geertz, C. (1974) '"From the native's point of view": On the nature of anthropological understanding.' *Bulletin of the American Academy of Arts and Sciences 28* 1, 26–45.

Heyl, E. (2001) 'Ethnographic Interviewing.' In P. Atkinson, A. Coffey, S. Delamont, J. Lofland and L. Lofland (eds) *Handbook of Ethnography.* London: Sage.

Hingley-Jones, H (2013) 'Emotion and relatedness as aspects of the identities of adolescents with severe learning disabilities: Contributions from "practice-near" social work research.' *Child and Family Social Work 18,* 4, 458–466.

Hunt, J. (1989) *Psychoanalytic Aspects of Fieldwork.* London: Sage University Paper.

Kennedy, R. (2000) 'Becoming a subject: Some theoretical and clinical issues.' *International Journal of Psychoanalysis 81*, 875– 891.

Klein, M. (1952) 'The Emotional Life of the Infant.' In M. Klein *Envy and Gratitude* (1988). London: Virago.

Kvale, S. (1996) *Inter Views: An Introduction to Qualitative Research Interviewing.* London: Sage.

Lesseliers, J., Van Hove, G. and Vanevelde, S. (2009) 'Regranting identity to the outgraced – narratives of persons with learning disabilities: Methodological considerations.' *Disability and Society 24,* 4, 411–423.

LeVine, R. and New, R. (2008) *Anthropology and Child Development: A Cross Cultural Reader.* Oxford: Blackwell.

Price, H. (2001) 'Emotional labour in the classroom: A psychoanalytic perspective.' *Journal of Social Work Practice 15,* 2, 161–180.

Price, H. and Cooper, A. (2012) 'In the Field: Psychoanalytic Observation and Epistemological realism.' In C. Urwin and J. Sternberg (eds) *Infant Observation and Research: Emotional Processes in Everyday Lives.* Didcot: Routledge.

Rustin, M. (2012) 'Infant Observation as a Method of Research.' In C. Urwin and J. Sternberg (eds) *Infant Observation and Research: Emotional Processes in Everyday Lives.* Hove: Routledge.

Silverman, D. (2000) *Doing Qualitative Research: A Practical Handbook.* London: Sage.

Simpson, D. (2004) 'Learning disability as a refuge from knowledge.' In D. Simpson and L. Miller (eds) *Unexpected Gains: Psychotherapy with People with Learning Disabilities.* London: Karnac.

Sinason, V. (1992) *Mental Handicap and the Human Condition: New Approaches from the Tavistock.* London: Free Association Books.

Spencer, J. (2001) 'Ethnography after Postmodernism.' In P. Atkinson, A. Coffey, S. Delamont, J. Lofland and L. Lofland (eds) *Handbook of Ethnography.* London: Sage.

Stalker, K. and Connors, C. (2003) 'Communicating with disabled children.' *Adoption and Fostering 27,* 1, 26–35.

Urwin, C. (2007) 'Doing infant observation differently? Researching the formation of mothering identities in an inner London borough.' *International Journal of Infant Observation 10,* 3, 239–251.

Urwin, C. and Sternberg, J. (eds) (2012) *Infant Observation and Research: Emotional Processes in Everyday Lives.* Hove: Routledge.

Wakelyn, J. (2012) 'A Study of Therapeutic Observation of an Infant in Foster Care.' In C. Urwin and J. Sternberg (eds) *Infant Observation and Research: Emotional Processes in Everyday Lives.* Didcot Parkway: Routledge.

Chapter 8

UNDERTAKING A CO-OPERATIVE INQUIRY IN A CHILDREN'S SOCIAL CARE SERVICE

PREREQUISITES, OPPORTUNITIES, COMPLEXITIES AND CHALLENGES IN ACHIEVING RELATIONSHIP-BASED RESEARCH

Gavin Swann

INTRODUCTION

This chapter describes the experience and learning of conducting a piece of action research within an organisation where I, the author, was employed as a senior manager. The aim of this chapter is to describe the experience and share the learning by identifying the prerequisites, opportunities, complexities and challenges of conducting research within your own organisation.

After providing a context, focus is placed on the identification of a collaborative research methodology that supports a relationship-based approach to research. I then concentrate on the factors that supported this methodology, paying particular attention to securing organisational support, recruiting 'the right' research participants and wider relationships at the boundary of the research. I then provide a contrast by analysing the complexities and challenges of a relationship-based research methodology. Here I concentrate on leadership, the exercise of power and dominant organisational and cultural constructions. I conclude with answers to the question: 'Is it possible to undertake relationship-based practice research in your own organisation?'

THE CHILDREN'S SOCIAL CARE SYSTEM IN THE UK

The Children's Social Care system is provided in the UK through Local Authorities via the Children Act 1989 and 2004, and the research took place in a local authority's Children's Social Care service. Children's Social Care is a local authority department with responsibility for assessing the needs of and providing support to vulnerable children in the community in line with statutory law and government guidance. Children's Social Care has a duty to safeguard and promote the wellbeing of children and young people. It provides services to children and young people assessed as being 'in need' for a variety of reasons, such as those:

- at risk of neglect or abuse (including domestic abuse)

- living in families experiencing acute stress

- with mental health problems

- whose parents are ill, disabled, learning disabled, mentally ill or substance misusing

- with caring responsibilities; and those looked after by the local authority (LA)

- children with disabilities.

All these vulnerable children and young people have unique experiences and circumstances, which must be taken into account when providing services. Children's Social Care works in partnership with them, their families and other agencies (police, health and education) to improve outcomes. Children's Social Care is a large service and is organised to provide community-based protective services via its Children-in-Need Service while supporting children in its care via its children-looked-after service. This research was initiated within the Children-in-Need service but evolved as the practice matured. The Children-in-Need Service employs over 120 staff, including

80 social work practitioners. These social workers provide services through Section 17 (child in need), Section 47 (child protection) and Section 31 (care proceedings) of the Children Act 1989.

THE RESEARCH CONTEXT

In 2009, I completed a small research activity entitled 'How do social workers think about men?' I concluded that men, as parents, as risks and as resources for children, are frequently excluded from statutory social work assessment and intervention. I determined that this exclusion is caused by a complex set of variables including the following:

- Negative assumptions of men are applied by social workers.

- Social workers' unconsciously project their experiences of their father (either idealised or denigrated) when working with fathers.

- Social workers, as a predominately female workforce, may have direct personal experience of male abuse and violence prejudicing their view, and social workers fear fathers' sexuality and physical and sexual attack by male clients.

- Additional variables for exclusion were also found to include a failure by social care organisations to support social workers in engaging fathers, a failure by some men to maintain their responsibility for their child, socio-demographic changes to contemporary society and the social construction of masculinity.

Armed with these research findings and the recommendations of the research to develop a set of practices to support the inclusion of men, an opportunity arose in my employing organisation to implement the research recommendations. In 2010, with organisational support, we established an action research project, which was integrated into the daily practice and systems of social workers and managers. Included in it was the formation of a co-operative inquiry group of social work practitioners who experimented with alternative techniques to include fathers. The co-operative inquiry process is grounded on participants involved in cycles of action and reflection over questions of common interest. Among the many suggested areas for exploration by the group was one that would form the foundation for the group: What techniques, approaches and practices can be developed to engage fathers in social work interventions?

The objective behind this experiment was to establish a change management project and integrate the project into social work practice and a professional doctorate, while creating a model that led to transformation in one area of practice. The research project was entitled: 'Breaking Down Barriers: Developing an Approach to Include Fathers in Children's Social Care' (Swann 2015).

The research methodology was a co-operative inquiry, 'book-ended' by a pre- and post-case file audit, which acted as a before and after comparison. The co-operative inquiry took place over an 18-month period. The group membership consisted of 12 social workers and managers (six male and six female) from across Children's Social Care (and two external partner agencies). When the co-operative inquiry group was formed, we agreed a series of aims and actions. We adopted a systematic process of experimentation and reflection. We would meet to agree areas of practice experimentation and then, over a period of six weeks, we would test different techniques in social work practice to include fathers. At the end of the six weeks we would convene for a three-hour reflective discussion to review our experiences of experimenting with new practice. From this reflective discussion we would agree what had worked, while generating the next set of techniques to be trialed. We followed this cycle of reflection, action and experimentation for a year and a half. In the reflective meetings we would listen and think about the experiences of each co-operative inquirer as we tested different inclusive practices throughout and at different hierarchical levels within the organisation. Collectively, we would identify from this reflective activity what methods worked, what methods needed to be further tested, and what alternative theories and practice testing strategies we might adopt. Every meeting was video and audio recorded, which allowed us to collect from 14 meetings and 78 weeks of experimentation a tried-and-tested 'body of knowledge' in one area of social work practice. The co-operative inquirers adopted 'a fatherhood strategy', which included identifying targets for engagement with fathers, and we refined systems to capture data on fathers. This data was used to further develop learning, quality assurance and services to fathers. The co-operative inquiry also comprehensively analysed 57 cases where fathers had been successfully engaged, allowing the group to develop a practice guide for social workers and managers in how to engage fathers. The research was supported by the senior management team of Children's Services and the Local Safeguarding Children's Board.[1] As the research gathered pace, the inclusion of fathers in wider services, such as Universal Health and Early Years Services, became a topic of conversation and interest across the council.

When the research began, I had been employed as a deputy head of service in Children's Social Care for two and a half years. In this time my position, role, authority, confidence and quality working relationships had become established and the preparatory research 'How do social workers think about men?' had helped to set the scene. Simply put, the research was a practice approach that centred upon the lived experiences of statutory frontline social work practitioners and studied how the anxieties and defences that dominate the system when working with fathers can be ameliorated. (Froggett and Briggs 2009; Whittaker 2011). This research methodology brought about a significant amount of learning. The methodology established that co-operative inquiry can create the conditions for changes in behaviours, practice and organisational sub-cultures. The methodology supported a 'system as a whole approach'. Practitioners meaningfully participated and were constantly consulted and involved, which contributed to the emergence of a learning organisation. The methodology empowered social workers, giving them the confidence to practise differently. The co-operative inquiry was integrated, over time, into the life, systems and culture of the organisation. Sustainability was achieved because practitioners participated in changing one area of practice. The research concluded that children and family social work is one of the few institutions to confront the perversities and abuses of traditional gender and power relations. Paternal alienation is a response to male abuse because it acts as a defence. At the conclusion of the co-operative

---

1   The Local Safeguarding Children's Board is an independently chaired statutory meeting involving a group of senior representatives from statutory and voluntary organisations whose role is to analyse situational or institutional issues that either cause or ameliorate risks to children in the borough. The Local Safeguarding Children's Board is also responsible for implementing the recommendations for any serious case review that is required in the borough. Those attending include senior managers from health (including the Director of Universal Health Services, the lead paediatrician for child protection, the lead nurses for child protection from both hospitals), probation, the voluntary sector, education welfare, schools, early years, the Director of Children's Services, the Police Borough Commander, Director of Child Protection and Quality Assurance Children's Social Care.

inquiry we had achieved an increase in fathers recorded on case files, a rise in fathers assessed and an increase in fathers attending child protection conferences and Looked After Reviews. Data triangulated from qualitative and quantitative activities indicated a rise in parental responsibility for fathers recorded on case files, an increase in contact arrangements and a significant increase in social workers considering the father's situation in on-going planning for children.

An unexpected independent evaluation of the research inquiry took place in January and February 2012 in the guise of a formal two-week Ofsted Inspection of Safeguarding and Looked After Services. The inspectors concluded:

> The LSCB [Local Safeguarding Children Board] makes very good use of audit to satisfy itself of safeguarding performance across the partnership. It monitors closely progress against priorities and the implementation of relevant action plans and these are continually reviewed and revised to ensure effective safeguarding services are in place across the partnership. Examples include the need to improve engagement with fathers has been identified and communicated to a range of agencies, and in consequence there has been an increase in assessments involving fathers and in the number of children placed with their fathers or with paternal extended families. (Ofsted 2012, p.18)

A THEORY TO SUPPORT RELATIONSHIP-BASED RESEARCH IN PRACTICE

A methodological literature review was undertaken to inform the research design as we needed a methodology that would operate within the milieu of a busy London children and families social work service. The review directed me towards co-operative inquiry, a relationship-based research methodology which indicated it would encourage participation from across different parts of the organisation.

Seventy case files were randomly audited prior to starting the co-operative inquiry and again once it concluded. The 'pre' audit provided the co-operative inquiry with 'baseline' data at the beginning of the inquiry. The case-file audit appealed to the senior management team and the organisational culture because it served to evaluate the impact of the 'Breaking Down Barriers' project. The case-file audits set the scene and legitimised the research activity; however, the main tool to gather data was co-operative inquiry.

As a social worker, researcher, student and manager, I understood that my research would be complex because of my multiple roles. I knew that the concepts of power, knowledge and oppression were all subjects of concern, which potentially gave me an advantageous and oppressive vantage point (Alexandrov 2009). I did not want to be undemocratic and design a unilateral research activity. I recognised from my many conversations with social workers that I needed a method that would meaningfully involve them, using a relational-based technique, in the development of social work practice. I wanted a method that would develop and empower social workers and serve our profession. These objectives further directed me towards co-operative inquiry, which 'involves two or more people researching a topic through their own experience of it, using a series of cycles in which they move between this experience and reflecting together on it' (Heron 1996, p.1).

Co-operative inquiry is understood (and explained here) as a process between action and reflection. It is a participative, person-centred method, which uses participants' own experiences and emotions as research instruments studying *with* people rather than conducting research *on* them. Crucially, co-operative inquiry includes participants within 'a mutually supportive collective endeavour' (Winter and Munn-Giddings 2003, p.32) and is described by Carr and Kemmis as a 'self-reflective community' (p.33). Seel (2008d) identifies that to achieve change and improve practice we must empower our workforce, while Stanley, Miller and Richardson-Foster (2011) argue that to challenge male abuse, social workers must feel confident and empowered. Co-operative inquiry was a method that potentially could support empowerment theory in addition to the research aims.

Co-operative inquiry is also a very appealing method when one considers the context and environment of Children's Social Care, as it recognises multiple roles, it demystifies research, utilises practitioner expertise and builds an organisationally based culture of inquiry while off-setting hierarchical and power relationships. The preparatory research and literature identified inherent resistance to the research aims. Co-operative inquiry is a methodology that subtly ameliorates resistance by encouraging talking skills and emotional literacy in working relationships. The co-operative inquiry integrated Jacobs' (2010) recommendations in responding to resistance as a way of deconstructing defences: by identifying and naming the resistance and then attempting to explain it through the appreciation of the social workers' anxiety, identifying what is being resisted and asking social workers to corroborate or refute the explanation or ask social workers what feelings are being resisted (Trevithick 2011). I also applied in the co-operative inquiry Schneider *et al.*'s (1998) theory of change to achieve human potential, as it rests on a number of assumptions, which I also held.[2]

The rest of this chapter focuses on the prerequisites, challenges and complexities when establishing and implementing a practice research project in social work.

PREREQUISITES TO SUPPORT RELATIONSHIP-BASED PRACTICE RESEARCH

Securing organisational support

I went about establishing the co-operative inquiry by first securing senior management and organisational support for the project.[3] Powerful organisational 'players' needed to be persuaded of the prospective benefits of the inquiry while conversely be convinced it did not present a threat to what Obholzer (2002a/2002b) describes as the primary task. It was crucial to gain the support of the senior management team within Children's Social Care and of the wider 'integrated' Assistant Directors of Children's Services, otherwise the research would have quickly floundered. Leonard (2005), citing numerous other academics on change in organisations, argues that transformational change cannot be achieved without the support of good corporate leadership.

---

2   i. People crave growth and development and can be creative when permitted such opportunities.
    ii. People place significance on interpersonal interaction (with peers and supervisors). The formal and informal nature of these relationships is a prominent characteristic of organisational life.
    iii. People require encouragement, collaboration and confidence to perform successfully.

3   Senior managers are confronted by a myriad of new policies, procedures and initiatives and changing and competing priorities. For example, at the time of the research there was significant uncertainty caused by the rationalisation of budgets and the subsequent reduction in resources and service re-organisation. These conditions were not conducive to committing organisational support, social work and management time and resources to an 18-month research inquiry.

Positively, 'the roots' of support came from the original preparatory research. My line manager agreed to continue to support further activity on the understanding that the organisation of the work was completed outside of office hours. This situation changed one year into the inquiry when the project became mainstreamed into the Children-in-Need and Safeguarding Children's Board Service Plans.

I presented a summary of the original research to the senior management teams of both Children's Social Care (of which I am a member) and Children's Services. I focused the presentation on the gap in practice and the potential benefits to the organisation and practitioners. A passionate discussion followed, with both management teams unanimously agreeing that further work should be undertaken – to quote one manager, 'to address this obvious flaw in the management of risk'.

During this time, I portrayed myself, as Meyerson and Scully (1995) describe, as a 'tempered radical'. Coghlan and Brannick (in Mead 2002, p.25) point out that 'doing research in and on your own organisation is particularly political, indeed it might [even] be considered subversive'. This is an important point when undertaking practice research in one's organisation. I was able to use my well-established professional relationships and my status and position as 'currency' within the organisation to negotiate and secure tangible organisational support including:

- authority to proceed with the inquiry
- authority for staff to participate in a practice research project
- publicity across digital and print journals within the council
- access to other forums such as the Corporate Equalities forum, the Safeguarding Children's Board, and senior management teams of Universal Health Services, Police, Early Years Services and Education
- access to data, information and IT systems
- resources, including £5000 to support the research activity and a research assistant for one day a fortnight.

This investment of time and energy in gaining organisational support proved pivotal. I was also offered encouragement, advice and guidance by peers within my own management team. This allowed additional reflection when meeting barriers to the research, particularly during the setting up phase, and also an on-going 'space' to discuss the development of the research. Conversely and anecdotally, this level of organisational support can add unnecessary pressures, particularly in relation to expectations about meaningful results.

I also needed to recognise my role as an inside researcher. Research such as this mixed methodology diverges from traditional notions of scientifically sound research where the researcher is an 'objective outsider' examining subjects external to his or herself (Denzin and Lincoln 2011). As professionals we have completed a study of our own practices and work setting; this is also termed 'practitioner research'. The co-operative inquiry was a collaborative research effort and as such we were all actively involved in carrying out research as recommended by Titchen and Binnie (1993).

Professional relationships, networks and recruiting research participants

After securing senior management support, I turned to my well-established professional relationships and networks in the organisation and the surrounding multi-agency landscape, to identify potential allies and supporters for the research. Over the course of the research these allies would support the study by providing or facilitating access (especially access to forums locally and nationally), advice and resources or, more notably, advancing systems, policies and procedural changes. I also developed relationships with national organisations such as the Fatherhood Institute, the Domestic Violence Intervention Project and Respect, all of whom were interested in the research aims.

Once organisational support was secured and resources and a methodology had been identified, I put out what Heron (1996, p.40) terms 'an initiator's call' for 'potential participants to join a broad inquiry about including fathers in social work practice'. The initial call was broad as it was important that, from the very beginning, potential participants had a clear message that they would define the focus of inquiry. I employed several strategies to recruit participants. Positive remnants of the preparatory 2009 research remained, with some social workers who participated in the original research reporting that they would be interested in continuing their involvement should the research evolve. The original research inquiry had started an organisational debate about the inclusion of fathers and it felt as if our work remained unfinished.

I used my networking and negotiating skills to identify potential participants who I knew could greatly contribute to a process of facilitated emergence in the organisation. As we had identified that psychological and organisational defences significantly contributed to the exclusion of fathers, this left me keen to attract social workers and managers who thought pyschodynamically and systemically. I also wanted the inquiry to have a balance of inquirers in terms of representatives from each social work team, experience of statutory social work, position and function within the organisation, ethnicity and gender. As I had learnt from the original 2009 research, I felt it essential for the research's validity, legitimacy and outcomes that we should achieve an equilibrium within the composition of the group. In the original research I had two male supervisors and I felt this led to an imbalance of perspectives. I hoped that our diversity would lead to conversations about difference, although there was never any expectation that female or co-inquirers from ethnic minorities were expected to support the inquiry group to learn about feminist or racist practices (Dominelli 1988).

I sent a blanket email to every social worker and manager employed within the Children-in-Need Service, launching the inquiry and inviting potential participants to an induction meeting. I attached a summary of the original research, a link to the research proposal and a first draft copy of a potential contract of participation to provoke discussion. I also emailed those who had already expressed an interest in attending with a few reflections on topics to be discussed. I also sent a reminder to every social worker within the service the day before the first induction meeting, inviting attendance.

From the very beginning of the inquiry three principles were at the forefront of the research:

1. Initiating and supporting the participants' understanding of the methodology so they felt ownership.

2. The emergence of participative decision making and genuine collaboration, meaning the co-operative inquiry would become collaborative.

3. The formation of an ambience within the group where pain and anxiety aroused by the inquiry could be recognised, openly acknowledged and processed through reflective discussion.

(Heron 1996)

The induction of potential participations had to be well organised because it would provide the platform to articulate, integrate and role model these three principles from the beginning of the research process. The induction was the foundation for the research inquiry and it was crucial that potential participants felt that they understood the method, the decision-making process and felt safe enough to commit to the research.

The first induction meeting took place in a large meeting room within the Children-in-Need Service. We met for three hours. The induction was designed to mirror the co-operative inquiry method and to attract participation by showing those who attended a very different way of facilitating practice development. The primary outcome I wanted from the first induction meeting was to 'induct, select, inform and agree the focus of the inquiry' (Heron 1996, p.62).

At the end of the induction meeting an anonymous feedback questionnaire was circulated to participants who fed-back that 'they were excited to be involved in a project that was directly linked to practice development' but indicated that attendees 'did not fully understand the concepts surrounding the co-operative inquiry methodology'. Despite this, a total of seven people agreed to participate.

Adhering to the principles of co-operative inquiry, I felt it was important to organise a second induction meeting, which was arranged for an entire day three weeks later in a meeting room in the Town Hall, a separate building from the Children-in-Need Service. Forty-eight hours after the conclusion of the second induction/first reflection meeting the group agreed, paraphrasing McArdle (2002), the following terms of words:

We are a co-operative inquiry of 12 with numerous others [allies] on the peripheries. We know who we are. We have established and started to develop a group identity, a group consciousness and a collective understanding. Importantly, we have an agreed name: 'Breaking Down Barriers'. We are six men and six women, we have an age range of 32 to 53, we are all qualified social workers, we are four managers and eight social workers, and we are all educated to a minimum of a masters level. We are made up of three black British women, two black African women, two black British men, one Turkish British male, one Canadian white woman and three white British males; and we are based within the Children-in-Need Service and the Safeguarding and Quality Assurance, of Children's Social Care, and two external partners: Domestic Violence Intervention Project and Respect. We have agreed an ethical framework and a set of validity procedures, (both subject to review). We are using co-operative inquiry to explore what systems and practices exclude fathers in social work and we are identifying methods which encourage the inclusion of fathers within social work practice.

Foulkes (in Seager and Thummel 2009) argues that groups are most effective in terms of analysis when they reflect great diversity of psychopathologies, gender, age and cultural backgrounds, which is what we attempted here. The inquiry was successfully launched because we negotiated with multiple stakeholders. There are a series of hierarchies and layers of accountability within Children's Social Care which needed to be identified, respected and positively 'traversed'. The inquiry was also able to informally recruit senior managers who were 'supporters' and allies of the inquiry but who remained on its boundary. These 'supporters' had different expectations and demands and it was crucial to maintain a sophisticated level of communication through the initiation phase but also through the entire life of the project. Indeed, it was crucial to continually nurture these 'supporters' as well as identify new supporters and allies as the project matured (Charles and Glennie 2002).

I specifically targeted some of the most respected social workers and managers in the organisation (those who I believed would excel in a self-organised system) to participate in the research. I knew most of the research participants and identified those who could accept ambiguity while being innovative and creative. We recognised that we all had different roles within the organisation, depending on where we sat in the hierarchy. This was unique and, as I now recognise, crucial to advancing the project aims. I wanted co-inquirers to be representative of the organisational hierarchy as the barriers to inclusion were at every level of the organisation. I also wanted managers as participants as this would allow greater influence in bringing about organisational change (Seel 2008a).

The participants represented or were able to influence most parts of the systems we were working within. As the inquiry matured and as participants felt confident and empowered, the inquiry integrated itself into the business-as-usual activity of Children's Social Care. This integration proved pivotal as participants used their relationships to influence others in the organisation to change practice. Participants were able to lead conversations in team meetings and in formal activities such as legal planning meetings and child protection conferences. These conversations, coupled with changing systems and a consistent communication strategy, meant that the project infiltrated into organisational language via the social relations: 'With a name [Breaking Down Barriers], an identity, a regular time slot and a physical space, participants' ideas were validated as to the primary purpose of the project' (Barrett 2009, p.233).

I postulate that these project characteristics contributed to a change in the organisational sub-culture.

Wider relations and research

Presenting to the Local Safeguarding Children Board (LSCB) was a defining moment in the life of the inquiry because it allowed conversations about the inclusion of fathers to happen among professionals in many other settings. Senior leaders from across the safeguarding partnership asked to be involved because all recognised there was a significant gap in practice. The positive reaction from LSCB members ignited the project and the co-operative inquiry members, as well as colleagues in Children's Social Care. This was a 'transformational dialogue' as was the presentation of the project at the Department of Education as part of the Munro Review into Child Protection. This acted as the tipping point of the project, releasing energy into the system, which was now perceived by most people in the organisation as having authority, legitimacy and power. The inquiry was given renewed energy and our aims became possible – for example, no longer did I need to think about when it was strategically appropriate to talk about fathers.

As the inquiry evolved, it became a significant part of each inquirer's life as colleagues spoke informally about the increasing profile of the research, allowing participants to take up additional roles. 'Critical mass' was generated through the maturation of relationships in the group.

In observing the co-operative inquiry group, it was possible to see how their patterns of behaviour and the group dynamics changed as co-inquirers became familiar with one another. 'Surface' defensive behaviours slowly diminished, evidencing greater collaboration. Indeed, as the inquiry became more integrated into organisational life, the co-inquirers' roles changed, blurring expectations and easing transition between the roles of participants, as researchers and as practitioners. In turn, the integration of the project's aims into the daily business of the organisation (a key to the success of the research), influenced beliefs and attitudes among workers, a crucial dynamic for bringing about change in the organisation (Malin 2000; Rothbard, Philips and Dumas 2005).

This is what some of the co-inquirers said of the method:

It was our method and our research we were not just the subjects. We chose it, we designed it and I felt we, as practitioners, were at the centre of it.

We had the power to ask what we wanted to know and we had some resources to find out.

I understood it, it was flexible and it appealed to me because of my value base as a social worker.

I liked the cycle of action and reflection because we could measure every few weeks whether practice was changing.

It was good to work with one of our senior managers so differently. He was nearly one of us.

The co-operative inquiry created a space for working in confidence, for taking risks, for dialogue and discussion among co-inquirers where differing perceptions were clarified. This allowed co-inquirers to develop mature relationships with one another. The group developed over time as we became even more accustomed to one another in our new knowledge. This evolution led to changes in group behaviour and allowed for greater sophistication in analysis due to familiarisation and trust. The co-operative inquiry process challenged co-inquirers' feelings of isolation by bringing different ways of thinking to 'a space to reflect over the needs of children, families and the profession' (as quoted by one of the co-inquirers within the research). The methodology built trust and confidence in relationships among the co-inquirers and between co-inquirers and the department (Cooper, Hetherington and Katz 2003).

Alongside these developments, there were an increasing number of 'allies' in the research. These allies included a range of senior and middle managers as well as social workers, who were essential as they offered resources, behind-the-scenes support and encouragement, supporting the objectives of the inquiry as well as advancing the aims of the research.

THE COMPLEXITIES AND CHALLENGES OF UNDERTAKING RELATIONSHIP-BASED PRACTICE RESEARCH

A number of complexities came to light during the research.

Leadership and the exercise of power

I had a central role in the creation of the group. I knew there was a need for a group, I approached most inquirers prior to the induction and I had a professional relationship with each. This meant that when we met, each co-inquirer shared a common experience: my invitation for them to join the group. Other common relationships existed in the group – for example, as supervisors or as members of other developmental groups such as the newly qualified programme. This meant that throughout the project I was perceived as the leader of the inquiry, particularly as leadership responsibility is prioritised during the initial stages. With this leadership came power, which was needed to establish the inquiry but which hindered the reflective processes and relationships because I was perceived as 'the boss'. Power was ever-present throughout the life of the co-operative inquiry. Naively, I had attempted to find a balance in power, or in what I understood as power at the time, by structuring the group with an equal distribution of power and an equal voice for women and men. I firmly yet naively believed that this equal gender mix would counter the power of language and limit the replication of the oppression of women by men in wider society. In a further bid to manage the influence of power, we established co-facilitation of each reflective meeting. No matter what, my voice in the group remained significant, it shaped the process, it energised but also restricted.

My influence was present from the start. I had already developed an idea of who I wanted as members and the function of the group. I had identified the problem and believed with the support of others that I could go some way to resolve it. I used my energy, determination, my position, my 'currency' and my evaluation of the problem to establish the group and I kept the group going with my enthusiasm. I chose people I knew would thrive in self-organising systems. Conversely, I now recognise that these issues also acted to constrain the group as I established a leadership role and influenced the group's functioning. In undertaking a practice research project in my own organisation, I failed to recognise that I had a multiplicity of roles – roles that I thought I was keen to transfer to other participants although my journal reflections evidenced that during the early stages of the inquiry I was particularly split over the loss of power and control of the project. For example, I wrote that 'transferring the facilitator role to other co-inquirers concerned me greatly as I believed this would lead to a loss of direction and a breakdown in the group process'.

I was determined and felt powerful 'paternal' feelings of responsibility as the inquiry initiator, to create an inquiry that was safe, protected and sheltered. I was continually aware that I needed to 'let go', although I ignored this awareness. I knew I needed to promote a feeling of collective ownership of the research and shed my own concepts of ownership as this would further encourage authentic collaboration. We discussed the issue of leadership in the group and we agreed to take it in turns to facilitate each reflective meeting. Each co-inquirer was encouraged to develop their own skills and insight as they needed to become well-honed instruments of research. This was challenging in an organisational culture that had an overt focus on process (Mead 2002).

During reflective meetings I would experience feelings of fear, dread and a lack of confidence. I was anxious I would not be able to establish a group or drive forward the research aims. I felt vulnerable within the organisation and among peers, advocating for a perceived radical change in practice that was potentially threatening to managers' and workers' very survival. I felt responsible to provide a safe, meaningful space for co-inquirers and yet I felt de-skilled, especially during the early reflective meetings, thinking I was unable to contain and process anxiety, projection, transference and counter-transference.

I was also conscious of what Armstrong, Bazalgette and Hutton (1994, p.2) term the 'organisation in the mind', which they describe as the 'mental picture of the institution in its context which is informing the managers' experience, shaping their behaviour and influencing their working relationships both overtly and covertly'. Early in the life of the co-operative inquiry, co-inquirers participated in a reflective exercise where we attempted to identify the emotional meaning and reality of the organisation for each co-inquiry. We were able to identify risk with the concomitant need to prioritise the need for systems of safety. I understand that this was an essential component of completing the organisation's core task, although the process remained flawed because I facilitated the exercise only once. On reflection, I believe it would have been much more beneficial if an independent person had consulted and facilitated this exercise throughout the life of the project.

I now recognise that I compensated for my feelings of powerlessness by trying to gain power from others in the group. Power, according to Foucault (1980), is located in the positions people occupy rather than in people themselves. I held power in terms of my organisational position, which was further reinforced because I initiated the research and had considerable knowledge of the subject. I unconsciously, yet purposefully, put myself in a position of 'knowing better', which allowed me to impose my reality and maintain my position of power. This recreated existing power relations. I also believe, again using a 'Foucaultian' (1979) lens, that other co-inquirers also replicated the existing power relations and through projection and identification denigrated the quality of reflection because we re-enacted the dominant male discourse, sustaining institutional power as an unconscious contribution to maintain the status quo (Chambon, Irving and Epstein 1999; Gutting 1995).

One way we countered the negatives of power relations was to share knowledge as widely as possible across the inquiry group and later across the organisation in order to raise consciousness. We had to include a plan to disseminate knowledge, raise awareness and liberate through education in what Gaventa and Cornwall (2009, p.72) describe as 'the promotion of a critical consciousness'.

DOMINANT ORGANISATIONAL CULTURES
AND CONSTRUCTIONS

A further challenge to the research was the organisational culture, which remained an ever-present influence within the research activities. Indeed, it had a palpable presence throughout the inquiry. I now believe that this dominant organisational culture and the hierarchies in co-inquirers' minds that surrounded the research, influenced the group's functions, individual and collective thinking and subsequently the research findings (Dwivedi and Harper 2007). In writing up the research, I realised that the conscious and unconscious hierarchical power relations and dominant organisational culture were a constant dimension of the project and required an on-going cycle of reflection in order to regularly reflect on how it was influencing the project – something we simply did not do.

In hindsight, I now realise the research was an attempt to upset and to think differently about traditional power relations and therefore the dominant cultures and constructs operating in our organisation. The application of feminist thought went some way to ameliorate the worst of the oppressions because it pushed me to examine my own multiple identities, particularly my masculinity and how this influenced my management and researcher identity within the context of the organisation and the inquiry. I have also learnt more about my own identity and the need to expose silencing mechanisms, especially when they intersect with other oppressions.

Despite having other co-inquirers facilitate, I found myself wanting to direct and manage the group, and I had to regularly request co-inquirers to challenge me over this. My over-involvement was also evident in the number of actions assigned to me at the end of each meeting. I found myself needing (or wanting) to intercede to identify emotional responses, additional tasks or research findings. I positioned myself as 'a central person' throughout the life of the research. I have had this view confirmed by an external observer, who perceived me as having enhanced status in the group. I think the degree of influence I maintained over the group was significant, impacting upon individuals' behaviour and the outcome of the research, and was in opposition to the purity of the co-operative inquiry model as advanced by Bradbury and Reason (2009), Douglas (2000) and Heron (1996).

This was then additionally complicated by gender, which can never be avoided. Gender cannot be transcended as it is one of the most important categorisers, structuring internal and external experiences, and so is a basic method of perception. Consequently, gender and sexual difference could not have been denied in the group as they fuelled what was said and thought about in the group. During the research, we did not consider the insidious clandestine nature of patriarchal power and control and how it would affect group interaction. It is relevant to point out that writing about gender and sexual difference is not a neutral activity as I use the categories to organise experience. It has certainly brought me head to head with my own investments and desires.

IS IT POSSIBLE TO UNDERTAKE RELATIONSHIP-BASED PRACTICE RESEARCH IN YOUR OWN ORGANISATION?

There is no 'one size fits all' approach to social work and practice development. Each practitioner or researcher needs to design a bespoke plan contingent on the characteristics, circumstances, relationships and culture within their own organisations (Pawson 2006).

The Breaking Down Barriers research project had a broad appeal as the research topic affected all social workers and managers in the organisation while the themes also appealed to other professions, such as health visitors, midwives and educationalists. This bestowed the project with potential longevity, while the collaborative nature of the project gave inquirers the capacity to accommodate different ideologies. We adapted our research and our strategies, allowing for it to fit into every level and 'cog' of the functioning system of Children's Social Care and exploiting every chance to maximise the research opportunity. For example, we had 'change agents' and 'father inclusive champions' positioned across the organisation. We encouraged a 'sub-cultural shift' within the organisation's culture to allow social workers and managers to have conversations about fathers and fear (Heron 1996, p.145). This occurred through a commitment to the principles of Senge's (1990) learning organisation, particularly through collaboration, which is a proven method to empower workers (Smith 2001).

In part the research achieved a level of transformation because it took place within the correct conditions with a series of relationships already established. What also supported the research was that the infrastructure of the organisation was frequently modernised and the operating systems continually updated. There was a commitment to engaging with all workers across the hierarchy. These attributes provided solid foundations for the project.

The organisation has a particular culture, which emanated throughout the co-inquiry as we, unconsciously, duplicated the 'cultural way of doing and being' in the inquiry (Gaventa and Cornwall 2009, p.56). Children's Social Care is fast-paced where expectations are high over standards and quality. In order to assimilate into the organisation, the inquiry functioned and mirrored this culture. This developed what Gaventa and Cornwall (2009, p.58) describe as 'a mobilisation of biases', in favour of a certain type of exploration while suppressing other forms of reflection. This meant some topics were included in discussion while others were 'organised out'. For example, we failed to speak about difference, particularly gender, in the group in any meaningful way, preferring to accept the group's view that our agreed validity processes and procedures – for example, mixed gendered co-facilitation – combatted the pervasive nature of power relations. The project needed to have greater depth to be able to realise that, as members of society, we would replicate power relations and social inequalities in the inquiry. By assimilating to the organisational culture, the inquiry achieved much, but it failed to be truly reflective and missed further opportunities to advance father inclusion, particularly in relation to generating data about diversity in ethnicity, sexuality and class.

We recruited a group of co-inquirers who were motivated, committed and faithful to the task, and all played a pivotal role co-operating across the organisation to advance the inquiry's aims. We had to involve everyone in the service. This was essential for sustainability. We had senior management support, we integrated the research into the everyday life of the organisation, infiltrating its systems, processes and procedures, and we used a methodology that was concomitant with our social work ethics, values and ways of working; indeed, it is a methodology that by design encourages participation. The Breaking Down Barriers project became a well-known nomenclature across the organisation. Its work could be found across the service and its members were a common sight and sound across the organisation.

I have discovered that co-operative inquiry is an important tool within the 'social work tool bag' as it is a methodology to help us recognise defensive behaviours. This will encourage managers to foster an environment that stimulates creativity, inventiveness and enterprise from within. Co-operative inquiry should be used to analyse practice difficulties in other areas of social work as well as be used to consider wider barriers such as racism.

The co-operative inquirers were keen that the research be replicated. With this in mind the experience of this research informs us that when researching one's own organisation the work must always consider and plan for the roles of power and authority and these must be regularly reflected upon. Clearly then, the entire research process would be very different if a female senior manager in Children's Social Care had established a similar project. It would have been driven with a different set of sympathies. I recognise now I should have jointly launched and conducted this research with a female senior manager.

The co-operative inquiry taught me about the pervasive role of gender relations. Establishing and running a co-operative inquiry has led me to argue that as members of society, our individual social constructions of our gendered roles unconsciously determine, in the context of this research, social workers' and organisations' behaviour. I base this on the research findings but also the experience of the co-operative inquiry, which bore witness to the re-enactment of gendered identities and thus power relations that were palpably present throughout the research.

I had attempted to find a balance in power (in what I understood as power at the time) by structuring the group as equally mixed. I firmly yet naively believed that this equal gender mix would counter the power of language and limit the replication of the oppression of women by men in wider society. Within the context of this research, I was aware that the use of language mirrored gender differences within the group. For example, in research completed by Dutton and Nicholls (2005) some female participants use the language of care while male participants use the language of managerialism. In a further bid to manage the influence of power, from March 2011 we established co-facilitation with two co-inquirers (one male and one female). No matter what, my voice in the group remained significant, it shaped the process, it energised but also restricted and I need to identify why.

I now recognise that I compensated for my feelings of powerlessness by trying to gain power from others in the group. I felt my identity and self-esteem weakened through a loss of power and my subordination to others and so I adopted alternative strategies to oppose and reassert hegemony.

I have questioned whether the increasing abilities and skills of the inquirers stirred up feelings of envy as my hegemonic position was threatened, which then evoked in me the need to control by exerting power. I have reflected whether I attempted to control the inquirers through unconscious, indirect envious attack by not facilitating as well and by blocking creative ideas. This may have inhibited emergence although I believe I have the capacity to desist from envious attacks as it is a major managerial asset to facilitate the development of your staff (Obholzer 1996).

My current managerial identity was highly influential as I felt I had the experience, ability, professional position and seniority (bestowed by the organisation and, as I later discovered, by the group) to take risks. The change needed required active leadership. I used my energy, enthusiasm and determination to establish and maintain group direction, and the inquiry that emerged was influenced and led by me. This is a methodological limitation and, despite the persistent encouragement of co-facilitation, my own and the group's need for dynamic leadership remained. On reflection I realised that my role, as the organising manager, was to take ownership, which also meant there was implicit power and authority in the inquiry. I, with support and feedback, acted as 'the custodian of the design' (Heron 1996).

A significant challenge to the inquiry and my ability to reflect was my attempt, as a practitioner researcher, to undertake a complex piece of research within Children's Social Care. We endeavoured to create a reflective space within the whirlwind emotional experience and bombardment of child protection work. We punctuated this maelstrom by meeting for three hours every six weeks within our office. How could I have created a mental space for the inquiry when our minds were consumed by the stresses and the emotional reactions of child abuse? On reflection, our working environment prevented thought. For example, I believe that the organisational pressures and counter-transference at times led me to provide co-inquirers with what Copely and Forryan (1986, p.169), describe as 'pseudo-listening' and 'pseudo-containment'. I now recognise that children's specialist services 'lends itself to this type of functioning' (Horne *et al.* 2006, p.7).

CONCLUSION

The research we conducted in our organisation did bring about practice change and altered the organisational sub-culture to include a previously excluded group. The research was successful because it was based on relationships. In this circumstance the theory of practice-based research was founded on securing long-term senior management support, and on developing, attending to and relying on relationships and networks, particularly recruiting research participants who were committed to contributing to practice development. There are a number of complexities and challenges in undertaking relationship-based practice research, particularly in the conscious and unconscious exercise of power, which involved identifying and negotiating with the dominant organisational cultures and constructions. The experience of the co-operative inquiry bore witness to the re-enactment of gendered identities and thus power relations were palpably present throughout the research. So it is possible to complete practice-based research if one is sensitive and plans are established to manage what is thought but not said.

REFERENCES

Alexandrov, H. (2009) 'Experiencing knowledge: The vicissitudes of a research journey.' In S. Clarke and P. Hogget (eds.) *Researching Beneath the Surface: Psycho-Social Research, Methods in Practice.* London: Karmac.

Armstrong, D., Bazalgette, J. and Hutton, J. (1994) What does management really mean? *How psych-analytic and systemic thinking interact to illuminate the management of institutions.* Presented to the International Consulting Conference. The Group Institute. South Bank University 28–30 January 1994.

Barrett, P., A. (2009) 'The Early Mothering Project: What Happened When Words "Action Research" Came to Life for a Group of Midwives.' In P. Reason and H. Bradbury *The Handbook of Action Research.* London: Sage.

Carr, W. and Kemmis, S. (2004) *Becoming Critical: Education, Knowledge and Action Research.* London: Routledge.

Chambon, A., Irving, A. and Epstein, L. (1999) *Reading Foucault for Social Work.* New York: Columbia.

Charles, M. and Glennie, S. (2002) 'Co-operative Inquiry: Changing Inter-professional Practice.' In P. Reason (ed.) *Special Issue: The Practice of Co-operative Inquiry: Systemic Practice and Action Research*. Bath: Bath University.

Cooper, A., Hetherington, R. and Katz, I. (2003) *The Risk Factor: Making the Child Protection System Work for Children*. London: Demos.

Copley, B., Forryan, B. and O'Neill, L. (1986) 'Play therapy and counselling work with children.' *British Journal of Occupational Therapy 50*, 413–416.

Denzin, N. K. and Lincoln, Y. S. (2011) *Handbook of Qualitative Research*. London: Sage.

Dominelli, L (1988) *Anti-Racist Social Work Practice 2nd edition*. Basingstoke: Macmillan.

Douglas, T. (2000) *Basic Groupwork*. London: Routledge.

Dutton, D. G. and Nicholls, T. L. (2005) 'The Gender Paradigm in Domestic Violence Research and Theory: Part 1 – The Conflict of Theory and Data.' *Aggression & Violent Behaviour 10*, 680–714.

Dwivedi, K. D. and Harper, P. B. (2007) *Promoting the Emotional Well-being of Children and Adolescents and Preventing their Mental Ill Health*. London and Philadelphia, PA: Jessica Kingsley Publishers.

Foucault, M. (1979) *The History of Sexuality: Part 1*. London: Allen Lane.

Foucault, M. Gordon C. (1980) *Power and Knowledge*. New York: Pantheon Books.

Froggett, L. and Briggs, S. (2009) 'Editorial.' *Journal of Social Work Practice 23*, 4, 377–382.

Gaventa, J. and Cornwall, A. (2009) 'Power and Knowledge.' in P. Reason and H. Bradbury, *The Handbook of Action Research*. London: Sage.

Gutting, G. (1995) T*he Cambridge Companion to Foucault*. Cambridge: Cambridge University Press.

Heron, J. (1996) *Co-operative Inquiry: Research into the Human Condition*. London: Sage.

Horne, A. *et al.* (2006) In A. Horne and M. Lanyado (eds) *Winnicott's Children*. Independent Psychoanalytic Approaches with Children and Adolescents. London: Routledge.

Jacobs, P. (2010) 'Charged particle multiplicity measurement in proton–proton collisions.' *The European Physical Journal of Particles and Fields* 68, 3–4, 345–354.

Jarvis, P. (1999) *The Practitioner-Researcher: Developing Theory from Practice*. High and Adult Education Series. San Francisco, CA: Jossey-Bass.

Leonard, A. (2005) 'Exploring Challenges to Transformational Leadership Communication about Employment Equity.' *Transformational Change Management and Change Communication*. South Africa: University of Pretoria.

Malin, N. (2000) *Professional, boundaries and the workplace*. London: Routledge.

Mead, G. (2002) 'Developing Ourselves as Police Leaders: How can we inquire collaboratively in a hierarchical organisation?' In P. Reason (ed.) (2002) *Special Issue: The Practice of Co-operative Inquiry: Systemic Practice and Action Research*. Bath: Bath University.

McArdle, K. L. (2002) 'Establishing a co-operative inquiry group: the perspective of a "first-timer" inquirer. In P. Reason (ed.) *Special Issue: The practice of Co-operative Inquiry: Systemic Practice and Action Research*. Bath: Bath University.

Meyerson, D. E. and Scully, M. A. (1995) 'Tempered Radicalism and the politics of ambivalence and courage.' *Organisational Science 6*, 5, 585–600.

Obholzer, A. (2002a) 'Authority, Power and Leadership: Contributions from Group Relations Training.' In A. Obholzer and V. Roberts (eds) *The Unconscious at Work: Individual and Organisational Stress in the Human Service*. London: Routledge.

Obholzer, A. (2002b) 'Managing Anxieties in Public Sector Organisations.' In A. Obholzer and V. Roberts (eds) *The Unconscious at Work: Individual and Organisational Stress in the Human Service*. London: Routledge.

Obholzer, A. (1996) 'Psychoanalytic Contributions to Authority and Leadership Issues.' *Leadership and Organisation Developmental Journal 17*, 6, 53–56.

Ofsted (2012) Inspection of safeguarding and looked after children services: report from Care Quality Commission and Ofsted.

Pawson, R. (2006) *Evidence Based Policy*. London: Sage.

Reason, P. and Bradbury, H. (2009) *The Handbook of Action Research*. London: Sage.

Rothbard, N., Philips, K. and Dumas, T. (2005) 'Managing Multiple Roles: Work-Family Policies & Individuals' Desires for Segmentation.' *Organisation Science Volume 16*, 3, 243–258.

Schneider *et al.* (1998) 'Personality and organisations: A test of the homogeneity of personal hypothesis.' *Journal of Applied Psychology 83*, 3, 462–470.

Seager, M. and Thummel, U., (2009) 'Group analysis. Chocolates and flowers? You must be joking! Of men and tenderness in group therapy.' *The Group Analytic Society.* London: Sage.

Seel, R. (2008a) *Complexity and Organisational Development: An Introduction.* Available at www.newparadigm.co.uk/complexity.htm

Seel, R. (2008b) *Culture and Complexities. New Insights on Organisational Change.* Available at www.newparadigm.co.uk/culture-complex.htm

Seel, R. (2008c) *Organisational Culture Check List.* Available at www.newparadigm.co.uk/checklist.htm

Seel, R. (2008d) *Nature of Change: The Nature of Organisational Change.* Available at www.newparadigm.co.uk/nature_of_change.html

Senge, P (1990) *The Fifth Discipline: The art and Practice of the Learning Organisation.* London: Random House.

Smith, M. K. (2001) *Peter Senge and the Learning Organisation. The Encyclopaedia of Informed Education.* Available at www.infed.org/thinkers/argyris.htm, accessed 23 September 2015.

Swan, G. (2015) 'Breaking Down Barriers: Engaging Fathers in Children's Social Care.' Unpublished doctoral thesis, University of East London, Tavistock and Portman NHS Foundation Trust.

Stanley, N., Miller, P., Richardson-Foster, H. and Thomson, G. (2011) 'A stop-start response: Social services' interventions with children and families notified following domestic violence incidents.' *British Journal of Social Work 41*, 296–313.

Titchen, A. and Binnie, A. (1993) 'A Unified Action Research Strategy in Nursing.' *Educational Action Research 1*, 1, 25–33.

Trevithick, P. (2011) 'Understanding defences and defensiveness in social work.' Special Issue: Defence and Defensiveness. *Journal of Social Work Practice 25*, 4, 389–412.

Winter, R. and Munn-Giddings, C. (2003) *A Handbook for Action Research in Health and Social Care.* London and New York: Routledge.

Chapter 9

CRITICAL REFLECTION ON FICTION
INCREASING PRACTITIONER REFLEXIVITY, MAKING KNOWLEDGE AND ENHANCING PRACTICE

Katarina Fagerström

INTRODUCTION

From my practice experience, I can recall how skilful children and young people were in hiding or diminishing their problems. This easily misled my colleagues and me. By sticking to readymade explanations of clients' situations, professionals miss the opportunity to see or listen to the signals that clients give. Even for experienced practitioners it is a demanding task to recognise problems at an early stage and service users can experience disappointment in relation to professionals' blindness (Fagerström 2005). In this chapter I will discuss my experience of using critical reflection in research and the potential of using fiction as a source for learning and knowledge making in groups of professionals.

Drawing on action research, in this chapter I analyse how knowledge is worked out and processed in focus groups of professionals. My interest is particularly in studying how using fictional novels and autobiographical literature (subsequently referred to for reasons of brevity as fictional novels) can promote critical reflection in social work. Another focus is on how knowledge is made in groups. The empirical material for this study consists of 27 written reflections by 27 group members and four audiotaped 90-minute focus group conversations, all focused on thinking about how issues with substance misuse are identified and responded to. As an illustrative example, I present the educational model used for critical reflection in four focus group sessions, where I used fictional novels to stimulate the systemic, dialogic and reflexive knowledge making processes. My overall aim in these sessions was to create a space for the practitioners' reflections on their own assumptions and values and to share experiences and knowledge for developing the practice of recognising, at an early stage, substance misuse problems in families. Finally, I move on to discussing the potential of reading fiction for transformative learning and knowledge making and I analyse how this kind of reflective model for inter-professional collaboration in social work could contribute to knowledge production in social work.

MOVING FROM A PRACTITIONER'S POSITION TO A RESEARCHER'S POSITION IN AN ACTION RESEARCH FRAMEWORK

Becoming a researcher was a new experience for me, one in which I could use my working experiences and practice wisdom to conduct action research. As a researcher I firmly believe that research results must primarily be considered through the first person and with active verbs, and, as Chard (2014, p.39) has put it, 'the observer's inevitable presence [should be] acknowledged, and should be written about in the first person, not the third, giving us an insight into who these observers are'. With this understanding, my voice(s) are also heard and present in the form of a first person position throughout the text. Methodologically, I used the literature of action research (Burns 2007; Heikkinen, Rovio and Syrjälä 2007; Reason and Bradbury 2008) and a mix of systemic, constructionist, reflexive, collaborative and dialogic literature from both practice and research (Hedges 2010; McNamee and Hoskin 2012; Parton and O'Byrne 2000; Simon and Chard 2014) to inform the design of the action research project.

The action research process was interwoven within a development project of three parallel group work leadership courses that I had arranged. The courses were divided into three modules: autumn (five days), winter (three days) and spring (three days) and structured around three groups (nine, six and five members in each), comprising in total

20 group members from the fields of substance misuse treatment, school social work and child welfare services. For the purposes of the research the leadership groups were also the focus groups as similar elements exist when conducting dialogue in both focus groups and when teaching group leadership or leading therapeutic or dialogic groups. In the circle of action research, I positioned myself as a group member, a teacher and a researcher. Thus my research object was the knowledge that emerged from the conversations I had with the practitioners who became my co-researchers in the focus groups.

Reflexivity is an important dimension of agency and a crucial component of qualitative research. Fook and Askeland (2007) define it as an ability to recognise our own influence, especially as knowledge creators and makers; it is the perspectives we apply when selecting particular aspects of knowledge, through which we make our judgements, that are most important (Juhila 2006; Taylor and White 2000). Reflection in dialogue involves listening to both our inner and outer voices, and learning from others' reflections and perspectives.

A FOUR SESSION RESEARCH WORKSHOP REFLECTING ON NOVELS

An exercise from a group work leadership course where the members were reading and writing reflections on fictional novels was developed into a four-session research workshop that was piloted one year later. The model was influenced by Fook's critical reflection model (Fook and Gardner 2007), taking into account issues of power (both structural and personal), and also by Ruch's (2009) relationship-based model of reflection, especially the notions of process, systemic thinking and organisational learning. I have developed the theoretical frames of the model further by introducing influences from Bakhtinian ideas of dialogue and dialogical space, which I explore below (Bakhtin 1991).

The group comprised seven professionals: a social worker, a family worker and a secretary (who came from the fields of family work in child welfare services, substance misuse treatment and school social work and had formed a previous focus group) were joined by a psychologist, a psychiatrist and a preventive substance misuse worker. The position I took up as the facilitator and researcher in the workshop required me to create a safe and relaxed environment in which the dialogues could take place. Most importantly, it was vital that the structure of the sessions was clearly set out. The participants were obliged to attend all of the sessions and the idea was to leave work preoccupations, as far as is possible, outside the workshop and to show respect towards the other participants. The workshop follows the key points for Open Dialogues and Anticipations (Arnkil and Seikkula 2015), where it is essential to foster a dialogical space instead of pursuing strategic interventions aimed at changing others. This calls for respecting the uniqueness of others without any conditions. Following this pattern, the group members present and respond in the here-and-now, instead of the facilitator guiding the process to realise normative goals. This enhances the possibility of each person being heard, which is the core principle of dialogical relationships. Practitioners learn from their reflections on how they manage to relate to the clients and families, rather than how they manage to change them. This also applies to the focus group reflection process, where the objective is to collaborate with the focus group members, instead of convincing the others of their own perspectives. In this regard, dialogue is not debate.

The workshop was turned into a reflective research evaluation process comprising four expanding sequences (see Figure 9.1):

1. During the first session, the group members were introduced to each other and they discussed and agreed which novels to read with content relevant to working in the field of substance misuse. Before the second session, members read the book and wrote down a reflection on it. This was then sent to three agreed members in the group. They wrote down their own reflection of the received reflections and sent them back to those who wrote them. So, every group member received three reflection notes written by other group members about their reflection and then finally they each wrote a reflective summary based on all the reflection notes in question.

2. In the second session, the group continued the dialogue about the books, the written reflections and the notes they received. The members reflected upon the characters in the novels, described the problems in the person's life and discussed how the person could be understood and helped. The group discussions were documented on video.

3. The third session began with video-stimulated recall, where the group watched recorded excerpts from the previous

group discussion. Group members identified and reflected on the assumptions, values, power issues, new perspectives and ideas that were raised in the videotaped conversations. Additionally, they explored what was missing. Finally, a self-critical reflection on their own influence on the conversation and their ability to listen to other group members' perspectives was observed and reflected upon.

4. In the fourth session, the group members reflected on what they had learned from each other, and on possible changes in their own understanding and reasoning about families with substance misuse-related problems. They also reflected on how their own assumptions, values and knowledge were transformed into their own practice.

The model is also influenced by David Kolb's (1984) experiential learning cycle, and Schön's (1983) model of reflective practice. Kolb's (1984) model of experiential learning describes the reflective process with the stages of *concrete experience* (here manifested as reading the novel), *reflective observation* (writing a reflection about it, sending it to group members and receiving reflection notes on one's own written reflection), *abstract conceptualisation* (dialogue in the focus group about the novel, reflections and exchanges of experiences and theoretical perspectives) and *active experimentation* (the fourth focus group conversation about how to put the experiences gained from the workshop into practice). An emotional or affective component of reflection is originally acknowledged as important in different models of reflection, first by Dewey (1933) and later by Boud, Keogn and Walker (1987).

Several models have been developed that take aspects of organisational learning and contextuality into account. Järvinen, Koivisto and Poikela (2000) have a combined cycle of learning with processes of knowledge production for individuals and communities. Models that explain how knowledge is produced in the context of an institution take on an institutionalised nature. Intuition starts from the individual and needs a group to be its interpreter and transmitter. After that, the received knowledge can be integrated as the property of the whole organisation. Group learning cannot be described without considering the individual, just as organisational learning cannot be explained without considering individuals and groups.

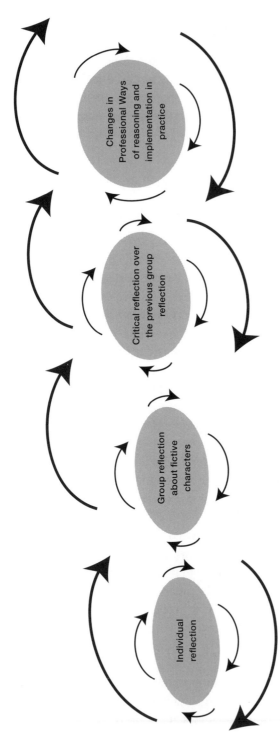

Figure 9.1: From fictive voices to reflexive practice – four sessions workshop

1. Written reflections based on novels about families with substance abuse.

2. Three sets of notes written by the other group members on each individual's reflection.

Written comment on the three sets of notes from each of the group members.

Recorded focus groups, dialogue about the characters in the novels and reflections on the interpreted problems in their lives.

3. Recorded recall on episodes from the previous group session.

Critical reflection on the co-construction of group

4. Dialogue on possible changes in ways of reasoning about families with substance abuse (e.g. how attitudes and knowledge are implemented in practice).

THE CAPACITY OF FICTION TO PROMOTE EXPERIENTIAL UNDERSTANDING

Novels and film material have previously been used in professional education and social work for the purposes of widening professional perspectives. Fiction produces openness to ideas and the possibilities of change (Taylor and White 2006). Furthermore, fiction concerns the language of the novel, which is neither professional language nor that of a particular profession. Communication in inter-professional networks, often a source of misunderstanding, needs to be premised on a shared language as a means of overcoming the cultural and language differences that exist between groups (Wenger, McDermott and Poikela 2002). Using fiction can helpfully surface these tensions to enhance practice and inform research.

The importance of using fiction in education has been discussed, for example, by the philosopher Martha Nussbaum (2010), who criticises educational programmes in Western countries as being eager for materialistic wealth, while neglecting the important skills of the humanities. Only critical thinking gives an opportunity to undertake independent action and offers intellectual resistance to blind tradition and the authority of power. She emphasises that the humanities help to develop empathy. Reading literature enriches a person's view of reality and also contributes to their moral growth as fiction offers a chance to see the world in a richer, more complex and more nuanced way. In his dissertation 'Why should physicians read?' Altzén (2010, p.245) emphasises that reading novels is of the greatest ethical importance for physicians. Naturally, this also goes for all relationship-based professions, including social work.

A novel invites the reader to change their perspective, to appreciate a context as being a series of events seen from the perspectives of several different people or the perspective of a person who may be very different from the reader. Russian linguist Michael Bakhtin specifically analysed Dostoyevsky's work and has stressed the polyphony of the novel. Bakhtin (1984) writes that the multitude of independent and un-united voices and minds – the true polyphony of full voices – actually constitutes the basic characteristic of Dostoyevsky's novels. Novelist Milan Kundera (1986) argues that a novel examines not reality, but existence. Existence is not only what has occurred, but also the whole realm of human possibilities, everything that one can become and everything one is capable of. Novelists draw up the map of existence by discovering human possibilities; hence, both the character and his world must be understood as possibilities. Ahlzén (2010, p.270) claims that there is a difference of emphasis between Bakhtin and Kundera, the former addressing the more formal aspects of the novel, and the latter the ideas that are expressed. Both, however, share the same conviction: that the novel may offer a narrow opening of freedom and potentiality in a world of determinism. Interesting similarities can be found between Bakhtin (1984) and Kundera's (1986) descriptions of a deterministic world and the writing of Healy (2014) or Parton and O'Byrne (2000) in relation to the discourses that narrowly define outcomes and evidence-based practices associated with modern developments in social work contexts. These ideas are aligned with ideals of objectivity, rationality, individualism and linear notions of progress in a world of determinism.

Both reading fiction and working from a systemic perspective are approaches that tolerate ambiguity and engage conversations that invite alternative perspectives. Central concepts for systemic thinking are 'curiosity' (Cecchin 1987) and 'not-knowing' (Anderson 1990; Anderson and Goolishian 1992). From the field of organisational learning, Senge (1990) argues that systems thinking allows individuals to move from seeing parts to seeing wholes and from seeing people as helpless reactors to seeing them as active participants, capable of creating change (Redmond 2004). It is useful to look at things systemically because it helps us to make connections that we would otherwise not have made (Burns 2007).

There is, on the other hand, a paradox in whole systems thinking. Burns (2007) brings up the fact that we can only ever see a part of the whole. Kemmis (2001) emphasises that systems theory and many of the developments of post-modern and post-structuralist theory rightly persuade us that this notion of a social whole is illusory. There are no 'whole families', 'whole' organisations, 'whole' societies, 'whole' systems or 'whole states' that are the subjects of social theory or practice. There are just interwoven, interlocking, overlapping networks of social relationships, which galvanise power and discourses in different directions and in different ways in relation to the personal, social and cultural realms.

Feedback-loops are central in systems theory, and in dialogic terms it is responsiveness that keeps the conversational system going. Dialogue is more than just talk or people exchanging words in a room.

The more a word is used in our speech, the more contexts it gathers and its meanings proliferate with each encounter. According to Bakhtin (1984), dialogue compels difference, uncertainty, playfulness, surprise and open-endedness as necessary, positive and productive aspects of the human condition. He also makes an important distinction between explanation and understanding. Explanation, in Bakhtin's terms, is monologic and premised on the assumption that we come to know something first through empirical investigation and then proceed to explain our findings to others. Explanation is abstract and quite independent of its addressee, because only one active subject, the explainer, is involved. Understanding occurs where there is an exchange, a response, an answer back, perhaps also resistance (Irving and Young 2002).

In Bakhtinian terms, the nature of learning and knowledge making are social and participatory activities founded on dialogue, thereby the nature of education is about negotiated meaning rather than information transmission. The most important thing about people is not what is contained within them, but what transpires between them (McNamee and Hosking 2012, pp.41–42). It is *in* the relationship that knowledge is produced.

ANALYSING CRITICALLY REFLECTIVE
DIALOGUES IN RESEARCH FOCUS GROUPS

In analysing dialogue in focus groups (Marková *et al.* 2007) note that it is easier to work with topical episodes of sequences of talk that are internally coherent. Topics do not simply follow one another as autonomous units in a sequence; rather they develop out of interactions between prior, present and projected future topics, and the transitions are often shaded.

In this chapter I have chosen the episodes of dialogues about one particular book, which was the most discussed novel in all of the focus groups. The Swedish author Åsa Linderborg's novel, [*Mig Äger Ingen Nobody Owns Me*], published in 2007, generated dialogue in the focus groups on interesting topics that seem to be key in recognising and understanding children in the context of individuals with drink-related difficulties and their families. The novel is a true story about the author's childhood in the city of Västerås, Sweden. Today Åsa Linderborg is a famous journalist in Sweden and she grew up with her single-parent father at the beginning of the 1970s. Her parents separated when Åsa was four years old and her mother left Åsa with the father. The author describes her father as caring and loving, even though at times they did not have sheets on their beds or food in the fridge. The father worked hard at the factory and his alcohol problem increased as the years passed. As a teenager, Åsa moved in with her mother when the drinking problem was dominating all parts of her father's life.

In the focus group conversation I was involved as a collaborating and participating voice. In one of the groups the members discussed differences in relation to the text, based on whether you had read the novel or if you had just read a group member's reflection on it. The group members who had read the book could recognise the father's warm and loving relationship with Åsa and became annoyed when other group members doubted this. Some members of the group who had not read the book asked if the girl behaved like her father's wife. We in the group who had read the book were convinced that this was not the case. In the conversation in the focus group the members came to the conclusion that this could be compared with how you perceive clients: it is different if you meet them to how it is if you only read about them in files; and especially you have power in documenting your work.

Although I mostly followed the conversation in a listening position, the excerpt below shows that at times I actively participated in the conversation. I have changed the names of the group members and kept my own name.

> *Katarina:* I feel I want to interrupt here. What do you think Marina, what would be the best thing to do for the whole, if Åsa was your client? What would you decide to do here?

> *Marina:* Mmm. Damned difficult to answer…because… What is the best for the whole? … Well…

> *Katarina:* You can think for a while. When I read the novel I got the impression that this father was warm and he managed well as a father. There was no confusion that he might have been like a husband to Åsa. In the text I think you could read that he really acted like a responsible father. And I thought about the expectations on him. There was much pressure on him about how

to behave. And he wanted to be a good father. Somehow I got the impression that Åsa's mother just had to sacrifice her daughter, because she thought her ex-husband would totally break down if she took her away from him. And one can imagine what would have happened to Åsa if her father had a breakdown. The mother must have thought of this.

Marina: But think of how critical we are towards the children's services, that they don't do anything, that they should be more active, that they should do... How many of us would think it would be ok that the mother argues in this way? That the father will have a breakdown if I take the child away from him. Is it better that the child stays with the drinking father?

Katarina: That is why I ask, 'What is best for the whole?'

Marina: Good question. Mmm. I already see here how blind we become, depending whose side we are on. Where is the neutrality? We are sucked in on an emotional level as to whose side we take!

In this exchange I was emotionally involved and convinced that the father did not treat Åsa as his wife. I was also in the teacher's position where I tried to steer the conversation back to a balance between the discourses of child and parent sensitivity. Even if I clearly chose to look at the relationship between the father and Åsa from a parent-sensitive position, I felt that the voice of the child-sensitive discourse was also heard.

WHAT KIND OF KNOWLEDGE EMERGES FROM CRITICAL REFLECTION AND DIALOGUES IN FOCUS GROUPS?

The aim of gathering the focus groups in the workshop was to create relationships and challenge working cultures, so that people could learn to value each other's personal and professional experiences and expertise, and recognise each other's work. Ghaye (2005) notes that dialogue both within teams and across professions moves the process of reflection beyond the individual and is informed by a concept that Mezirow (1991) refers to as perspective transformation. Tsang (2007) describes dialogue as being both internal and external, drawing attention to the work of Burbules (1993) to emphasise that power differences need to be acknowledged and that dialogue between individuals must be supported by mutual respect and a commitment to the process (Karban and Smith 2010).

Critical reflection on one's own assumptions and stereotypes

In one of the focus groups, while Helena was presenting the novel, Margareta, who had not read the novel, asked questions about the little girl Åsa who lived with her father with substance-misuse difficulties. According to self-help literature (Woilitz 1990), children have certain traits, where they take or get assigned roles in families where substance misuse is a problem. They become the 'silent child', 'the rebel', 'the hero' or 'the clown'. I think this is how professionals involved in substance misuse treatment often categorise children in relation to families where substance misuse is a problem.

> *Margareta:* Can you see if she has taken one of these roles, as she comes from an alcoholic family? Children usually take these roles...
>
> *Helena:* In what phase, do you mean?
>
> *Margareta:* In some phase of her childhood?
>
> *Helena:* Well, maybe she is this nifty girl, perhaps...
>
> *Margareta:* Can you recognise this in school work, for instance? How did all the practical things work at home...who took care of it all? Was it the father who took care of the household?
>
> *Helena:* Somehow I think that the father did all that, despite the drinking. I get the picture that she was not responsible for the household, as some children become...more...but I did not get that impression. She...somehow...concentrated on her own things... I do not know really...

Åsa's story does not fit the stereotypical description of the child living in a family where substance misuse is a problem. The writings on roles in such families have helped many people to understand why they behave like they do, but fixed ideas can be limiting. If we do not listen to children and already have readymade explanations in our heads, then we might miss important messages.

All of the focus groups had participants who had experiences of heavy drinking in their own childhood. They were aware of their personal history and some of them had worked on this issue in psychotherapy. Reading the novels and discussing them, however, opened up new inner reflective processes in their personal life. As Fook puts it (2010, p.40), 'Once individuals become aware of the hidden power of ideas they have absorbed unwittingly from their social contexts, they are then freed to make choices on their own terms.' In this sense, individuals are freed to change their social operation at the level of their personal experience.

Dialogical relational practitioners respond to utterances with genuine interest in what the person has to say, avoiding any suggestion that someone may have said something wrong. They adapt to the emerging natural rhythm of the conversation. As the process enables participants to find their voices, they also become respondents to themselves. Hearing their own words repeated respectfully and responded to widens the possibility to understand more of what they themselves have said (Arnkil and Seikkula 2015).

Child and parent sensitivity

Networks of professionals involved in helping families with substance misuse-related problems often have conflicts concerning the goals for individual family members and the family as a whole. This is especially so when there are strong emotions involved.

The novel provoked the group to discuss the split between seeing the problem from an adult or a child's perspective. One participant wanted to emphasise that Åsa had the right to be a child. Another participant agreed, but also talked about sympathising with the father's struggle as a parent. She reflected on how during a weekend group for parents with drinking difficulties (the children were in their own groups during the weekend), she was surprised by how openly the parents talked about their struggle with their drinking problem. She had previously worked in children's welfare services and realised how different the relationship was when she was in a position where she did not have the power to take the children into custody. When she heard the parents' stories in this group, she felt a new empathy for them, although she had a very clear opinion that in all cases it is important to look at the child's needs first.

The concept of the group leader course was based on systemic thinking, which means 'taking into account the whole' (i.e. the family in its environment, and the network of professionals involved), and sought meaning in the complex patterns of inter-relationships between people and groups of people (Packham and Sriskandarajah 2005). An inability to understand systems dynamics results in what appears to be a good description of single-loop learning, where we are led into cycles of blame and self-defence: the enemy is always out there and problems are always caused by someone else (Redmond 2004). In all of the focus groups, the child welfare services became the scapegoat when the members discussed what to do with the children of parents who do not stop drinking. When the conversation continued, the process moved in a more constructive and reflexive direction, where they began to talk about what they could do themselves, how they played a part in the network of co-operating professionals, and how they concretely collaborated with child protection.

Systemic family therapy has been criticised for gathering family members around the misusing parent, and for the children's needs being put aside for the needs of the substance misusing parent (Itäpuisto 2013). The professionals from the field of substance misuse treatment tend to forget the children in the family, or see these children as the biggest motive for parents to stop drinking or taking drugs. The child welfare services often lack expertise in substance misuse issues and want to rescue the children from the parents. In doing so, they risk becoming insensitive to the children's loyalty and love towards their parents. Professionals seldom recognise misuse early, so the problems usually become more serious and complicated (Itäpuisto 2005, 2013; Fagerström 2005).

Trifnoff et al. (2010) have developed the concept of child and parent sensitivity to take into consideration both the child's and the misusing parent's needs (Itäpuisto 2013). This can be aligned to what constructionist therapist Harlene Anderson (1997, p.95) calls 'multipartiality', a stance where a therapist takes all sides simultaneously. In family therapy and group work this is a facilitative position, which promotes a process that keeps all voices in motion and supports contribution. Central to this therapeutic stance is a therapist's (also a teacher's and researcher's) honest and sincere capacity to be receptive, to invite, respect and hear and to be engaged in every story. This is as important in work with clients and in co-operation within professional networks as it is in relationship-based research. The facilitator of the family therapy session, group session or focus group conversation wants each person in the group to feel that his or her version is as important as any other.

Individual and structural perspectives

In the written reflections on the novel there was an episode of polite dialogue between two group members about two different scientific perspectives.

Lisa: Even the sociologist in me read the book with pleasure, because it isn't a biography in a narrow sense. It is a description of a fascinating family, a description of class and a society that undergoes big changes. Linderborg does not only focus on the individual, she also writes about the societal circumstances, about inequality. What I appreciate most is that she avoids psychologising too much about the father's drinking problem. Instead she tries to understand him as a human being and an individual, and as a controversial person with many sides.

Respecting the dialogical principle that every utterance calls for a response, Clarissa responds to Lisa's reflection elegantly by telling her that she is very curious about her reflection and recognises new things in her own way of thinking.

Lisa: writes that what she likes most in *Mig Äger Ingen* is that it avoids psychologising the father's alcoholism. As a psychologist I became very curious about this reflection and what is meant by 'psychologising' and how this differs from 'understanding (the father) as a controversial person with many sides'. I get the impression that 'psychologise' in this context is perceived as a reduction, but I became uncertain as to whether this means a psychological perspective in general. I am fascinated because this reflection makes me realise how strongly I myself focus on the dependency problem as an expression of an individual dynamic, where class and society are naturally important, but seldom so primary as they seem to be in this reflection written by a sociologist.

Answering does not mean giving an explanation or interpretation, but rather demonstrating in a response that one has noticed what has been said, and when possible, opened up new points of view on what has been said.

Even if critical social work is traditionally seen as being synonymous with a structural approach, social work in general has developed more individualistic approaches to practice. It is important to integrate theoretical frameworks to social problems, so as to avoid a perspective that is only appreciated on either an individualistic or structural level. Thus, it is crucial for social work to develop tools that analyse all levels simultaneously (Hertz 2012).

The reflections about the novel can be seen as a dialogue between individualistic and structural perspectives. From the example above, we can see that dialogue can also be seen as discourses competing for their place in the centre, and in so doing forcing other discourses to the margins (Baxter 2011; Marková et al. 2007). Through critical reflection these power struggles are identified on all systemic levels, from the personal on the micro level to societal structures on the macro level, and this was seen in the group discussions. In knowledge making social workers have to choose, make judgments and use their agency in the here and now. According to Taylor and White (2000), choosing among different versions is the core of the expertise in social work. Every client relationship and situation is unique. Theories, methods and professional experience that social workers use are interpreted in a new way for this special situation (Juhila 2006).

CONCLUSIONS AND IMPLICATIONS

Summing up, it appears that the critical reflection and dialogue that took place in the focus groups of professionals in this action research project helped group members to question their own assumptions and stereotypes about parents who misused drink, and their children. While it can be helpful to recognise certain traits of children's relationships to adults with substance misuse difficulties, it is even more important to relate to every child as a unique individual from a curious and not-knowing stance. The dialogue with colleagues from different contexts and professions helped the members to realise the consequences of reflexivity and how influential professional positioning is in working with parents who misuse drink. Reflecting openly and transparently about one's positioning with clients and colleagues makes expectations more realistic and releases tensions, which in turn makes collaboration easier in inter-professional networks.

Critical reflection helped the focus group members to discover the competing discourses behind different perspectives, such as child sensitivity versus parent sensitivity. It is difficult to get a picture of the whole situation or to be neutral with respect to all voices, and this goes for children and parents, as well as the interactions between professionals. By being curious with an intention to understand and see all sides, it is easier to make sure that every voice involved has the feeling of being heard.

The importance of the multiplicity of voices also came up in the focus groups when looking at substance misuse as a problem on an individual level, as well as it being a more structural, societal problem. By way of critical reflective dialogue, the members took into account both the individual and societal aspects of substance misuse. In general, dialogue and systemic thinking promote knowledge that is based on both aspects, and perspectives that promote collaboration in the professional network, instead of a one-sided, either-or form of specialist expertise where someone is right and the rest are wrong.

According to the focus group members' feedback, it was surprising how relaxing they found the rhythm of the workshop. They forgot about their workloads and were inspired by the conversations and reflections that took place. In a peaceful and accommodating atmosphere it was easy to adopt a not-knowing position and be open to other participants' ideas and experiences. As Karvinen-Niinikoski (2009) puts it, when safe and containing reflective forums for social workers to stop and think are available, then critical reflection will work in helping social workers to become subjects of their own agency and to see the meaning of professional discretion in promoting good creative and proactive social work. Thus, they might also be gaining the experience of 'having a say' and feeling more satisfied and motivated to stay in their career path. However, she also warns of the importance of how workshops are conducted in the organisation: 'However, if critical reflection is left to occasional use depending on the organisational "good will" for a "culture or climate for critical reflection" (Fook and Askeland 2007) it may work in just the opposite way' (Karvinen-Niinikoski 2009).

This action research process has inspired me to develop new forms of models for using fiction – both novels and films – as pedagogical approaches to teach critical reflection to social work students and practitioners and as research methods to expand existing knowledge. It is crucial to see these four session workshops as a tool for organisational learning and knowledge production, and definitely not as an easy time to discuss literature during working hours and an opportunity to get a short rest from work. The aim is not only to raise an awareness of one's own assumptions and positions, but also to put this awareness into action and to develop practice in changing contexts. Linking to this, however, Karvinen-Niinikoski (2009) warns that an insistence on transformation and political emancipation in times of unexpected change (and the critical reflection this may entail) might also turn into a self-made pressure trap, where we become exploited by our own idealism and simultaneously feel unable to act in the complexity of our times. Under such conditions, remaining critically alert and curious as researchers, pedagogues and practitioners, committed to engaged in knowledge making, and practice enhancement, is of the utmost importance.

REFERENCES

Ahlzén, R. (2010) *Why should physicians read? Understanding clinical judgement and its relation to literary experience.* Unpublished Doctoral Thesis. Durham: University of Durham.

Anderson, H. (1990) 'Then and now: From knowing to not-knowing.' *Contemporary Family Therapy Journal, 12,* 193–198.

Anderson, H. (1997) *Conversation, Language, and Possibilities. A Postmodern Approach to Therapy.* New York: Basic Books.

Anderson, H. and Goolishian, H. (1992) 'The Client is the Expert: A Not-knowing Approach to Therapy.' In S. McNamee and K. Gergen (eds) *Social Construction and the Therapeutic Process.* Newbury Park, CA: Sage.

Arnkil, T. E. and Seikkula, J. (2015) 'Developing dialogicity in relational practices: Reflecting on experience from open dialogues.' *Australian and New Zeeland Journal of Family Therapy 36,* 142–154.

Bakhtin, M. (1984) *Problems of Dostoevsky's Poetics* Theory and History of Literature: Volume 8. Manchester: Manchester University Press.

Bakhtin, M. (1991) *Dostojevskijs poetik.* Stockholm: Anthropos.

Baxter, L. A. (2011) *Voicing Relationships. A Dialogic Perspective.* London: Sage.

Boud, D., Keogn, R. and Walker, D. (1987) *Reflection: Turning Experience into Learning.* London: Kogan Page.

Burbules, N. C. (1993) *Dialogue in Teaching: Theory and Practice.* New York: Teachers College.

Burns, D. (2007) *Systemic Action Research: A Strategy for Whole System Change.* Bristol: The Policy Press.

Cecchin, G. (1987) 'Hypothesizing, circularity, and neutrality revisited: An invitation to curiosity.' *Family Process 26,* 405–414.

Chard, A. (2014) 'Orientations: Systemic Approaches to Research Practice.' In G. Simon and A. Chard *Systemic Inquiry: Innovations in Reflexive Practice Research.* Farnhill: Everything is Connected Press.

Dewey, J. (1933) *How We Think: A Restatement of the Relation of Reflective Thinking to the Educative Process* (Revised edition). Boston, MA: D. C. Heath and Co.

Fagerström, K. (2005) *Att upptäcka och bemöta alcohol- och drogmissbruk – Samtal med döttrar uppvuxna i familjer med missbruksproblem.* (Avhandling pro gradu). Helsinki: Helsingfors Universitet.

Fook, J. (2010) 'Beyond Reflective Practice: Reworking the "Critical" in Critical Reflection.' In H. Bradbury, N. Frost, S. Kilminster and Zukas, M. (eds) *Beyond Reflective Practice: New Approaches to Professional Lifelong Learning.* Abingdon: Routledge.

Fook, J. and Askeland, G. (2007) 'Challenges of critical reflection: Nothing ventured, nothing gained.' *Social Work Education 26,* 5, 520–533.

Fook, J. and Gardner, F. (2007) *Practising Critical Reflection – A Resource Handbook.* Berkshire: Open University Press.

Ghaye, T. (2005) *Building the reflective healthcare organisation.* Malden, MA: Oxford.

Healy, K. (2014) *Social Work Theories in Context.* Basingstoke: Palgrave Mcmillan.

Hedges, F. (2010) *Reflexivity in Therapeutic Practice.* London: Palgrave Macmillan.

Heikkinen, H., Rovio, E. and Syrjälä, L. (eds) (2007) *Toiminnasta tietoon: Toimintatutkimuksen menetelmät ja lähestymistavat.* Helsinki, Kansanvalistusseura.

Hertz, M. (2012) *Kritiskt Socialt [Arbete Critical Social Work].* Malmö: Liber Ab.

Irving, A. and Young, T. (2002) 'Paradigms for pluralism: Michael Bakhtin and social work practice.' *Social Work 47,* 1, 19–29.

Itäpuisto, M. (2005) 'Kokemuksia alkoholiongelmaisten vanhempien kanssa eletystä lapsuudesta.' Kuopion yliopiston julkaisuja E *Yhteiskuntatieteet* 124.

Itäpuisto, M. (2013) 'Päihdehoidon lapsi– ja vanhemmuus sensitiivisyys.' *Yhteiskuntapolitiikka 5,* 78, 533–543.

Järvinen, A., Koivisto, T. and Poikela E. (2000) *Oppiminen Työssä Ja Työyhteisössä.* Juva: WSOY.

Juhila, K. (2006) *Sosiaalityöntekijöinä Ja Asiakkaina. Sosiaalityön Yhteiskunnalliset Tehtävät Ja Paikat.* [As Social Workers and Clients. The Societal Tasks and Places for Social Work.] Tampee: Vastapaino.

Karban, K. and Smith, S. (2010) 'Developing Critical Reflection within an Inter-professional Learning Programme.' In H. Bradbury, N. Frost, S. Kilminster and M. Zukas *Beyond Reflective Practice:* New Approaches to Professional Lifelong Learning. Abingdon: Routledge.

Karvinen-Niinikoski, S. (2009) 'Promises and pressures of critical reflection for social work coping in change.' *European Journal of Social Work 12,* 3, 333–348.

Kemmis, S. (2001) 'Exploring the Relevance of Critical Theory for AR.' in P. Reason and H. Bradbury, *The Handbook of Action Research.* London: Sage.

Kolb, D. A. (1984) *Experiential Learning: Experience as the Source of Learning and Development* (Volume 1). Englewood Cliffs, NJ: Prentice-Hall.

Kundera, M. (1986) *Romankonsten.* Original title: *L'Art du Roman.* Stockholm: Bonniers Grafiska Industrier.

Linderborg, Å. (2007) *Mig Äger Ingen.* Stockholm: Atlas Pocket.

Markova, I., Linell, P., Grossen, M. and Orvig, A. (2007) *Dialogue in Focus Groups: Exploring Socially Shared Knowledge.* London: Equinox Publishing Ltd.

McNamee, S. and Hoskin, M. (2012) *Research and Social Change: A Relational Constructionist Approach.* London: Routledge.

Mezirow, J. (1991) *Transformative Dimensions of Adult Learning.* San Fransisco: Jossey

Nussbaum, M. (2010) *Not for Profit: Why Democracy Needs the Humanities.* Princeton: Princeton University Press.

Packham, R. G. and Sriskandarajah, N. (2005) 'Systemic action research for post graduate education.' *Agriculture and Rural Development in Systems Research and Behavioural Science 22,* 119–30.

Parton, N. and O'Byrne, P. (2000) *Constructive Social Work: Towards a New Practice.* London: Macmillan.

Reason, P. and Bradbury, H. (2008) *The SAGE Handbook of Action Research: Participative Inquiry and Practice.* London: Sage Publications.

Redmond, B. (2004) 'Reflecting on Practice: Exploring Individual and Organisational Learning through a Reflective Teaching Model.' In N. Gould and M. Baldwin (eds) *Social Work, Critical Reflection and The Learning Organisation.* Aldershot: Ashgate Publishing Limited.

Ruch, G. (2009) 'Identifying "the critical" in a relationship-based model of reflection.' *European Journal of Social Work 12,* 3, 349–362.

Sampson, E. (1993) *Celebrating the Other: A Dialogic Account of Human Nature.* Boulder: Westview Press.

Schön, D. (1983) *The Reflective Practitioner: How Professionals Think in Action.* New York: Basic Books.

Senge, P. (1990) *The Fifth Discipline: The Art and Practice of the Learning Organisation.* London: Century.

Simon, G. and Chard, A. (2014) *Systemic Inquiry: Innovations in Reflexive Practice Research.* Farnhill: Everything is Connected Press.

Taylor, C. and White, S. (2000) *Practising Reflexivity in Health and Welfare: Making Knowledge.* Buckingham: Open University Press.

Taylor, C. and White, S. (2006) 'Knowledge and reasoning in social work: Educating for humane judgement.' *British Journal of Social Work 36,* 937–954.

Trifnoff, A., Duraisingam, V., Roche, A. and Pidd, K. (2010) *Taking First Steps: What Family Sensitive Practice Means for Alcohol and Other Drug Workers: A Survey Report.* Adelaide: Flinders University National Centre for Education and Training on Addiction.

Tsang, A. K. T. (2007) *Learning to Change Lives: The Strategic Skills in Learning and Development System.* Toronto: University of Toronto Press.

Wenger, E., McDermott, R. and Snyder, W. M. (2002) *Cultivating Communities of Practice.* Boston: Harvard Business Review Press.

Woilitz, J. G. (1990) *Adult Children of Alcoholics.* Deerfield Beach: Health Communications Inc.

Chapter 10

EXPLORING RELATIONSHIPS AND EMOTIONS THROUGH REFLEXIVE SECONDARY DATA ANALYSIS

PEER SUPPORTERS', PROFESSIONALS' AND CLIENTS' EXPERIENCES OF A FINNISH STREET-LEVEL SUBSTANCE MISUSE CLINIC

Elina Virokannas

INTRODUCTION

How and why do social scientists choose the focus of their studies? How do they select participants or the contexts of observation? What are their motivations? If there were no obligations to study certain subjects but one could freely decide what to do, would it be personal or professional interests that guide one's choices? Or is it all just coincidence? In the end, do we know what we want our written legacy in academic papers and books to be and is it possible to make the world a better place through research articles?

In the field of social work research, I believe it is imperative that we conduct and promote research that enhances social justice and generates research-related benefits for participants (Peled and Leichtentritt 2002). The aspiration to promote social justice is perhaps the factor that most effectively connects the diversity of social work research traditions (see e.g. Banks 2012). As a social work researcher, my primary interest lies in developing a better understanding of the life situations and experiences of the marginalised people who are clients of social work services, in order both to improve social work practice and to promote social justice. This approach has always felt right for me and underpins all the research choices I have made.

In this chapter I focus on the relationships between peer supporters, professionals and clients at the Finnish street-level health and social care project called 'Katuklinikka' [Street Clinic]. The aim of the Street Clinic project is to reach the most marginalised substance users and to help them receive the social and health services they need. I have chosen the Street Clinic as my focus, partly due to my passion for the drug-related issues I have studied throughout my career, and partly due to several coincidences. I first heard about the Street Clinic three years ago from my sister, who worked as a project leader in a larger project 'Osis', which oversees the Street Clinic. At the same time, I was organising a course called 'Social work and substance abuse' at the University of Helsinki. I asked my sister to visit the course with a peer supporter. They agreed and the visit was a success.

The peer supporter's message was simple but effective: drug users are people just like any others and they have a right to be treated with human dignity. He talked about his own addiction, HIV-infection and the consequences he has to deal with for the rest of his life. However, he wanted to work with other drug users and affect the negative attitudes they often encounter. Listening to someone who has lived through substance addiction is a very different experience to theorising about it. The peer supporter's experiences were helpful in teaching the social work students how to work face-to-face with substance users and what it means to be stigmatised and unable to get help. This experience confirmed for me the importance of utilising experience-based knowledge in social work education.

My sister and the peer supporter visited my course at the same time as the Street Clinic was starting up. About two and half years later I learned that they had gathered data in which peer supporters wrote about their work at the Street Clinic. The data consisted of open-ended qualitative questionnaires that were conducted to develop the practices of the Street Clinic. I immediately sensed that the data would provide significant material for a research project using secondary analysis. It was valuable and interesting data because of the scarcity of empirical research that focuses on how professionals and peers co-operate in social work practice and particularly because of the perspective of the peer supporter, which is noticeably absent in existing research. The principles and fieldwork practices of the Street Clinic were unique as there are no other projects in Finland that have worked in a similar way. I was interested, therefore, in learning more.

I received the research data after the management team of Osis and the Street Clinic team had granted permission for its release: Acquiring research data that I was not familiar with was at first rather peculiar, as previously I have collected data, such as interviews and observations, myself. Working with this kind of secondary data has both benefits and challenges for a researcher. I found it refreshing to be able to start working with the data without being personally involved in gathering it, but conversely my lack of familiarity with it made it harder to 'get inside' it. After familiarising myself with it, however, I noticed that the peer supporters used a range of expressions for emotions when they articulated their work as peer supporters. Partly this was due to the questionnaire, in which feelings were specifically asked about. Expressions of emotions were connected to their relationships with other people as well as to how they identified themselves as peers. In this study, therefore, I have approached relationship-based practice, first, through analysing how peer supporters expressed the emotions that arose from their relationships with the professionals and people who misused substances, whom they referred to as 'clients'. Second, adopting a reflexive stance in the research process, I reflect on my researcher engagement and the feelings I experienced while reading the peer supporters' stories.

My way to approach emotions is to look at how emotions are expressed and connected to different relationships. To be more specific, my aim is not to analyse so-called 'real emotions'. I do not have access to what occurred in the peer-supporters' minds and hearts but I do not deny the significance of people's experience of their emotions and feelings. Just like Gergen (2009), I found the performances of internal states, such as thinking and feelings (both pleasurable and painful), as relational actions: 'All words gain their intelligibility – their capacity to communicate – within coordinated action' (Gergen 2009, p.70).

The need to understand the role emotions play in practitioner–user interaction in the field of social work, or any other professional helping context, has been highlighted in the literature (Ruch, Turney and Ward 2010). For example, Rajan-Rankin (2013) has studied the lived experiences of social work students in managing emotions and developing resilience. She states that acceptance of emotions as an integral part of one's own self-hood is an essential aspect of becoming a professional. The same goes for research work. Social scientists are inevitably part of the society they study and cannot be free from preconceptions and preferences. According to interpretative phenomenological analysis, the capacity as a researcher to reflect on one's preconceptions is an essential part of understanding research subjects (Smith, Flowers and Larking 2009). Thus, in my data analysis I use discursive methods (Wood and Kroger 2000) to analyse the expression of emotions. Yet, as I reflect on my own emotional responses and engagements with methodological issues throughout the chapter, my orientation is phenomenological.

EXPERIENCE-BASED KNOWLEDGE AND THE IDEA OF PEER SUPPORT

Knowledge learned from personal experience differs significantly from knowledge based on training, evidence or research. In the context of social and health care services, the importance of service user involvement and service users being seen as a source of knowledge have, in recent years, become increasingly recognised as important components of effective practice (Beresford, Adshead and Croft 2007; Fox 2011; Nelson 2012; Warren 2007). Nelson (2012) states that for social work to claim to be anti-oppressive or anti-discriminatory it must take service user involvement seriously. At the same time, this approach has received criticism with McLaughlin (2009, p.1107) suggesting that 'the act of involving service users has become more important than providing more effective services'. Merely the act of involvement is not enough if user knowledge remains as fashionable jargon only. According to Beresford (2010), user knowledge is treated as being less important than other viewpoints involved in the political and policy process. People who have direct experience of problems are seen to be too close to the problems and that is why their knowledge is treated as being less reliable.

The concept of the service user can also be seen as problematic. Service users are often presented as a homogenous group with shared needs, without problematising which service the users are being referred to. Users of social and health care services, however, have diverse needs and expectations and the 'failure to recognize value pluralism' can result in negativity and disconnection (Simmons 2009, p.58). For example, people who use services because of their illegal drug abuse encounter strong prejudices and resistance from service providers (e.g. Paylor, Measham and Asher 2012).

For the purposes of this chapter I have used the term 'peer supporter' because that was the term used at the Street Clinic. In the Finnish context, peer support is seen as being based on shared life experiences (Nylund 2000). People with similar life situations or problems can gather together, and have the potential to become organised and advocate shared goals. For example, the disabled people's movement and the mental health service users' movement highlight the importance of people speaking and acting for themselves and having an impact on the support and services they receive (Beresford 2009). However, at the Street Clinic the concept of peer supporter has started to develop its own life as a sign of belonging to 'us' in a positive way. For them, it was not important to consider the definition of peer support – it was simply important to belong to it.

THE PRINCIPLES AND PRACTICE OF THE STREET CLINIC

The Street Clinic commenced at the beginning of 2011 as a part of the larger three-year project called Osis, the funding for which comes from Finland's Slot Machine Association (RAY). Osis is organised by two partners, the A-Clinic Foundation and the Family Supported Drug Rehabilitation Association (OHT), with the A-Clinic Foundation having responsibility for the Street Clinic. The aim of the project is to develop and strengthen peer activity and to create new methods and models for the co-operation of peers and professionals in order to improve the inclusion and wellbeing of marginalised populations.

The principles of the Street Clinic are shared by the Drop-In Needle Exchange programme (Vinkki). The practice is based on a policy of harm reduction, which aims to reduce the harmful consequences of drug use, such as infections due to syringe sharing (see e.g. Tammi 2007). The Street Clinic provides low-threshold services, such as the opportunity to receive health and social services in drug users' homes or wherever they are. The work is intended to be client-centred and to address each client's personal needs and wishes.

The Street Clinic team consists of both professional workers (one full-time social work qualified project worker, a part-time doctor and a part time counsellor) and peer supporters. On the project documents a peer is defined as follows:

> a person who has experienced situations similar to drug users. A peer has 'inside knowledge' through his or her experience that can have a positive result in providing services. In addition to experiential knowledge, peers can bring credibility and trust to an agency in ways that regular service providers may find difficult because users may distrust and avoid contact with 'official helpers'.

Peer supporters do not have to be permanently drug-free as long as they are able to be sober and co-operate when working at the project. The clients of the Street Clinic are people who engage in heavy drug use and who are not using the social and health services they are entitled to. They do not even use the services provided by the needle exchange programme. They frequently have a multitude of problems in all areas of their lives. In addition, mistrust of professionals and the official system of service delivery is strong. In the United Kingdom, peer-led services have been set up primarily as aftercare services for people who have left treatment (Nelson 2012), whereas at the Street Clinic peer supporters try to motivate and encourage substance users to take part in health and social care services.

Between August 2011 and May 2014, approximately 100 peer workers were involved in the project. Some of them had been involved in the Street Clinic since the beginning of the project, while others took part occasionally or just informed other peer supporters about drug-using friends who needed help. The total number of clients reached approximately 600 and there were 1300 appointments.

The fieldwork and house calls began in August 2011. The Street Clinic team offers treatment for minor ailments, testing for sexually transmitted diseases, hepatitis C and HIV. It provides counselling on contraception, sexual health and the insertion of contraceptive implants. Needle exchange is offered all the time. Use of the Street Clinic's services is voluntary and anonymous, except vaccination for hepatitis A and B, which cannot be received anonymously because Finnish law requires personal data for vaccinations.

It is not necessarily known beforehand how many people will be present at the house calls. It could be that a peer supporter has contact with one client – a middle-aged woman, for example – and when the team arrives the client's adult daughter is also present, along with her friend and her friend's partner. They all might have needs for different services, including medical, financial and social ones. The team attempts to map out the needs and the life situations of clients. They give counselling on accessing social services and obtaining the necessary treatment. Later, when the client has an appointment, such as an evaluation for opioid substitution therapy, the peer supporter might accompany the client when going to services (see Virokannas 2014).

THE DATA: THE PEOPLE BEHIND THE QUESTIONNAIRE

People always tell their story to someone. Research interviews, for example, are seen as interactional contexts where interviewees transform their experiences into comprehensible narratives with the help of an interviewer (see Holstein and Gubrium 2007; Miller and Glassner 2004). In addition, when people complete questionnaires, they have assumptions about who is receiving their answers and the reasons why the questions are being asked. In the case of the Street Clinic, it could be seen in several instances that the completed qualitative questionnaires were directed primarily towards the project workers. The word '*you*' was sometimes used to refer to a project worker, or there were greetings or other signs that could be interpreted as referring to the worker.

The data consisted of 89 descriptions of house calls or other activities, written by 11 peer supporters. The episodes concerned descriptions of visits to a client's home or day centres, or the experience of accompanying clients to different services. The data were gathered from the beginning of the project (autumn 2011 to spring 2014). The questionnaire included five sections: 1) why a place was visited 2) what was done 3) what the peer supporter experienced his or her role to be 4) how the peer supporter felt the co-operation with professionals or other peer supporters and 5) how the peer supporter felt afterwards.

The data were mostly hand written and I spent several days making literal transcriptions.[1] Instead of, for example, listening to people's voices from audiotape, I familiarised myself with different handwriting styles, different types of papers (e.g. grid paper) and special characters that could be understood as signs of emotions. I can only imagine how different the papers would have looked if they had been directed at a researcher who was unfamiliar to the writers. They would probably not exist at all. Of the peer supporters, I knew two from before. For the rest of them, based on their writings, I imagined some kind of face and shape. Because the tone of their stories was mostly informal, emotional and familiar, it was easy to think of them as acquaintances and empathise with their stories. At the same time, I knew I would not be able to get full *insight* (for more on this concept, see Lunabba, Chapter 6, in this book) into the peer supporters' accounts because, on a personal level, their life was unfamiliar to me.

My expectations were later realised when I went to the Street Clinic's office to present and talk with some of the peer supporters about my research work. The idea of visiting the Street Clinic emerged as soon as I had received the data and realised that I could not write about these people without asking them if I had understood them correctly. After finishing my preliminary analysis (Virokannas 2014), I asked the peer supporters and project workers to read and comment on my analysis. All the project workers read the manuscript and sent me corrections concerning some details or concepts. At the meeting there were about 10 peer supporters present (half of whom had participated in data production) and some of them had read my manuscript beforehand. Others simply wanted to listen to my presentation and took part in the conversation based on my presentation.

Rarely, if ever, have I had such an appreciative and enthusiastic audience. They did not want to change anything. I got feedback that I had correctly understood the point of the Street Clinic and the idea of peer support. One of them pointed out a few lines from my manuscript that he felt were the most important part of my research and I agreed

---

1   The transcribed data consist of 45 single-spaced A4 sheets. The length of the episodes varies from a few lines to two pages. I have changed names, places and some other details to ensure the anonymity of the peer supporters and clients. The professionals of Street Clinic have given permission to use their real names. Peer supporters were instructed to reply to the questionnaire as soon as possible after house calls or other activities. On average, their answers were received in one to three days. Most of the peer supporters did not reply at all and those who did were the most active ones.

with him. Still, I hesitate to say that I can fully understand the life of people with a history of heavy drug use. Nor is such a deep connection necessary as long as there is enough sensitivity and a willingness to understand.

ANALYSING THE DATA: WORKING SYSTEMATICALLY WITH INTUITION

Explaining the analysis process to others is difficult. The more I have worked as a researcher and analysed different data, the more I realise that I work by intuition. The ideas for analysis usually appear when I first read a new set of data. On subsequent readings I come across new ideas and the problem becomes which ones to choose and start work with. This intuition, of course, is informed by my reading of numerous methodology books and studies as well as by knowledge of different analytical tools. But is there any point in referring to some of the methodology books or researchers when explaining my own way of doing things? Or should I try to explain it in my own words? Writing the analysis is the most enjoyable stage in the research process for me, but I find I prefer to skip explaining how I have done it.

In the case of this project I did a different type of data analysis than I am accustomed to, as the analysis is the second one to be undertaken on the Street Clinic data. The first one (Virokannas 2014) deals with how peers describe and perceive their work with drug users and what kinds of membership categories are constructed in their collaboration with professional helpers. In the course of doing this I noticed the large number of expressions of emotion but did not concentrate on the emotions because I was focusing on membership categories. However, I could not shake off the desire to analyse how expressions of emotions are connected to relationships between peers, drug users and professionals. This desire became the basis for this new study from the same data.

This time I began my data analysis by looking at the variation of emotions the peer supporters expressed in their written descriptions. I selected all the episodes concerning emotions and divided them up, based on the relationship the emotion was connected to. For example, I distinguished emotions concerning the Street Clinic professionals and other professionals from emotions connected to other peers and drug users. I noticed that expressions of emotions connected to the Street

Clinic professionals were, without exception, positive and emotions connected to other professionals were more ambivalent. In addition, there were different nuances or meanings associated with the positive as well as the negative expressions.

The dominant feature in the data was that emotions connected to drug users (or clients) varied from enormous satisfaction to feelings of immense disappointment and failure. I have selected extracts from the larger body of the data to illustrate the main emotional nuances as follows. I analysed each selected passage in terms of what was being done in the situation and how the expressions of emotion were structured to perform various functions and achieve various results (see Wood and Kroger 2000). Alongside this analysis, I reflected on my own emotions associated with these extracts.

Respect and acceptance among the Street Clinic team

When peers described teamwork with the professionals at the Street Clinic they expressed many positive emotions connected to their motivation to work as peer supporters. In the extract below, Susanna describes her first house call as a Street Clinic peer. The visit took place at a residential unit for homeless people and the team consisted of a project worker, doctor, peer supporter and social work student.

> We worked as a team so well! We just decided which room Maarit (the doctor) and Liisa (the project worker) would take and started to exchange needles with a student. I felt like I have always done this since I did not have to ask or explain anything to anyone. Everyone knew what to do. Surely we are all professionals in our own field! Really good feelings! This is what I want to do in the future too. I hope it will work out as soon as possible…? (Susanna)

Susanna's description is consistently positive and enthusiastic. It was easy to be a part of the Street Clinic team and she felt accepted, needed and skilful. She also shows respect to the other team members – 'surely we are all professionals in our own field'. She expresses a strong willingness to continue working as a peer supporter in the future, and the last sentence of her questionnaire answer is formulated as a request for a chance to continue as a peer supporter.

Receiving appreciation and respect as well as becoming trusted were identified as important in a number of responses. Just like Susanna, Mari emphasises the importance of respecting different skills and knowledge. The next extract is part of a description about a house call to a long-time friend of Mari's who is an intravenous drug user. During the visit, Mari encourages her friend to accept help from the Street Clinic doctor. She observes the traffic by other drug users inside and outside of her friend's apartment, while professionals map out her friend's life situation and arrange treatment and services.

> I felt our teamwork was really nice, rewarding and confidential and every one of us appreciated and respected the others' skills and knowledge in our own field. The atmosphere was relaxed and peaceful.

Both Susanna and Mari described their emotions as shared: everyone in the team respected the others. Team members have different skills and they are all equally useful. The use of 'we' and 'us' is strong in both extracts and the positioning of oneself involved in something meaningful seems to be connected to expressions of positive feelings.

During the house calls, peer supporters described their role as team members as equal to that of the professionals. However, when planning the house calls or other practices, the professionals were defined as supervisors who have power to decide how the team work (Virokannas 2014). In the next extract, Susanna has been working at the Street Clinic for four months and she describes how she handles some of the Street Clinic's practices independently:

> Part of my responsibility was to get the women from their home to the 'office' at least somehow on time. ... I went through beforehand with Liisa what I am supposed to do and she told me she will have to leave almost immediately after we arrive [at the Street Clinic's office]. That was clear. Besides, the more responsibility Liisa gives me, the more satisfied I am!

Along with feelings of respect and acceptance, feelings of becoming trusted and gaining responsibility were expressed as being important. The relationship between peer supporter and professional seems to be clear: the project worker supervises the peer supporter and decides on the amount of responsibility the peer supporter will assume.

At first reading, the peer supporters' descriptions of how great and agreeable the teamwork with peers and professionals was made me sceptical: is this accurate or are the peer supporters exaggerating the positive aspects of their relationships? However, the repetition of the

183

descriptions, as well as mention being made of negative examples, began to convince me that the Street Clinic really had managed to create a trusting, positive context for teamwork. As the analysis shows, however, such positivity does not mean that the collaboration was free from problems.

Frustration over being rejected by other professionals and officials

The relationships between the peer supporters and the Street Clinic's professionals were overwhelmingly positive compared with the emotions connected to other professionals, which were distinctly ambivalent. Peer supporters interacted with other professionals and officials when they accompanied clients to different services such as health-care centres, the dentist, social work office or different evaluation or in-patient units. If everything went well, emotions were not expressed in their answers at all, while negative emotions were referred to when the peer supporters encountered difficulties and obstacles.

In the next extract, Susanna failed to accompany on time a client from the service centre where the client lived to a clinic appointment. The reason for being late was that the service centre personnel did not let Susanna in to pick the client up:

> I was so annoyed because we didn't make it on time to the clinic, and it was not nice to leave a confused person there [in front of the closed clinic] even though her boyfriend was with us. The most irritating thing was that I was not allowed to pick her up from the service centre. I tried but nobody opened the door even though I rang the bell and said that I was a Street Clinic peer supporter. I couldn't tell them anything else other than that I was supposed to pick a client up for a lab appointment, and they said: 'She'll come if she's in there. And if she has told you on the phone that she will come, you just have to wait there at the front of the centre.' ARRRGH! Well, there was no shortage of company out front; there were really wild stories, depending on the teller. We would have been on time for the clinic if only they had let me in to pick her up from inside. I was so frustrated. The client needed support and help really badly.

Susanna's account illustrates how failing to be at the laboratory on time aroused several negative feelings, including frustration. She had to leave the client on the street with her boyfriend instead of proceeding to the client's treatment. She could have managed to get the client on time to the clinic if the service centre personnel had not rejected her attempts to get in. She told staff she was a Street Clinic peer supporter but was treated more like the other drug users and was left at the front of the building to stand with them. In other words, the doors of the service centre stayed closed to her just like they did to other substance users.

There were other similar stories in the data; for example, where a peer supporter and their client had arrived on time to the outpatient health unit but the personnel refused, for no apparent reason, to let them in. These episodes are related with expressions of powerlessness and disappointment. For example, Pete describes how he accompanied a client to a substance abuse rehabilitation clinic. The client wanted him to be present at the meeting with professionals but he was denied entry:

> They just would not let me in with Mika [the client]. Nonsense! Was this what the rehab clinic wanted?

Relationships between peer supporters and other officials differed significantly from relationships with the Street Clinic professionals. And so did emotions connected to these relationships. Along with rejection, Pete expressed confusion because he was not sure who wanted to exclude him from the meeting. Performing a socially valued role in the team, receiving approval for one's skills and expertise, and having tasks, which included taking responsibility, were connected to very different emotions for the peer supporters compared with the rejection and stigmatisation associated with the relationships with other professionals. In addition, the power structures in the relationships differed from being equal members of the team to being unilaterally oppressed by the inexplicable will of others. These results are similar to those found by Simmons (2009) in his study of service user expectations regarding how they would like to be treated: People felt more positive about their identifications as service users and more connected to services if they were treated with courtesy and respect and their knowledge was valued. In addition, fairness, equity and the clarity of rules were important.

On a personal level, descriptions of the actions of other authorities provoked feelings of anger and sadness in me. It seems obvious that people prefer kind, respectful treatment to being shut out and stigmatised. In several cases, the difference is about minor things, such as being polite and expressing no prejudices. Peer supporters work hard to help their drug-using friends, and professionals only need to do their part: to let people come in and give them the services they need and have the right to receive. I find myself wondering why such a simple element of the relationship is made so difficult.

Relationships with drug users: feeling useful and failing to help

Peer supporters expressed a variety of emotions when describing their work and the relationships with people who were misusing drugs. A desire to help their drug-using friends or acquaintances was strongly present in their descriptions. In addition to feelings of being accepted as part of the team, feeling oneself to be useful was expressed as being significant.

> Our house call left me in very good mood and I felt I had succeeded. I got the feeling that our visit was really useful for clients on a concrete level, not just empty promises that will never come true. (Mari)

> At short notice we came to XX [a part of the city] because one young person had just the day before shot up with HIV-positive paraphernalia. I got really good feelings because the fellow got a shot at the hospital. (Pete)

Both Mari and Pete described the positive emotions they experienced as a result of successful house calls. The clients received help from the Street Clinic team and in the latter case they probably managed to save a client from an HIV infection. In some descriptions simply getting a client on time to a rehab session or doctor's appointment was considered to be an achievement that made the peer supporter happy.

> The client had been late three times so this was certainly the last possible time she got from the rehab clinic...I felt my role to be really important because I knew the client and I knew she trusted me and she trusted that I would be there and support her... Really good and successful [feelings]. (Pia)

In Pia's extract the personal relationship between her and the client is identified as being important. Knowing each other and the assumed trust the client has for Pia is considered to be essential when trying to get the client to the treatment appointment. Positive feelings are connected to this successful personal relationship. For example, for social workers, gaining this kind of trust might be impossible because there is no shared experience and the starting point for the relationship might be mutually suspicious (see, for example, Paylor *et al.* 2012).

In all the previous episodes the desire to help is a self-evident starting point for house calls and appointments. When everything goes well and clients obviously benefit from the Street Clinic's practices, peer supporters express strong positive feelings. On the other hand, not all appointments with clients caused positive emotions. There were several descriptions of failure to accompany a client to treatment or witnessing unexpected drug use in face-to-face meetings. In these cases where help was refused or could not be provided, the expressions of disappointment were strong.

> I was really pissed off because I knew the client was in very bad shape and, furthermore, she is a very young girl and we did not get her to rehab. Well, I hope Liisa [the project worker] and Maarit [the doctor] manage to motivate her to start rehab. (Susanna)

Failure to get a client to rehab is expressed as being especially trying in Susanna's extract because the client is young, she is a girl and in bad shape. This time, it was not the professionals who were the obstacle to receiving treatment. Instead, it was the client herself. In other parts of her description, Susanna explains that the client was not at home, did not answer her phone and had simply vanished. However, Susanna says she hopes that Street Clinic's professionals will manage to help the girl in the future even though she, as a peer supporter, failed.

The situations in which clients did not answer the phone or were not home when it was time to leave with a peer supporter for treatment were the most common cases in which peer supporters expressed feelings of frustration. Peer supporters also expressed frustration, anger or sadness if a client was intoxicated, offered them drugs or used drugs in front of them.

> I went to [a part of the city] to bring him tools because he did not have a bus ticket and his leg was broken. He visits Vinkki but quite rarely. We talked for a long time… There were bad feelings because

the guy began to shoot up right away. Otherwise everything was okay. (Harri)

Harri brought clean injection equipment to his friend whose leg was broken. Even though it is obvious that the equipment was needed for shooting up, Harri was disappointed that his friend could not wait until their face-to-face meeting was over. In another part of the data, Olli, an experienced peer supporter, said that if he sees someone shooting up, he approaches them and gives advice on how to inject safely. However, seeing someone shooting up created certain emotions in peer supporters. Even if the purpose of the Street Clinic is not to get people to stop using drugs but to promote their health, there could be an unspoken desire that over time the clients would reduce their use.

The emotions connected to failure to help varied from sadness and disappointment to frustration and anger. Feelings of anger were more common in situations where the authorities or service system were considered as the reason for failure. Frustration was expressed because of both the service system and clients' behaviour. Sadness was connected to a client's poor conditions and missed treatment appointments. For example, Mari described her feelings after several house calls:

> Feeling a bit depressed and also sad because some people must live their lives in such dirty and inadequate living conditions. And some clients are in such bad health that they are unable to take care of their personal hygiene.

As a researcher who is only connected to professionals and peer supporters but not the drug-using clients, I can only imagine the conditions some people are living in. It could be that even if I were a trained social worker, I could not manage to deal with situations where the need for help is obvious but help is not available. In addition, most of the clients are peer supporters' friends and not just some unknown 'clients'. The Street Clinic professionals paid significant attention to how the peer supporters manage, but still the risk of burnout for them is real.

Conflicting emotions

The last type of emotions peer workers expressed in the data concerns conflicting emotions. By this I am referring to situations in which peer supporters wonder if they have worked out or evaluated situations correctly or if they should have done something differently. In the following extract, Mari considers a house call that was interrupted, on her request, because of the risk of violence. During the house call, there had been people coming and going and at some point one couple had started to quarrel loudly. Mari fetched the project worker from a separate room and suggested that she and the other peer supporters leave instantly. Afterwards, she reflected on her feelings:

> I felt a bit confused. I mean, did I do the right thing in that situation when I suggested that we leave? I mean, did I possibly overreact to the risk of violence toward us?

Peer supporters had a tremendous amount of responsibility for evaluating situations and risks connected to them during the house calls. On the one hand, they were proud to have such responsibility, but on the other, it could be stressful to make quick decisions under uncertain circumstances. This kind of reflection on confused emotions and ethical dilemmas is common to social workers in a range of work situations (e.g. Dolgoff, Loewenberg and Harrington 2009). Unlike peer supporters, professionals are trained to deal with confusion. Outside of the excerpted passage, Mari said that she received help from the project worker in handling her conflicting emotions. However, if this kind of help had not been available, the peer supporter might not have managed to continue.

The other kind of situation that raised expressions of conflicting emotions was connected to a case in which the peer supporter was able to help a client to some extent but the life situation of the client remained sad:

> I was surprised how little things made the client grateful. She said she could not believe that she had been picked up from home, accompanied to treatment and even after that there was someone holding her hand if needed. I was a bit confused: there were good feelings because I had managed to help her, but on the other hand it was clear that the client was not used to getting, not to mention asking for, help. (Susanna)

Susanna explained that she was touched by a client who was very grateful for help she received from her peer supporter. She got the feeling that this client was not used to receiving or asking for help but had instead given up any hope of improving her life. This extract touched me especially as well. Susanna thinks that the help she was able to give to the client was slight, when actually she gave everything: real caring, looking and seeing the human being behind the drug user, letting herself be touched and assisting in every practical way she could. It is moving to see such humility concerning one's own abilities to help combined with an unquestionable willingness to help, even when one's own life situation might not be free from troubles. It is clear that people with no power or resources care for each other in ways that we, as educated professionals who have power and the capacity to act, do not.

CONCLUSION

My previous research work with drug issues has focused on under-age young people being treated for drug abuse and mothers who have abused illegal drugs and received treatment and social welfare services. Studying peer supporters' street-level work with heavy drug users has opened up a totally new perspective, since the young people and mothers I interviewed before had all received professional help. The awareness of the fact that there are people living in such poor health and social conditions right in my neighbourhood troubles me. The totality of the lack of resources and the negativity of attitudes among service providers feels unbearable. It does not feel right to stay in the position of an 'objective' researcher who pretends to have no emotions at all.

The new research experience, other than sharing my own feelings while analysing the data, has been working with data that I have not collected personally. In the end, I did not find it problematic to work with secondary data. Especially due to my analytic methods, it was good to concentrate on the data by itself: I wanted to look at the *expressions* of emotions, not emotions as such. Naturally, there is a risk of misinterpretation if a researcher does not know the context of data. That's why it was helpful to see the Street Clinic office, meet some of the peer supporters and talk about my analysis and interpretations with them. In addition, being acquaintanted with one peer supporter, Olli, gave me some background knowledge and made the situations illustrated in the data more concrete.

On the ideological level, there is broad agreement that service user involvement is an important element in the development of effective drug treatment as well as other social and health services (see, for example, Beresford *et al.* 2007; Nelson 2012; Paylor *et al.* 2012). However, how the involvement is enabled and arranged on a practical level is emphasised less. My contribution to that lack of knowledge is that emotions seem to play an important role in face-to-face interaction between service providers and users.

As the analysis showed, the repertoire of expressed emotions was wide, and disappointments and frustration as well as feelings of success and happiness could be extremely strong. Strong emotions entail the risk of burnout but they could also be a key strength of the work. In addition, situations where peer supporters' drug-using friends injected or offered drugs might be emotionally hard for peer supporters because of their own background of substance use.

What makes the peer supporters' accounts interesting from the perspective of social work practice is the silent knowledge that is based on several years' experience of living in a stigmatised subculture. Through their stories, it is somehow possible to see the social and health care system from an outsider's point of view. However, the shift in perspective might be painful because the view could give rise to a hopelessness that tempts one to look away and give up.

On the other hand, my analysis raised many positive emotions, because it is evident that there is a strong willingness to help, humanity and dimensions of reciprocity between both drug users and professionals. I strongly agree with Fox (2011, p.173) when she states: 'true partnership working requires an element of reciprocity'. Professionals such as social workers can learn from their clients or they themselves may have difficult experiences. Doel and Best (2008) have studied how the expression of these types of experiences by professionals were beneficial for their face-to-face work with clients. Expressing and sharing emotions does not have to be seen as unprofessional but could be used as a tool of reciprocity. As I have illustrated, writing this chapter and working with the data has raised some strong emotions in me as a researcher and as a social work educator. Instead of trying to be objective, I have acknowledged that I empathise with peer supporters' work and admire the work the Street Clinic does. At the same time, while I might not have insight into drug users' everyday reality, I know enough to understand that the service system has a lot to improve on. Social work professionals and members of society both have much to address in their own attitudes. For me it is natural to hug Olli, the experienced peer supporter, and have a chat when I see him, but when I see 'a drug user' in a subway I may easily change my stance. One starting place is the idea that letting service users or peer supporters do something meaningful could create reciprocity. Their experiences and knowledge are to be valued. They deserve responsibility and their skills should be taken seriously. However, it must be remembered that peer supporters are volunteers who also need support in dealing with confusing emotions as well as in their work.

I started this chapter by asking if it is it possible to make the world a better place through research articles. I cannot, of course, answer that question definitively, but if I lacked all hope, there would be no point in writing this or any other text.

REFERENCES

Banks, S. (2012) *Ethics and Values in Social Work, 4th edition.* Basingstoke: Palgrave Macmillan.

Beresford, P. (2009) 'Differentiated Consumers? A Differentiated View from a Service User Perspective.' In R. Simmons, M. Powell and I. Greener (eds) *The Consumer in Public Services: Choice, Values and Difference.* Bristol: Policy Press.

Beresford, P. (2010) 'Re-examining relationships between experience, knowledge, ideas and research: A key role for recipients of state welfare and their movements.' *Social Work and Society 8,* 1, 6–21.

Beresford, P., Adshead, L. and Croft, S. (2007) *Palliative Care, Social Work and Service Users: Making Life Possible.* London and Philadelphia, PA: Jessica Kingsley Publishers.

Doel, M. and Best, L. (2008) *Experiencing Social Work: Learning from Service Users.* London: Sage Publications.

Dolgoff, R., Loewenberg, R. M. and Harrington, D. (2009) *Ethical Decisions for Social Work Practice, 8th edition.* Belmont: Thomson Brooks/Cole.

Fox, J. (2011) '"The view from inside": Understanding service user involvement in health and social care education.' *Disability and Society 26,* 2, 169–177.

Gergen, K. J. (2009) *Relational Being: Beyond Self and Community.* Oxford and New York: Oxford University Press.

Holstein, J. A. and Gubrium, J. F. (2007) 'Context: Working it up, down, and across.' In C. Seale, G. Gobo, J. F. Gubrium and D. Silverman (eds) *Qualitative Research Practice: Concise Paperback Edition.* London: Sage.

McLaughlin, H. (2009) 'What's in a Name: "Client", "Patient", "Customer", "Consumer", "Expert by Experience", "Service User"—What's Next?' *British Journal of Social Work 39,* 6, 1101–1117.

Miller, J. and Glassner, B. (2004) 'The "Inside" and the "Outside": Finding Realities in Interviews.' In D. Silverman (ed) *Qualitative Research: Theory, Method and Practice, 2nd edition.* London: Sage.

Nelson, A. (2012) *Social Work with Substance Users.* London: Sage.

Nylund, M. (2000) *Varieties of Mutual Support and Voluntary Action: A Study of Finnish Self-Help Groups and Volunteers.* Helsinki: Hakapaino.

Paylor, I., Measham, F. and Asher, H. (2012) *Social Work and Drug Use.* Berkshire: Open University Press.

Peled, E. and Leichtentritt, R. (2002) 'The ethics of qualitative social work research.' *Qualitative Social Work 1*, 2, 145–169.

Rajan-Rankin, S. (2013) 'Self-Identity, Embodiment and the Development of Emotional Resilience.' *The British Journal of Social Work.* doi: 10.1093/bjsw/bct083.

Ruch, G., Turney, D. and Ward, A. (eds) (2010) *Relationship-based Social Work: Getting to the Heart of Practice.* London: Jessica Kingsley Publishers.

Simmons, R. (2009) 'Understanding the "Differentiated Consumer" in Public Services.' In R. Simmons, M. Powell and I. Greener (eds) *The Consumer in Public Services: Choice, Values and Difference.* Bristol: Policy Press.

Smith, J. A., Flowers, P. and Larkin, M. (2009) *Interpretative Phenomenological Analysis: Theory, Method, Research.* London: Sage.

Tammi, T. (2007) *Medicalising Prohibition: Harm reduction in Finnish and international drug policy.* Helsinki: Stakes Research Report 161.

Virokannas, E. (2014) 'Vertaisten ja ammattilaisten jäsenyyskategoriat huumeidenkäyttäjille suunnatussa katuklinikkatyössä'. *Yhteiskuntapolitiikka 79*, 6, 657–668.

Warren, J. (2007) *Service User and Carer Participation in Social Work.* Glasgow: Learning Matters.

Wood, L. A. and Kroger, R. O. (2000) *Doing Discourse Analysis: Methods for Studying Action in Talk and Text.* London: Sage.

Chapter 11

DESIGNING A QUALITATIVE RESEARCH STUDY
GIVING FATHERS WITH CANCER A VOICE
Kathleen Sheridan Russell

INTRODUCTION

Curiosity is often the driving force behind practice-based research. Social workers and practitioners are interested in learning more about the experience of their service users. Whether they want to learn about what hospice services are available for homeless men, why parent support groups are not well attended or how communities view crime, the underlying driving force behind the author's research is curiosity. The key then is to channel this curiosity into a clear, thoughtful study with a definite and specific research question (Robson 2011). Moreover, in an era driven by funding, outcome measurement and choices between different theoretical practices, social work is dominated by the demands of evidence-based practice; therefore, how the researcher asks the questions and defines the parameters is often vital in obtaining funding as well as ethical and scientific approval (Briggs 2005).

Having worked as an oncology social worker for over 20 years, counselling cancer patients and their families, I was curious to learn more about the experiences of fathers who have cancer. I had worked with young mothers with breast cancer and had read numerous articles about their experiences but knew little about what it was like from the perspective of fathers. I also knew that often male cancer patients may be reluctant to openly and candidly discuss their feelings about their experiences. Yet I wanted to truly learn what their experience was like: What were their worries? Were they primarily worried about their children or did they also still worry about their self-image? In the case of testicular cancer in particular, was their masculinity challenged by the surgical treatment of an orchidectomy (the surgical removal of the affected testicle), and how might this impact on their experience of being a father.

I suspected that in order to truly find answers to these questions I would need more than a standard questionnaire. Hence, I was determined to find a research method that would allow me to recruit and interview men in a medical context while also enabling me to explore their concerns in a deeper way.

With this in mind, in this chapter I will present how I managed to design my study: moving from the initial curiosity, to the decision to use qualitative methods in general, to specific psycho-social methodologies in particular. In order to understand why I chose to utilise qualitative methodology it is helpful to review some of the essential premises of qualitative studies and why this was deemed the appropriate methodology to investigate this issue, even though I was conducting the research in a hospital setting where quantitative approaches are deemed to be 'scientific' and 'the norm'.

Finally, as it is now widely recognised in social science research, in order to do justice to the understanding of the participant's experience, researchers must also acknowledge their own part in the process. Therefore, I will conclude the chapter by reviewing how reflexivity in this study became a vital tool in identifying areas of concern for the participants that might have been missed had I only analysed the verbatim interview transcripts. I hope that this chapter will then inspire practitioners to move from being curious to developing a research project of their own.

DEVELOPING AND FORMULATING A RESEARCH STUDY

As an oncology social worker, I was asked to consult on a project to develop an intervention for families when a father has cancer. In particular, a child and family team at a mental health facility was considering offering family sessions to fathers with testicular cancer. While numerous studies have been conducted when the mother is the cancer patient and a variety of interventions – both individual and family – have been developed, the majority of these studies and interventions address the family needs when the mother has breast cancer (Barnes *et al.* 2000; Friedman *et al.* 1988; Lewis *et al.* 1989; Walsh, Manuel and Avis 2005). However, research and interventions designed exclusively from the perspective of men who are fathers is very limited. Given my experience of counselling individual men with cancer, I questioned whether a family intervention was the optimal modality for these patients. I was curious as to whether a family intervention would in fact address the major areas of psycho-social concerns and individual anxieties for these men. The team agreed this would be an important phenomenon to explore before we began the process of planning an intervention.

It was decided that in order to explore in depth the experience for men, it would be best to choose one type of cancer that primarily affects men who are most likely to have children. Thus, even though the sample size would be small, the study would be internally consistent with a coherent argument (Smith 1996). The most common cancer in the UK for men between the ages of 25 and 49 is testicular cancer (15%) (Orchid Cancer Appeal 2014). It also has an excellent prognosis (97.2% survival rate at five years' post diagnosis), and was deemed, therefore, to be the optimal diagnosis to investigate.

A substantial amount of research had already been conducted, which established that men with testicular cancer had a range of psycho-social concerns (Arai *et al.* 1996; Carpentier *et al.* 2011; Chapple and McPherson 2004; Dahl, Mykeletun and Fossa 2005; Gordon 1995; Incrocci, Bosch and Slob 1999; Moynihan 1987; Reiker *et al.* 1985; Schover and von Eschenbach 1984). However, this research has not specifically explored the concerns for *fathers* with cancer. Therefore, this study was designed to uniquely illuminate the particular experience of men who are fathers with cancer, with the ultimate aim to develop an intervention designed to meet the needs of this particular patient population.

A KEY QUESTION: QUALITATIVE OR QUANTITATIVE RESEARCH?

Having decided that the purpose of this study was to explore the areas of concern and individual anxieties of this population, the next decision was which methodology to employ: qualitative or quantitative? Working as a hospital social worker, I am surrounded by innovative and life-changing medical studies, most of which are quantitative in nature. Therefore, it is easy to question the benefits of studies that explore emotions rather than medical treatments. Yet it is important to keep the whole person in mind when considering the experience of patients. One of the roles of a social worker is to be a voice for our service users and to try to make a challenging time a bit easier. For this to happen, I believe it is vital to have a solid understanding of both qualitative and quantitative methodologies in order to justify the need to consider thoughts and feelings in an environment that places priority on scientific outcomes and quantitative studies.

Historically, within medical settings quantitative research has been the dominant paradigm, recently reinforced by the rapid expansion of interest in evidence-based interventions. It is not surprising then that social workers, as in other professions, are being bombarded with the demands of producing evidence-based practice (EBP) in order to receive funding, while also meeting regulatory audits and inspections (Briggs 2005). With limited resources and pressure, there is a desire to ensure that funds are being deployed in a way that can guarantee results. Moreover, the desire to investigate and focus on emotionality has historically been met with scepticism (Richardson 1996). Recently, however, this perspective has been seriously challenged with a shift to appreciating the value of understanding and exploring a phenomena in depth (Stake 2006). Needless to say, my study was not looking to establish empirical regularities or truths, nor was it interested in turning information into measurable and accurate data. Instead, I was interested in understanding the service users who have ideas about their own world and have also attached meaning to their experiences (Robson 2011).

Fortuitously, the cancer centre I was affiliated with, which primarily conducts quantitative medical research, does recognise the benefits of qualitative research. I was able to design my research to encompass qualitative paradigms, informed by social constructionism and constructivism, approaches that then addressed the methodological needs of my study to explore men's experience (Henwood 1996; Robson 2011). In particular, acknowledging the role of social constructionism in helping to define the concept of 'masculinity' was a major component of understanding men with testicular cancer (Moynihan 1998). Often, men facing a chronic or critical illness start to have self doubts about their masculinity (Charmaz 1995). Gordon, in his study on men with testicular cancer, found they employed different strategies to cope with the challenges it posed to their masculine identities. One strategy was to define their cancer ordeal as a means of reaffirming their version of masculinity, while the other strategy was to develop a new, less traditional, view of masculinity (Gordon 1995). Having an understanding of social constructionism, constructivism and how masculinity is one of the concepts constructed by communities was an essential ingredient in understanding how fathers with cancer face challenges to their masculinity.

While it is beneficial to understand the distinct theoretical models that underpin qualitative research, I also needed a more specific methodology to explore the lived experience of fathers with cancer. Hence, I recognised the need to find a particular methodological framework that would ensure that my research would meet the scientific criteria of data analysis expected within the medical community while also ensuring that the interview approach would allow deeper exploration of emotionality and inter-subjectivity.

CONDUCTING RESEARCH IN NON-SOCIAL WORK SETTINGS

Safeguarding a 'scientific' attitude

When developing my research study, I realised that not only did I need to determine the most effective and efficient way to acquire the data to answer my research question, but also I needed to consider the practical realities of conducting research within my organisation. In this section, I will outline the organisational hurdles that I was confronted with when preparing my research study and how the institutional requirements, combined with the research topic, led to my decision to utilise the Interpretative Phenomenological Analysis (IPA) methodology for data analysis. Moreover, throughout the whole process of designing a research study, I was also cognisant of the need to follow an ethical code of conduct, ensuring the emotional wellbeing of my participants.

In order to recruit the necessary participants for this study, I obtained the support of an oncologist at a large cancer centre, who kindly agreed to act as the Chief Investigator. However, there were still multiple obstacles to overcome: in particular, gaining approval from both the Research Ethics Committee (REC) and the Committee for Clinical Research. In the UK the role of Research Ethics Committees have been described as being 'the provision of support and advice to health professionals and patients on ethical issues arising from clinical practice or patient care' (Slowther et al. 2004, p.950). In other words, ethics committees are designed to support health professionals dealing with difficult ethical issues, as well as others affected by such cases. In practice, this will usually mean that the REC will provide a multi-disciplinary forum for the discussion of the issues of the study and will support the decision-making process of the health care professionals (McLean 2007). What was important here was the need to design the study in an ethical manner that would ensure the wellbeing of the participants as well as being approved by the REC.

The study, therefore, was designed to not only encourage the participants to share their experience in a safe, containing environment, but provisions were made to ensure that a participant could withdraw if he ever felt uncomfortable, given that research interviews may stir up uncomfortable material for them (Hollway and Jefferson 2000). Moreover, in the event that participants found that discussing their experience had raised issues that warranted further support, they were offered free psychological support. The need to address the ethical factors of identifying and providing additional support for the participants was just one of the logistical details that needed to be presented to the REC Committee, and written into an official 'protocol' – a full, detailed plan for the study that verifies the reliability and validity of potential findings. Of particular ethical note for this study was, first, the need to ensure fully informed consent and, as far as possible, to safeguard anonymity in light of the intimate biographical data being gathered. Second, in the event that a participant found discussing his experience upsetting, I had to be equipped to provide easily accessible and appropriate support (Smith, Flowers and Larkin 2009). Similarly, I had to be prepared to halt the interview if necessary.

This may seem obvious and straightforward but having recruited a participant, found a venue, driven to the interview and then spent close to two hours in a meeting, this can be more challenging for the researcher than one expects. Thus it is vital that the ethical principles are firmly established and the wellbeing of the participant is viewed as paramount in order to ensure that the whole research process falls within the established code of conduct.

Given the necessity of demonstrating to the two committees the reliability and validity of this study, it became evident that a 'scientific' attitude was needed. Although, historically, qualitative research has been criticised for failing to meet conventional scientific standards, it is now recognised that qualitative study can be viewed as scientific research with important and valid findings (Smith 1996), provided it adheres to the following 'quality criteria':

- it constitutes a *systematic consideration* of the nature of the observations and the role of the investigator

- it includes an openness to *scepticism*, to challenges to and to disconfirmation of subjective interpretations and assertions

- there is commitment to an *ethical code* of conduct.

What is particularly important here is the criteria of 'scepticism', which encourages subjecting ideas to disconfirmation and scrutiny. When searching for a qualitative methodology to analyse the data, I was determined to find a method that would allow for both the discussion and presentation of the lived experience of the participants as well as stand up to challenge. Qualitative researchers usually recognise that their assertions are open to dispute. They acknowledge that their findings carry opinion; however, they are hoping that their studies may 'not win over a critic but…be persuasive to critical friends' (Stake 2006, p.41). Therefore, I was determined to employ a specific analytic method that would allow me to incorporate a scientific attitude into my research project. The methodology that seemed to be the best fit was IPA.

Interpretative Phenomenological Analysis methodology

IPA is a qualitative research approach that is committed to the examination of how people make sense of their experiences. While it originated and is best known in the field of psychology, it is increasingly being chosen by other disciplines in human, health and social sciences (Smith *et al.* 2009). IPA has three distinct components, which are reflected in the name:

- *Phenomenological* – The study is concerned with the 'thing' itself, the researcher wants to learn about the lived experience of the participant in their own terms.

- *Interpretative* – This component of IPA is informed by hermeneutics theory of interpretation. The researchers take the view that the participant is trying to make sense of his experience. It is an interpretative endeavour of the researcher trying to make sense of the participant making sense of his experience.

- *Idiographic* – IPA is committed to the detailed examination of a particular case. IPA studies usually have a small number of participants and the aim is to reveal something of the lived experience of the participants.

(Smith *et al.* 2009)

In short, the IPA methodology wants an insider's perspective. The researcher wants to learn what it is like to stand in the participant's shoes. However, they are also standing alongside the participant and taking a look from a different angle and become reliant on interpretation. This methodology seemed the ideal approach to explore with the participants their experience of being a father with cancer. Moreover, it invited the incorporation of psychodynamic concepts as a means of interpreting the data and developing themes; and it allowed for a more comprehensive and insightful understanding of the participant's experience. Finally, it was ideal for a small sample size. This again blends well with psychoanalytically informed research, which is very strong in providing in-depth discussions of individual cases in a way that illuminates the internal world of the participant as well as allowing for case comparisons.

Another appealing quality of the IPA methodology, which reflected a scientific attitude, was the systematic process of analysing the data. In order to analyse data the IPA sets out a structure to develop themes that are grounded in specific examples from the data. There are five stages of the analysis process:

1. Read and re-read notes and transcripts.

2. Initial noting: examine the semantic context and language used; look at descriptive content; explore the conceptual content.

3. Develop emerging themes.

4. Search for connections across themes.

5. Look for patterns across cases.

(Smith *et al.* 2009)

Although this process is time-consuming and labour intensive, the researcher hopes to ensure that the identified themes accurately depict the participants' experiences. Moreover, this approach adheres to Robson's (2011) scientific attitude and systematically provides the 'evidence', which is directly linked to the interview text, that can be scrutinised by the sceptics.

What was missing, however, from the IPA methodology was guidance on how to conduct the interview. The standard approach to interviewing with either structured or semi-structured surveys seemed somewhat inadequate and inappropriate to social science research (Hollway and Jefferson 2000). Even with the IPA approach, which allows for interpretation of the data, the quality of the findings is directly linked to the quality of the interview itself. Thus, finding an interview approach that would generate rich data was vital in ensuring a relevant and informed study. Recent innovations in psycho-social methodology as developed by Hollway and Jefferson (2000) and Wengraf and Chamberlayne (2006) seemed to provide the key to tapping into the latent levels of personal meaning.

Psycho-social research

It is precisely because individuals have personal views about their world and attach latent levels of meaning to these ideas that within qualitative research there is traditionally a rejection of the view that truths can be established. Instead, the focus is shifted to take into account the uniqueness of individuals within their environment (Hollway and Jefferson 2000). With this perspective in mind, research that can facilitate the exploration of both the spoken and latent meanings for participants while incorporating concepts and principles from psychoanalytic theory is, therefore, well placed to bond the split between the 'individual' and 'society'. Hence, the emergence of the psycho-social study, which posits a need to understand both the inner and outer world of its subjects by combining specific interviewing techniques with a conceptual framework that draws on psychoanalytic concepts with a particular emphasis on the unconscious.

In a further effort to incorporate key fundamental principles of psychoanalytic theory into informed practice research, Hollway and Jefferson (2000) introduce the concept of the 'defended subject' in research studies. In order to better understand the defended subject, they suggest the incorporation of the fundamental psychoanalytic proposition that anxiety is inherent in the human condition and precipitates defences against threats that are largely unconscious. A core psychoanalytic concept is the premise that individuals' dynamic unconscious, which defends against anxiety, significantly influences individuals actions, lives and relations (Hollway and Jefferson 2000). Traditionally, psychoanalysis examines how individuals respond when feeling threatened and what defence mechanisms they employ as well as focusing on the emotionality and the process of relationships (Briggs 2005).

The concept of the defended subject is particularly relevant to the participants of this study, all of whom were facing a life-threatening illness. Cooper (1982) insightfully comments that for patients confronted with Hodgkin's disease (a form of cancer) 'somewhere, in even the most carefree or apparently coping personality, will lurk the fear of imminent death' (p.613). Thus, for men who may be employing defences to cope with some of the most primitive fears, including the fear of death itself, the prospect of being able to utilise a methodology that encourages the understanding of the defended subject seemed particularly relevant. Patients are repeatedly asked to provide their medical histories to a range of health care professionals; therefore, in a research interview, the respondent potentially could present a rehearsed set of generalisations to the researcher. In keeping with the defended subject approach, there is the possibility of the participant employing a defensive strategy utilising intellectualisation and avoidance to control potentially painful and frightening concerns (Hollway and Jefferson 2000). Hence, incorporating the concept of a defended subject provides me with a means to see past or 'below the surface' of the routine responses.

I have discussed how psycho-social research utilises these psychoanalytic concepts to explore the unconscious dynamics and defences at play. However, and what is vital, is that these concepts not only help us to understand the participant, they also shed light on the research process, like the analytic process, as a whole. Through a psychoanalytic lens it becomes clear that the research subject can only be known through the researcher, because together they are co-producers of meaning (Clarke and Hoggett 2009). In other words, the affective dynamics of the research encounter are influenced by what the social researcher and the participant bring to the interview. Thus, proponents of psycho-social research have established the need for a reflexive researcher who is engaged in sustained self-reflection throughout the research process (Hollway and Jefferson 2000). I will discuss my experience as a reflexive practitioner in more detail below.

Given my commitment to exploring both the conscious and unconscious communications of the interview, the choice of interview technique was a vital ingredient. I turned to Hollway and Jefferson's (2000) text, which presents four approaches to interviewing that are compatible with the areas of interest for psycho-social research. They include traditional approaches, feminist approaches, narrative approaches and clinical case study approaches. The first two work on the traditional question and answer structure, whereby the interviewer selects the topics and themes. This is not in keeping with the aim of my study, which was to explore the areas of concern and anxiety as presented by the participants, not the researcher. Traditional narrative approaches focus on the 'telling of the story'; subsequently, the actual life events may take precedence over developing an understanding of the individual telling the story. Hollway and Jefferson (2000) addressed this concern by developing their own interview process, which they called the 'Free Association Narrative Interview'. However, for the purpose of my study I turned to the clinical case study approach of interviewing. This approach is both consistent with the emphasis on reflexivity in the interview while also allowing for the development of an understanding of the unconscious dynamics at play, particularly the individual's defences against anxiety (Hollway and Jefferson 2000). This particular approach seemed to fit with the aim of my study.

Adopting a Biographic Narrative Interpretive Method approach

Having determined that the case study approach best fit the needs of my study, I was then fortunate enough to be introduced to the Biographic Narrative Interpretive Method (BNIM) developed by Wengraf and Chamberlayne. One of main strengths of the BNIM method is its ability to enable the researcher to explore the latent levels of meaning (Chamberlayne, Bornat and Wengraf 2000). Additionally, it encourages eliciting narratives from the participants in an uninterrupted way, thus helping to minimise the possibility that the facts of the story become more important than the person telling the story (Clarke and Hoggett 2009).

In the case of my study, I simply asked the men to tell me about their experiences of being fathers with cancer from the point they suspected something was wrong to date. This straightforward, open question enabled the participants to share not only the actual details of their case but also the larger context that was important to them. I did not interrupt the participants and let them share their experiences in their own distinctive way. This surprised most of the participants who were expecting a more formal semi-structured interview. I explained that I had chosen this particular type of interview approach because I was keen to learn about their unique experience.

The authors of the BNIM method argue that not only do we need to understand our personal histories; we also need to understand the context around them – both the psychological and the social. In order to encourage participants to explore their experience with the researcher, they developed a method that includes a specific interview process comprised of two sub-sessions. In the first sub-session, the participant is asked one question and then encouraged to take his time and answer the question in detail. The interviewer does not interrupt and allows him to take as long as he likes. In the second sub-session, the interviewer follows up with approximately 5–7 questions asking for the participant to elaborate on specific points. This very open first question invites the participants to describe and then explore their experience. Unlike structured interviews, by focusing on eliciting narratives the hope is that participants will express perspectives that may have been suppressed and reveal what is important to them.

This method was appealing for my research with cancer patients, who have become accustomed to telling their medical history to health care professionals, thus having a 'public account' that lacks emotion and personal details. An additional benefit is that this method encourages men to present what is important to them, not what the researcher thinks will be important. This proved to be extremely valuable in my study where men discussed topics and shared concerns that had not been anticipated.

The BNIM method has two distinct lines of interpreting and processing the data, one of which is the actual chronological events and the other is how the participant told the story. In order to analyse the interviews, the researcher engages a panel of 3–5 participants to help explore what issues and themes are particularly relevant to the individual. While I could see the benefits of this process in providing a very in-depth understanding of the participants, in order to meet the requirements of the two committees mentioned above the sample size needed to be ten men. Therefore, I knew that practically this process of data analysis was not feasible. Yet, I wanted to utilise the very effective interview method; therefore, I decided to employ the BNIM interview method combined with the IPA method of data analysis presented above.

The benefits of mixed methodologies: giving fathers a voice

I believe that there were definite advantages to employing two methodologies in this study. The beauty of the BNIM method of interviewing shone through with these men. By telling their story in their own way, in their own time, a rapport was developed between the participants and me; hence, the men confided some of their deepest concerns and anxieties.

Having completed an extensive literature review, I had anticipated some of the concerns and anxieties that would emerge for men who are fathers with cancer. In particular, I had expected them to share concerns about:

- lack of information
- frustration with the medical community
- concern for their children and role changes
- financial concerns and work-related problems.

However, other common themes emerged that I had not expected and found somewhat surprising, given that when I had first met the patients I had invited them to participate in a study about being a father with cancer. Therefore, to have them either verbally or nonverbally disclose some of their deepest fears and concerns was quite powerful and informative. In particular they shared with me concerns about:

- challenges to their sense of masculinity
- frustration at the lack of information particularly regarding prosthesis
- changes to their self-image
- fear of death and annihilation.

By allowing men to tell their story in their own way, it was interesting to note how often they returned to a particular topic. This was helpful in determining how important a particular theme was for the participant. For example, although most of the men confidently stated that they were never afraid of dying and that they knew the statistics were in their favour, they all repeated this numerous times. For example, one participant, Bob, explained early in the interview:

> Of course, I knew I would be fine. I never worried about dying or anything like that. The consultant said I had a 97 per cent chance of survival so I just thought I have to get through the surgery.

However, later he went on to say:

> When this young medic told me I had a 93 per cent survival rate I was really pissed. I thought, 'Don't they teach you anything?' When I challenged him, he got real defensive. But that really shook me up. I mean you worry about these things, right? Doesn't he get that?

The participant raised the topic of survival rates and statistics several more times. Clearly, this participant was more worried about 'dying or anything like that' than he first admitted. This example demonstrates the ability of the BNIM interview method to allow the participant to reveal significant personal meaning (Hollway and Jefferson 2000).

Additionally, one of the expectations and benefits of the IPA method of data analysis is to include interpretation. For example, by looking at the content, the choice of words and the number of times the participant returned to the topic, the depth of this participant's fears emerge. For instance, his choice of words shows anger and frustration, referring to the 'young medic' when he means a doctor, and using the strong word choice of 'pissed', suggested he was projecting his own anger onto this doctor. Additionally, he changes verb tenses, implying a contradiction that not only was he worrying about dying during his cancer experience but he is still frightened now. These clues in the text support the hypothesis developed during the interview that this participant was much angrier and frightened than he was verbalising. In accordance with the concept of the defended subject utilising defences such as denial, intellectualisation and projection, I proposed there was an underlying deep fear of death and annihilation.

Above I have presented the two methodologies to elicit and analyse data that were incorporated in this study to help understand the participants. Relatively recently in the field of social science research, the researcher's feelings have begun to be recognised as another form of data (Hollway and Jefferson 2000). Rather than the researcher attempting to remain objective and ignoring personal feelings, there is a shift towards the utilisation of the researcher's feelings and subjectivity (Jervis 2009). From this is derived the idea of the reflexive, and defended researcher (Hollway and Jefferson 2000), which also became a very important tool in developing a comprehensive understanding of the participants in my study. My experiences of reflexivity in the research process were particularly enhanced by attendance at research supervision groups, which were an integral component of the doctoral programme that the research was being completed under. The group sought to explore research data and to bring 'many minds' to it in order to surface unconscious dimensions and to unsettle hidden assumptions underpinning the data analysis process.

REFLEXIVITY AND A FATHER'S EXPERIENCE

The gradual shift in social science research to include rather than ignore the researcher's emotional responses, has opened up richer ways of conceptualising and incorporating reflexivity into understanding the research environment (Price and Cooper 2012). The researcher needs to be open to considering the unconscious dynamics, communications and defences of *both* the participant and the researcher and their co-construction of the research environment. Thus, at the heart of the psycho-social research model is the reflexive practitioner who is engaged in self-reflection, emotional involvement and affective relationships with the participant (Hollway and Jefferson 2000). In order to give meaning to the emotional responses felt by the researcher, it is helpful to draw on psychoanalytic concepts such as countertransference, containment and projective identification.

Price and Cooper (2012) utilise the work of Steiner (1980) to explain how psychoanalytically attuned researchers can make sense of the conscious and unconscious material brought to the research environment. They explain that within everyone there is frustration and anxiety associated with experience. These frustrations can be communicated by the client in words and narratives or by projections in the form of action or feelings. In the analytic environment, the analyst would experience feelings of 'countertransference', which help them to develop an awareness of the content of the client's psyche. In the analytic sphere, and now in the research environment, countertransference has become recognised as a phenomenon that facilitates understanding (Jervis 2009). The analyst, therefore, has two modes of communicating with the client: the narrative or words, and the emotional countertransference, which can then be related to an experience or psychic process. The job of the analyst is to make interpretations and link up the two (Price and Cooper 2012). Similarly, the reflexive researcher will also be exposed to double communications and to the participants' primitive and unprocessed psychic material, in the form of the defended subject as described above. With the help of supervision and peer support, the researcher should be able to explore the material as well as understand some of the feelings stirred up in the countertransference.

Closely linked to the concept of countertransference are Klein's (1946) notions of projective identification, an unconscious process whereby unwanted parts of the self are 'split' off and projected into another person who then takes in and identifies with these parts (Jervis 2009). Projective identification, according to Bion (1959), is a form of communicating emotions and experiences started in infancy and then used throughout life. Projective identification can be a powerful means of communicating what is happening in an individual's psyche. Bion (1959) emphasised the need for individuals to be able to project the unbearable and incomprehensible feelings and experiences, which then necessitates someone being able to receive or 'contain' these disturbing emotions (Jervis 2009, p.147). The concept of containment thus is based on the premise of an unconscious inter-subjectivity when emotions are passed between people (Hollway and Jefferson 2000). If the person receiving the projections finds them too unbearable, they may reject them or deny them. If, on the other hand, they can contain them and 'detoxify' them, the individual initially projecting the feelings may feel recognised and understood (Hollway and Jefferson 2000). One can see the value of a researcher who understands these concepts, because it provides the research participant the opportunity to not only verbally share but also emotionally communicate their experiences.

Not only is a reflective researcher in a position to develop a comprehensive understanding of the research encounter, Hollway and Jefferson (2000) also believe that the participant may benefit from participating in the study. They postulate that interviewees warm to the idea of a narrative interview because they appreciate having the experience of being paid attention and taken seriously. Moreover, precisely because the participants feel that their stories were interesting, relevant and valued, they are inclined to discuss even discomforting events (Hollway and Jefferson 2000). In other words, by providing a containing environment, the participants find the interview process to be a beneficial experience.

Similarly, in my own experience of interviewing men, when I was recruiting the participants and informed them that the interview would last approximately two hours, they all commented that they would not have that much to say. However, not one interview lasted less than two hours and one was three and a half. Additionally, once I had turned off the voice recorder and the official interview was complete, I found the men were even more willing to elaborate on their concerns and ask for practical support, particularly around how to communicate with their children. I attribute this to having established a trusting and containing relationship during the interview process. And what of the participant who spoke for three and a half hours? This was Bob, the participant quoted above. By further reviewing elements of his case, both the benefits of the reflexive practitioner as well as the need for supervision become apparent.

Above I described how Bob started the interview by claiming that he was confident in his positive prognosis because of the impressive statistics. However, I quickly began to speculate that in fact his fears were greater than he wanted to admit. My suspicions were founded on the fact that he returned to the topic of cancer statistics numerous times *and* because of his choice of words and tenses. Later in the interview he also shared his fears of leaving his wife and children and how they would cope without him. Additionally, and profoundly, as a researcher and with the help of a research supervision group, I felt the intensity of his fears. In order to explain this I need to set the context of the interview.

I met with Bob in his home, which was an hour's drive for me on a day when it was snowing. I was facing the window and as Bob continued to talk, I watched the snow pile up on his country lane. I became distracted and agitated and was relieved when after three and a half hours Bob said he had no more to say. When we were reviewing this case in supervision, my colleagues noticed that I was uncharacteristically unsympathetic to this participant and was almost angry. My colleagues encouraged me to explore these feelings. I commented that in this particular interview I had felt trapped and out of control; whereas with the other participants I had been able to keep to our schedule, with this participant I had felt stuck. It was only when offered this reflexive space that I was able to ponder my responses. I needed the help of others not emotionally connected with the participant to formulate an understanding of the unprocessed and unconscious aspects of the material and then to link it to the conscious data (Price and Cooper 2012).

I was aware of Klein's (1946) discussion on the development of infants where she describes disintegration and the fear of annihilation as one of the most primitive states. She writes about the infant's ego and the anxiety which is:

> a fear of annihilation (death) and takes the form of the fear of persecution...[this fear is] experienced as an uncontrollable overpowering object...the anxiety of being destroyed from within. (Klein 1946, pp.4–5)

Hence, I intellectually knew it was highly likely that men confronted with cancer would be experiencing a profound fear of death and annihilation. And yet it was not until I felt trapped and out of control that I began to fathom the depth of this fear. Through the group supervision discussion it became clear that Bob had projected his unbearable fears onto me. I truly felt out of control of my own situation and angry. Clearly, I was not in a life-threatening situation;

however, what is important to note is that by exploring my reactions I was able to acknowledge my own feelings and defences and further begin to comprehend the depth of Bob's fears. I had been the unconscious recipient of Bob's projections. By paying attention to my uncharacteristic responses, we were able to discover that Bob had communicated how he was truly feeling without actually verbalising it (Jervis 2009).

Having the opportunity to explore in a supervision group this interpretation that Bob had projected his fears onto me, provided a containing environment for myself where I could separate my own feelings that had been evoked while also developing an interpretation of Bob's responses. When using reflexivity, it is important to guard against bad interpretations and to assist with good ones (Hollway and Jefferson 2000). It is essential that the researcher seeks additional material to support assumptions based on their emotional responses (Jervis 2009). Thus, not only did I support my interpretation that Bob was deeply frightened with Kleinian theory as well as the consensus of my peer support, but additionally I relied on other research studies that also found that men facing chronic and life-threatening illness are frightened and angry (Charmaz 1995; Cooper 1982; Dahl *et al.* 2005; Gordon 1995). Moreover, by exploring in depth my response to Bob, who was my third participant out of ten, I was more sensitive and receptive to similar unconscious communications in future interviews.

One other key aspect that should be mentioned when discussing the importance of reflexivity within a psycho-social study is that I was a female researcher interviewing all male participants. A thorough discussion of how this may have impacted on the interviews is beyond the scope of this paper and requires a more detailed discussion of masculinity. Suffice it here to acknowledge that being a female researcher may have enhanced the male participants' need to enact their masculinity (McCaughan *et al.* 2012). Moreover, what this also highlights is the necessity of the researchers to acknowledge the multiple conscious and unconscious components that are at play within the research environment.

CONCLUSION

Above I have presented a brief but hopefully good enough description of the development and implementation of a research study. It was far more time consuming, intellectually taxing and emotionally draining than I had ever anticipated. Yet, it was worth it. What motivated me to start the project was my curiosity about the experience of what it was like for men who are fathers with cancer. What kept me going during the long haul were the participants themselves. They had candidly shared with me their experiences and, therefore, I was determined to see the process through. I found the combination of the BNIM and IPA methods with psychoanalytic theory a powerful and comprehensive formula for exploring both the psycho-social concerns as well as the individual anxieties that were sometimes hidden 'below the surface'. Additionally, having a supportive supervisor and peer support system enabled me to utilise reflexivity to further understand the unconscious dynamics and communications that were also at play. Hopefully, by sharing my findings from the study more health and social care professionals will understand the unique experience these men are confronted with and be able to incorporate this knowledge into their working relationships. Moreover, I have found what I suspected from the start, a family support group is probably not the best form of intervention for these men. Now onto the next project, developing a more appropriate, research informed intervention based on the findings of this study.

REFERENCES

Arai, Y., Kawakita, M., Hida, S., Terachi, T., Okadu, U. and Yoshida, O. (1996) 'Psychosocial aspect in long-term survivors of testicular cancer.' *Journal of Urology, 155,* 574–578.

Barnes, J., Kroll, L., Burke, O., Lee, J., Jones, A. and Stein, A. (2000) 'Qualitative interview study of communication between parents and children about maternal breast cancer.' *British Medical Journal 321,* 7259, 479–82.

Bion, W. R. (1959) 'Attacks on Linking.' Reprinted (1993) in *Second Thoughts.* London: Karnac.

Briggs, S. (2005) 'Psychoanalytic Research in the Era of Evidence-based Practice'. In M. Bower (ed) *Psychoanalytic Theory for Social Work Practice: Thinking under Fire.* London: Routledge.

Carpentier, M. Y., Fortenberry, J. D., Ott, M. A., Brames, M. J. and Einhorn, L. H. (2011) 'Perceptions of masculinity and self-image in adolescent and young adult testicular cancer survivors: Implications for romantic and sexual relationships.' *Psycho-Oncology 20,* 7, 738–745.

Chamberlayne, P., Bornat, J. and Wengraf, T. (2000) *The Turn to Biographical Methods in Social Science.* Routledge: London.

Chapple, A. and McPherson, C. (2004) 'The decision to have prosthesis: A qualitative study of men with testicular cancer.' *Psycho-Oncology 13,* 9, 654–664.

Charmaz, K. (1995) 'Identity Dilemmas of Chronically Ill Men.' In D. Sabo and D. F. Gordon (eds) *Men's Health and Illness: Gender, Power and the Body.* London: Sage Publications.

Clarke, S. and Hoggett, P. (2009) *Researching Beneath the Surface: Psycho-Social Research Methods in Practice.* London: Karnac.

Cooper, A. (1982) 'Disabilities and how to live them.' *The Lancet 1,* 621–613.

Dahl, A. A., Mykeletun A. and Fossa S. D. (2005) 'Quality of life in survivors of testicular cancer.' *Urology Oncology 10,* 23, 193–200.

Friedman, L. C., Baer, P. E., Nelson, D. V., Lane, M., Smith, F. E. and Dworkin, R. J. (1988) 'Women with breast cancer: Perception of family functioning and adjustment to illness.' *Psychosomatic Medicine 50,* 529–540.

Fuller, R. and Petch, A. (1995) *Practitioner Research: The Reflexive Social Worker.* Milton Keynes: Open University Press.

Gordon, D. F. (1995) 'Testicular Cancer and Masculinity.' In D. Sabo and D. F. Gordon (eds) *Men's Health and Illness: Gender, Power and the Body.* London: Sage Publications.

Henwood, K. (1996) 'Qualitative Inquiry; Perspectives, Methods and Psychology.' In J. T. E. Richardson (ed) *Handbook of Qualitative Research Methods for Psychology and the Social Sciences.* Leicester: Biddles.

Hollway, W. and Jefferson, T. (2000) *'Doing Qualitative Research Differently: Free Association, Narrative and the Interview Method.'* London: Sage.

Incrocci, L., Bosch J. L. and Slob, A. K. (1999) 'Testicular prostheses: Body image and sexual functioning.' *British Journal of Urology International 84,* 1043–1045.

Jervis, S. (2009) 'The Use of Self as a Research Tool.' In S. Clarke and P. Hoggett (eds) *Researching Beneath the Surface: Psycho-Social Research Methods in Practice.* London: Karnac Books Ltd.

Klein, M. (1946) 'Notes on Some Schizoid Mechanisms.' In J. Mitchell (ed.) (1991) *The Selected Melanie Klein.* Harmondsworth: Penguin.

Lewis, F. M., Woods, N. F., Hough, E. E. and Bensley, L. S. (1989) 'The family's functioning with chronic illness in the mother: The spouse's perspective.' *Social Science Medicine 29,* 11, 1261–1269.

McCaughan, E., Prue, G., Parahoo, K., McIlfatrick, S. and McKenna, H. (2012) 'Exploring and comparing the experience and coping behaviour of men and women with colorectal cancer after chemotherapy treatment: A qualitative longitudinal study.' *Psycho-Oncology 21,* 1, 64–71.

McLean, S. A. M. (2007) 'What and who are clinical ethics committees for?' *Journal of Medical Ethics 33,* 9, 497–500.

Moynihan, C. (1987) 'Testicular cancer: The psychosocial problems of patients and their relatives.' *Cancer Survivors 6,* 477–510.

Moynihan, C. (1998) 'Theories in health care and research: Theories of masculinity.' *British Medical Journal 3,* 17, 1072–1075.

Orchid Cancer Appeal and Orchid Editorial Board (2014) *Male Cancer: Awareness, Diagnosis and Treatment.* London: Orchid Cancer Appeal.

Price, H. and Cooper, A. (2012) 'In the Field: Psychoanalytic Observation and Epistemological Realism.' In C. Urwin and J. Sternberg (eds) *Infant Observation and Research: Emotional Processes in Everyday Life.* Hove: Routledge.

Richardson, J.T.E. (ed.) (1996) *Handbook of Qualitative Research Methods for Psychology and the Social Sciences.* Leicester: Biddles.

Reiker, P. P., Edbril, S. D. and Garnick, M. G. (1985) 'Curative testis cancer therapy: Psychosocial sequelae.' *Journal of Clinical Oncology 3,* 8, 1117–1125.

Robson, C. (2011) *Real World Research: A Resource for Users of Social Research Methods in Applied Settings.* Chichester: John Wiley and Sons Ltd.

Schover, L. R. and von Eschenbach, A. C. (1984) 'Sexual and marital counseling with men treated for testicular cancer.' *Journal of Sex and Marital Therapy 10,* 29–40.

Slowther, A., Johnston C., Goodall, J. and Hope, T. (2004) 'Development of clinical ethics committees.' *British Medical Journal 328,* 7445, 950–952.

Smith, J. A. (1996) 'Evolving Issues for Qualitative Psychology.' In J. T. E. Richardson (ed.) *Handbook of Qualitative Research Methods for Psychology and the Social Sciences.* Leicester: Biddles.

Smith, J., Flowers, P. and Larkin, M. (2009) *Interpretative Phenomenological Analysis: Theory, Method and Research.* London: Sage Publications.

Stake, R. E. (2006) *Multiple Case Study Analysis.* New York: Guilford Press.

Steiner, J. (1980) *'Psychotic and non-psychotic parts of the personality in borderline patients.'* London: Tavistock Paper no. 8.

Walsh S. R., Manuel, J. C. and Avis, N. E. (2005) 'The impact of breast cancer on younger women's relationships with their partner and children.' *Families, Systems and Health 23*, 1, 80–93.

Chapter 12

GETTING TO THE HEART OF RELATIONSHIPS IN SOCIAL WORK RESEARCH IN PRACTICE

Ilse Julkunen and Gillian Ruch

A RELATIONAL OVERVIEW

It is not uncommon to hear people say somewhat ironically about their work: 'If it wasn't for the people I'd really enjoy it.' And something of this sentiment rings true in relation to experiences of conducting research. As this book attests, stories of the difficulties encountered when negotiating access, retaining participants or managing an ethically tricky encounter are not uncommon. Yet the key message of this book is that we need to make a virtue of these relationships and encounters, however challenging or frustrating they may prove to be. Indeed, all aspects of the research process are informative and critical components of high-quality research and research findings.

This book has approached relationships in research broadly from two perspectives: first, relationships as the core constituent of the research, engaged both in the field and in the analysis from a psycho-social stance; second, relationships as configured in practice research as a key component of the research design, delivery and dissemination processes. In both cases, how relationships are approached has a significant influence on the quality of the research and its outcomes.

The rich and diverse accounts of relationships from these two discrete and overlapping perspectives captured in this book provide ample evidence of their importance. In drawing together the ideas presented, it is possible to summarise the significance of relationships under three conceptual headings:

1. *Role/position:* Recognising the overlaps between the researcher and practitioner identities as a strength and potential limitation of research is a dynamic process, requiring constant scrutiny.

2. *Respect/power:* Relationships in research are imbued with sensitivities. Researchers need to assert their expertise but in ways that bring participants, particularly practitioners, with them; this includes colleagues as co-writers as a central feature of practice research.

3. *Reflection/process:* Relationships in research invite attention being paid to the process, as much as to the content of the research projects (i.e. to *how* data are gathered, as much as what they constitute).

This book has focused on research in professional practice and the multitude of experiences and perspectives of researchers, service users and practitioners in social work. Its emphasis has been on relationships as a key component of research and their importance for the co-creation of knowledge and change generation at the level of policy and practice. We have endeavoured to deepen and expand understanding of how research processes are conducted in ways that embrace the often invisible and sometimes unconscious aspects of relationships. By giving voice to researchers involved in practice-based research in social work we have sought to make more visible their subjectivity and reflexivity in the research process. Through their accounts of navigating their way through research that encompasses case studies, ethnographic studies, action research and co-operative inquiries, the researchers have made their choices and reflections visible for the reader.

THE PARALLEL CONCEPTUALISATION
OF THE 'INSIDE' AND THE 'OUTSIDE' IN
PRACTICE RESEARCH RELATIONSHIPS

The distinctive relationship-oriented approach of this book is influenced by different theoretical frameworks. Common to these diverse frameworks is a shared concern with the complex and contested ideas about the forms of relationships that are created in the research process and how these influence both the research process and research findings. These studies challenge subjectivity and push the limits of conventional scientific research in search of more applicable and more realisable solutions. They go beyond reflexive diaries and recording to explore both the 'inner' and 'outer' dimensions of research, reaching the different standpoints that Bourdieu in his *Theory of Practice* has so eloquently conceptualised:

> To do this, one has to situate oneself within real activity as such, that is in the practical relation to the world, the preoccupied, active presence in the world through which the world imposes its presence, with its urgencies, its things to be done and said, things made to be said, which directly govern words and deeds without ever unfolding as a spectacle. It is possible to step down from the sovereign viewpoint from which objectivist idealism orders the world, but without having to abandon to it the 'active aspect' of apprehension of the world by reducing knowledge to a mere recording. (Bourdieu 1990, p.52)

What Bourdieu points out is the 'active presence', which includes experiences of being both outside and inside of the human mind, a parallel perspective that this book has sought to reach. A distinctive trait in the studies represented in the preceding chapters is the professional identity of the authors. All have been, or still are, social work practitioners or closely connected to practice and deeply involved in researching aspects of social work practice that hold great meaning for them and which they are passionate about. The emotional engagement in the research process is strong and they challenge it theoretically and methodologically. It is evident that all researchers and social scientists make assumptions about action and interaction and that these assumptions greatly affect their conclusions, interpretations and procedures. Anselm Strauss (1993), along with other scientists, has urged explicitness and sensitivity towards the phenomena of study, but in his perhaps forgotten book *The Continual Permutation of Action* Strauss specifically pinpoints the importance of the body in research, arguing that: 'body as a condition for action, is so patently banal that social scientists implicitly assume it, but few follow through very far on its implication' (Strauss 1993, p.24).

Acknowledging the inner and outer dimensions of research has significant implications for research. The studies in this volume illustrate this and suggest too that such a dual focus approach may also have relevance for rethinking the processes through which social work practice theories are developed (see Healy 2000).

The practitioner researcher identity is a common element in the study and shows the complexity of this phenomenon. The studies address how the researcher as a subjective person is constructed in relation to the other. But can we simply talk about practitioner research as it only highlights the representation of one social category? What make the identities even more interesting and complex are the many more roles that are intertwined: the role of an educator, developer, researcher, woman, man, family member, collaborator. Harry Lunabba emphasises in this volume the importance of understanding the inter-sectionality of the self in terms of acknowledging how different categorical backgrounds can simultaneously portray various meanings in a particular social moment. We believe that, having explicated the assumptions and choices made, we can contribute to a growing awareness of the forgotten issue of the body in social work research and at the same time add to the understanding of its importance in social work practices. Judy Foster started off in her chapter with a provocative question: 'What happens to social workers' ability to think on the job?' Social work emanates out of the need for physical, mental and emotional presence. To be aware of your own emotions and connection to your body, does that mean that one is present? And how can learning to be more present in action? Laura Yliruka's study showed that feelings became an acceptable part of a child welfare social worker's professional identity. The Mirror enabled social workers to get in touch with their emotions, reflect on them together and carry out a personal way of working with their own clients, with better awareness of the presence of emotions – an excellent example of relationships and emotions being seen as a virtue as a help, not a hinderance, to effective practice.

THE BREADTH AND DEPTH OF PRACTICE RESEARCH RELATIONSHIPS

For a more orthodox researcher, research processes call for ways of thinking learnt from scientific research, systematisation and research logic, approved methodological practice and good background knowledge of the relevant literature. For a researcher involved in practice-based research, it means dialogues and interactions and being mindful of the *breadth* of relationships, in terms of who needs to be approached and in what way in order for the research to progress, and of the *depth* of the relationships with regard to the often intimate and sensitive issues they can evoke. As all the preceding chapters demonstrate, negotiating access, entering the research field and leaving it require attention and much reflection. The breadth of the relationships require acknowledgement of the consequences of these interactions and how some of these become an important part of the conditions influencing the process. Often it is a question of struggling with the methodology, as for instance in the cases of Gavin Swann's and Katarina Fagerström's research, where the developmental interventions as research approaches encompassed the complex relationship between pragmatic activity and social process. This makes visible the important principle of dialogue as part of the data-gathering process, which then follows through into the analysis.

The depth of the relationships again may emerge as ethical issues that are integral to the sensitive subjects being explored. With the focus on young people with disabilities, Helen Hingley-Jones' research, for instance, has elaborated on the choice of research methods aimed at capturing emotions and relatedness to gain an appreciation of the experiences of young people with a learning disability. Kathleen Russell's research into fathers' experiences of cancer is similarly attentive – first, to the sensitive issues associated with this experience that the research elicits; and, second, to the silent voice that this group has had up until now.

PRACTICE RESEARCH AS A SITUATIONAL ACTIVITY

Drawing on different theoretical ideas such as Bion's (1962) psychoanalytic concept of 'containment' and the social psychological concept of 'attunement' (see, for example, Scheff 2003) to make sense of the reflexive self-consciousness of our experience *or* on co-evolving action research and actor-relational approaches, it is possible to design and conduct research in ways that address the relational and emotional dimensions of the research process from the outset and throughout the research. Nonetheless, the studies involved show also how intricate the research processes are and how open the researcher needs to stay in order to be sensitive enough to the methodological and theoretical tunings of the research process. Göran Goldkuhl (2011) reminds us that ontological stances have epistemological implications. Without seeing the practices, he warns us, the social world becomes fragmented. The complexities embedded in social work practices urge us to trace the on-going dynamics that both reveal and form relationships in research. Studying social objects without considering their practice habitat is very risky and may imply confusion and misunderstanding. Judy Foster's ethnographic research into team cultures is a case in point. Judy's skilful eye and ear captured crucial organisational dynamics from the outset of her research engagement with the three teams, which had considerable significance for her understanding of the teams' everyday experiences, in general, and their capacity to 'keep thinking', in particular.

There is a considerable amount of knowledge and experience that actors bring into play in carrying out both routine and innovative action in practice, which should not be overlooked but rather embraced and examined. In some cases, such as Kathleen Russell's and Elina Virokannas' chapters, this has meant staying true to their initial curiosity and passion. It has involved taking on a flexible, open stance when negotiating a way to begin, looking for consent gained through working with the users and their families and peers, carefully considering how to get an insider perspective and learning what it is like to stand in the shoes of others, and initiating discussions to explore further with all the research stakeholders their interpretations of the research focus. This may eventually lead to an insightful understanding of the practice and the participants' experiences. Dealing with emotions goes beyond situational activity into what these reflections would mean to practice. Close observation of what is done in practice is pivotal, but an epistemology of practice may also comprise learning through experimentation and exploration of new ways to act (Goldkuhl 2011). Or as Layder (1997) has argued, close observation of what is done is not separate from projections into the future or into the overall structural environment that exists beyond the immediate situation or context.

TAKING FURTHER STEPS IN PRACTICE CHANGE AND IMPROVEMENT

For a researcher with a close relationship to practice, their interest goes beyond simply research outcomes. All of the chapters illustrate this distinctive characteristic of practice research, with some (e.g. Swann's, Yliruka's and Fagerstrom's chapters) having practice change as an integral component of their research design. For other authors ,the impact of their research on themselves, on those with whom they researched and the wider social work community was more or less visible, but one can be confident in saying that no one involved, directly or indirectly, in the research, would be unaffected or unchanged by it. The knowledge interest in social-work practice research lies in practices and their development. Thus, testing and validation of knowledge formation in practice was often an essential element in the studies involved. Pickering (1995, p.21) uses the term 'tuning' as a perceptive metaphor, which refers to when scientists tentatively construct the 'doings' in research. In the various studies involved in this book there was an emphasis on such 'tuning', through interaction and critical reflection and nuanced discussions between all the different stakeholders. Reflections were facilitated through a supportive environment that either consisted of supervisors or collaborative reflective forums. Critical reflection, for instance, helped participants to discover the competing discourses behind different perspectives, such as child sensitivity versus parent sensitivity. In some of the studies methodological tools were developed that served the purpose of organisational learning.

To acknowledge emotional and practical experiences we need reflective arenas. 'Arenas come into existence at every level of interaction, from the most microscopic to the most macroscopic and they relate to interaction from the most collective to the most individual' (Strauss 1993, p.74). Most of all, relationship-based practice research requires a research and learning community that values relationships and privileges a space for testing knowledge formation in practice.

REFERENCES

Bion, W. (1962) *Learning from Experience*. London: Heinemann.

Bourdieu, P. (1990) *The Logic of Practice*. Stanford, CA: Stanford University Press.

Goldkuhl G. (2011) 'The research practice of practice research: theorizing and situational inquiry.' *Systems, Signs & Actions 5*, 1, 7–29.

Healy, K. (2000) *Social Work Practices: Contemporary Perspectives on Change*. London: Sage.

Layder, D. (1997) *Modern Social Theory: Key Debates and New Directions*. London and New York: Routledge.

Pickering, A. (1995) *The Mangle of Practice: Time, Agency and Science*. Chicago, IL: Chicago University Press.

Scheff, T. (2003, August) *Looking Glass Selves: The Cooley/Goffman Conjecture*. Memorial Session for Ervin Goffman, ASA, Atlanta, GA.

Strauss, A. Strauss, A. L. (1993) *Continual Permutations of Action*. New Brunswick and London: Aldine Transaction.

CONTRIBUTOR BIOGRAPHIES

Katarina Fagerström has a masters in social science and is a doctoral student in social work. Her research concerns critical reflection, dialogue and knowledge making in groups and inter-professional networks and she is in the process of finalising her doctoral thesis on knowledge making in groups about recognising social problems at an early stage. Katarina works at Folkhälsan (a Swedish-speaking non-governmental organisation in the social welfare and health care sector in Finland) as an expert in preventive child care.

Judy Foster, after a decade of practice and management in generic social work, specialised in organising and providing effective training for all social work and social care employees, first locally and then nationally. Most recently, Judy has been a visiting lecturer on social work masters and doctoral programmes at the Tavistock Centre in London, where she completed her own doctorate in social work. In 2014 she presented her research methodology, outlined here, at the International Conference on Social Work Practice Research in New York.

Helen Hingley-Jones is an associate professor of social work (research and teaching) at Middlesex University, where she teaches from undergraduate to doctoral level. She has a practice background in child and family social work, specialising in work with disabled children and their families. Her research interests include psychosocial methodologies, learning disability and adolescent development, looked after children and observation in teaching and research.

Ilse Julkunen is a professor in practice research in social work, Head of Discipline at the Department of Social Research, University of Helsinki. Her research concerns youth and marginalisation and youth transitions from a comparative perspective. She is the scientific leader of the practice research milieu of the Mathilda Wrede Institute and is particularly interested in developing methodological and theoretical approaches in practice research. Together with Edgar Marthinsen, she has co-edited *Practice Research in Nordic Social Work. Knowledge Production in Transition* (Whiting and Birch, 2012).

Harry Lunabba is a senior lecturer in social work at the Swedish School of Social Science at the University of Helsinki. His teaching focuses on social work practices and his main research interests are in the field of ethnographic studies with youth and children and research concerning gender and social relationships.

Gillian Ruch is Professor of Social Work and works in the Department of Social Work and Social Care at the University of Sussex. She teaches and researches in the areas of child care social work and relationship-based and reflective practice and is committed to enhancing the wellbeing of children, families and practitioners. Her particular interests are in promoting psycho-social research methods and reflective forums that facilitate relationship-based practice. She co-edited, with Danielle Turney and Adrian Ward, *Relationship-based Social Work: Getting to the Heart of Practice*. This book is an accompanying complementary publication to that work.

Kathleen Sheridan Russell received her masters in social work from Columbia University in the USA and her professional doctorate in social work from The Tavistock Centre/University of East London. She began her career as a medical social worker at Memorial Sloan-Kettering Cancer Center in New York. Since moving to the UK, she has worked at several cancer charities including Cancer BACUP, The Cancer Counselling Trust and Orchid Cancer Appeal. She is currently a visiting lecturer at The Tavistock Centre and has presented her research at the conferences of the American Association of Oncology Social Workers and the British Psycho-Oncology Society.

Gavin Swann is a doctor of social work and is currently employed as Head of Children's Safeguarding in Children's Services in a London local authority. Gavin has worked in the field of child protection in the United Kingdom as well as internationally, working for UNICEF and other child rights organisations in the developing world for the past 17 years. Gavin teaches in the fields of assessment, child protection, family support, research methods, child sexual abuse and exploitation and work with fathers. Gavin has a particular interest in working with fathers; his doctoral thesis was entitled *Breaking Down Barriers: Engaging Fathers in Children's Social Care* (2015).

Laura Yliruka is a development manager of The Heikki Waris Institute in Helsinki, a joint research and development structure of municipalities in the Helsinki Metropolitan area and the discipline of social work at the University of Helsinki. Her research interests include social work expertise and innovations, evaluation and competence management, as well as working conditions in social work. Her recently published doctoral thesis focuses on how reflective structures in social work enhance expertise in social work.

Elina Virokannas is university lecturer in social work at the Department of Social Sciences and Philosophy at the University of Jyväskylä. Her recent research interests are related to the issues of substance use and motherhood, peer support and discourse analysis. Her teaching interests focus on qualitative research methods and the ethics of social work research.

SUBJECT INDEX

AUTHOR INDEX